Dalits in Indian Democracy

Dalits in Indian Democracy

A Study of Punjab Politics

Nirmal Singh

KALPAZ

First Published, 2018

Published by

Kalpaz Publications
C-30, Satyawati Nagar,
Delhi – 110052
E-mail: kalpaz@hotmail.com
Ph.: 9212142040

Printed at: G. Print Process, Delhi

Cataloging in Publication Data—DK
Courtesy: D.K. Agencies (P) Ltd. <docinfo@dkagencies.com>

Singh, Nirmal *(Professor of political science)*, **author.**
Dalits in Indian democracy : a study of Punjab politics / Nirmal Singh.
pages cm
Includes bibliographical references.
ISBN 9789386397317

1. Dalits—Political activity—India—Punjab. 2. Caste—Political aspects—India—Punjab. 3. Democracy—India—Punjab. 4. Political parties—India—Punjab. 5. Punjab (India)—Politics and government. I. Title.

LCC DS422.C3S56 2018 | DDC 305.56880954552 23

Dedicated

to

My Revered Mother

Contents

List of Abbreviations

AAP	Aam Aadmi Party
AISCF	All India Scheduled Castes' Federation
BAMCEF	All India Backward (SC, ST and OBC) and Minority Communities Employees Federation
BC	Backward Caste
BJP	Bharatiya Janata Party
BKD	Bahujan Kranti Dal
BSM	Bahujan Samaj Morcha
BSP (D)	Bahujan Samaj Party (Democratic)
BSP (K)	Bahujan Samaj Party (Kanshi Ram)
BSP	Bahujan Samaj Party
CM	Chief Minister
DS-4	Dalit Shoshit Samaj Sangharsh Samiti
ECI	Election Commission of India
ILP	Independent Labour Party
INC	Indian National Congress
MLA	Member of Legislative Assembly
MP	Member of Parliament
OBCs	Other Backward Classes
PEPSU	Patiala and East Punjab State Union
RPI	Republican Party of India
RSS	Rashtriya Swayamsevak Sangh
SAD	Shiromani Akali Dal

SC	Scheduled Caste
SGPC	Shiromani Gurudwara Prabandhak Committee
SP	Samajwadi Party
ST	Scheduled Tribe
UP	Uttar Pradesh
UPSCF	United Provinces Scheduled Castes' Federation
VHP	Vishwa Hindu Parishad

Foreword

The Indian democracy faces a large number of challenges. One finds conformism, graded inequality and ghettoisation through the length and breadth of India and any affront to the latter called forth immediate sanctions from vested interests. Those who strive for the democratic transformation of Indian society, irrespective of their political ideology, have to fight against the prevalent caste system. The present work provides valuable historical material on various Dalit movements and politics in Punjab with an insight into the history of casteism in India. It is based on an exploratory study of the experiences of Dalit community in India while providing special considerations to the Scheduled Castes (SCs) in the State of Punjab. It attempts to find out the caste-oriented features of Punjabi society which are unique and separate from the socio-cultural pattern of the other parts of India. It focuses on the exclusion of Dalits in socio-economic and political spheres, and tries to identify the spheres of exclusion, discrimination, practices and processes in which they manifest.

The study concentrates on the State of Punjab primarily due to the numerical strength of Dalit communities in the region. It also investigates the question as to why the Bahujan Samaj Party (BSP) has not been able to make a space in Punjab politics. Many social scientists feel puzzled when they attempt to find the reason as to why Dalits have remained at the margin despite their good strength. Studies undertaken in this regard reveal that the BSP draws its core support from the social group of Dalits. SCs comprise 16.6 per cent of total population in India. The distinguishing feature of Dalits in Punjab is that they constitute the largest proportion of the SC population, i.e., 31.9 per cent (2011 Census). In terms of population share, Punjab accounts for 4.4 per cent of the total SC population in India. In 2001 also, Punjab with 28.9 per cent of its population as SCs ranked highest in the country in terms of proportion. Recently, two more castes, namely, Mochi and Mahatam/Rai Sikh have been notified as SCs in Punjab. Today, it is estimated that the proportion of Dalits may have been above 32 per cent in the State of Punjab. In Punjab, Dalits comprise up to 42 per cent of the Doaba Region. Despite this high concentration of Dalit population, the BSP has not been successful in this region. This book explores this question quite earnestly. To unravel this puzzle, the book also provides a more nuanced understanding of the relationship between social cleavage and party support. For this purpose, two aspects have been examined; firstly, the nature of the party organisation and second, political strategy of the BSP. These are the two key factors that impinge on the success or failure of a political party. Despite the high percentage of Dalit population in Punjab, the inability of the BSP to gain electorally/politically can be attributed to the failure of the party in terms of its organisation and strategy.

The BSP is, generally, identified with the castes feel threatened by the increasing influence of Ad-Dharmis though the BSP is aimed at creating a broad front of Dalits' prospects of becoming an important player than the Congress and the Akali Dal. The major shift from grass roots level movement to the formal political participation in elections as a means to empowerment is quite visible among Dalits. The Congress and the SAD which have a sizeable support base among Dalits, weaken the support base of the BSP. By these factors, the BSP finds difficult to mobilise Dalit voters in the State of Punjab. The BSP's ideology concerned with Dalit oppression and discrimination does not find strong expression in the State of Punjab in view of the inclusive role of the Arya Samaj and the Sikhism. The Sikh Gurus' opposition to Brahminical fanaticism and *Varna* system reduced the oppressive nature of casteism in Punjab.

Dr Nirmal Singh's book, *Dalits in Indian Democracy: A Study of Punjab Politics,* offers an insight into the dynamics of Dalit politics with special reference to Punjab. It explores all the aspects leading to the formulation of Dalit politics in India. The question why the BSP has not been able to mark among Dalits in Punjab has not been addressed in the existing literature. In spite of the highest Dalit population it asks the question as to why the BSP has not been able to make a space in Punjab politics and empirically studies Dalit support base among the political parties like the Congress, the SAD and the BSP. Hence a study of this kind proposed here will not only fill the gap but may also provide a new insight with regard to the mobilisation, organisation and political strategy of any political party. Moreover, this study would also enrich our understanding of the party politics in India and will be more useful for the teachers, researchers and students.

Professor Emanual Nahar
Co-ordinator, Deptt. Political Science (USOL),
Director of Ambedkar Centre
and Centre for the Study of Social
Exclusion and Inclusive Policy (CSSEIP)
and Dean Student Welfare (DSW)
Punjab University, Chandigarh.

Preface

The encounter of democracy with caste is a historical process accommodating two sets of opposed values. There is a common understanding that caste is antagonistic to democracy. Indeed, the hierarchical universe of the caste system is theoretically at odds with the egalitarian requirements of substantive democracy. Caste in its principle has uniquely stratified the Indian society as compared to the other stratified societies in the world. Casteism has always been a major threat to the Indian democracy. It destabilises a democratic system. In fact, it is being used as a tool for narrow political gains. This evil is rooted so deep in the Indian political system that it has posed a challenge for all of us to get rid of it in the larger interests of the nation. This is, in fact, a regression from Ambedkar's analysis of the place of labour in the caste system........ Caste system is not merely division of labour; it is also a division of labourers..... It is a hierarchy in which the divisions of labour are graded one above the other (Ambedkar, 1987b: 354-55). For Dr Lohia, it is meaningless to talk of equality while maintaining separate castes. Castes have to be abolished. The political culture of our society is leading to more and more social contradictions. On the one hand, we aspire to become egalitarian society while, on the other, the caste culture negates this very aspiration. And what is more problematic we cannot become egalitarian without the help of this very caste culture, at least in the economic sense. Caste has for long been viewed as the defining reality of the Indian social structure. From early orientalists to contemporary sociologists and social anthropologists, almost everyone saw caste as the primary institutions around which the social life in India was organised. The mainstream theories of caste, for example, have almost unanimously worked with a *Varna* model of hierarchy. Politicisation of caste is also about assertion of certain kinds of collective identity. Dalit politics in India seems to be informed by a similar kind of understanding of caste.

Political parties are an indispensable link between the society and the institutions of Government. In traditional societies undergoing modernisation and political development, political parties have the double task of providing stable Government and of building new groups of people into the political process. The emergence of the BSP, its construction of the identity of Dalits, criticisms of the Hindu social order and promise of an alternative social justice has introduced much change in the social and political field. The BSP's ideology, particularly the need to construct a Dalit-Bahujan State and the idea that capture of political power is the key to social transformation, has a powerful appeal among SCs and BCs in the State of Punjab. In constructing the ideology of social justice, the political power is the key to social progress of Dalits. But this is different from those of Ambedkar being an adaptation of Ambedkerism to the political conditions in the North India countryside. The BSP is an Ambedkarite party, not only in ideological sense but also in political sense. It does not believe in social transformation or revolution. It wants merely some changes in the existing structure because the BSP's ideology of social justice is based upon a desire to compensate for centuries of historic injustice suffered at the hands of the upper castes.

Dalit assertions have been one of the most significant features of the society and polity of Punjab. In the context of Dalit politics, Punjab is an important State because it has the highest proportion of SCs in its total population. Low caste Sikhs are the only Dalits from non-Hindu religious communities listed among the SCs. Dalits in Punjab have experienced political power either through two main traditional political parties (the Congress and the SAD) or through the BSP which claims to be their representative. The BSP's core support comes from Dalits. Its vote share among them is one of the highest recorded for any large group in any State (Hasan, 2007: 20). The BSP has failed to make a significant impact in Punjab politics. In this context, the current field study of the BSP and Dalits in Doaba region of Punjab assumes greater significance. The social context of contemporary Punjab is of particular interests because of the numerical strength of SCs. In Punjab, Dalits comprise up to 42 per cent of the Doaba region, which consists the districts of Nawan Shahr, Kapurthala, Jalandhar and Hoshiarpur.

For this purpose, the book has been divided into six chapters. The first chapter explains and analyses the theology of caste system and the origin of untouchability in India. This chapter also discusses the theory of social justice and identity formation in India. The second chapter traces the history of the term "Dalit", Dalit movements. It also studies the socio-economic profile of Dalits and Dalits' politics especially in UP, Maharashtra and Tamil Nadu. Third chapter deals with the theoretical framework of the political parties, caste and political parties, emergence of Dalit political parties and the BSP and its organisation. The fourth chapter is devoted to the Dalits' movements in Punjab. This chapter explores the factors that have led to Dalits' mobility in socio-economic and religious terms in Punjab especially in the Doaba region. The fifth chapter is based on field survey and makes an attempt to look at the support base elicited by the Congress and the SAD in the Doaba region. It discusses the historical relationship between Dalits and the two main political parties, the Congress and the SAD. It focuses on the question as to why Dalits prefer to vote these political parties. The sixth chapter is also based on the field survey and investigates the dynamics of the BSP politics in Punjab. It explains the causes behind the failure of the BSP in the Doaba region. This book has a special relevance in the context of Indian democracy. It is an investigation into the question as to why the BSP has failed to make a dent in the Punjab politics despite the presence of a good number of Dalits in the State. Hence, it provides a new insight with regard to the mobilisation, organisation and political strategy of any political party in secular India State. Caste names are used in the book for academic analysis. Any offence caused by such an exercise is deeply regretted.

I shall be failing in my duty if I do not record my deep gratitude to all those who helped me in the pursuit of this work. The suggestions given by my well wishers have certainly helped me to improve this work and I feel indebted to them all. The idea of writing a book on the issue in hand was striking me for quite a long time, but the credit goes to Professor Emanual Nahar, co-ordinator in the department of Political Science, USOL, the director of Ambedkar Centre and CSSEIP and DSW, Punjab University, Chandigarh, who remained a greater source of inspiration and encouragement for me. This arduous task could not have been accomplished without his kind help, co-operation and scholarly guidance. I owe a deep debt of gratitude to Dr Kailash K. K, Department of Political Science, School of Social Sciences, University of Hyderabad, for his keen interest in this work and constructive criticism. I am also very grateful to Professor Ronki Ram, Shaheed Bhagat Singh Professor, Department of Political Science, Punjab University, Chandigarh, for his valuable thoughts and suggestions which helped me in the accomplishment of this book.

I am really thankful to the leaders of various political parties such as the BSP and its factions, the Congress and the SAD who spared their valuable time for the interviews conducted to collect the much needed information on the issue of Dalit politics in Punjab. I am also thankful to the BSP office workers and journalists who helped me in gathering information through their contacts and press clippings. I would like to express my gratitude to all the respondents from Dalit youth organisations especially Ambedkar Sena, Begampura Tiger Force, Ambedkar Force and the members of Ambedkar BAMCEF for their co-operation. I am beholden to the library staff of Punjab University, Chandigarh; Indian Council for Social Science Research (ICSSR), Panjab University, Chandigarh; Guru Nanak Dev University, Amritsar; Punjabi University, Patiala; Delhi University, Delhi; and Jawaharlal Nehru University, Delhi who assisted me to obtain the relevant reference-material.

I gratefully acknowledge the help extended to me by the faculty members of the department of Political Science, Panjab University, Chandigarh. I owe my sincere thanks and courteous gratitude to Professor P. S. Verma, Professor B. S. Brar, Professor Surinder K. Shukla, Professor Ashutosh Kumar, Professor Sanjay Chaturvedi, Professor Pampa Mukherjee, Dr Deepak Kumar, Dr Kamla and Dr Navjot Kaur for their timely help throughout the completion of this manuscript. I am also indebted to my friends Dr John Mao, Dr Balbir Kumar, Dr Sanjeev Ranjan, Vinod Kumar, Kamaldeep K. Aujla, Surender and Sanjeev Kumar in the completion of this book.

I sincerely acknowledge the great contribution of my family in the completion of this task. Indeed, all the members of my family have been a constant source of inspiration for me. I am beholden to my mother whose unflinching encouragement and blessings which worked as the guiding light for me in the darkest moments, have gone a long way in the completion of this task.

Chandigarh: February, 2018 **Dr Nirmal Singh**

List of Table

APPENDICES' TABLES

APPENDIX - I

APPENDIX - II

APPENDIX - III

APPENDIX - IV

Graph/Pie Chart

Chapter - 1

Caste and Democracy: Vision of an Egalitarian Society

The democratic experiment in India has been full of trial and error but it has survived despite some major onslaughts on its edifice. It has produced a large section of people who believe in democracy and have a strong motivation and interest in preserving it. Analysing democratic political processes in terms of caste has completely become commonplace in contemporary India. Caste communities are presented as determining electoral outcomes; and they work as pressure groups and influence the governance agenda of the Indian State at the local, regional and national level. Caste considerations also tend to structure political parties, their leadership, and programmes. The post-independence political leadership took a clear position against giving it any legitimate place in the political organisation of the new democratic nation (Kaviraj, 1997: 58-59). Articulating the then mainstream position on the subject, in his well known book *The Discovery of India,* Pandit Jawaharlal Nehru wrote in 1946: "*The caste system and much that goes with it are wholly incompatible, reactionary, restrictive, and barriers to progress. There can no equality in status and opportunity within its framework, nor there be political democracy*" (1992: 257).

The first law minister of independent India, B.R. Ambedkar, was more emphatic on Indianness. "I want all people to be Indian first, Indian last and nothing else but Indians," Ambedkar said, outlining his vision from an India where caste community and creed no longer define an individual. *'You cannot build anything on the foundation of caste. You cannot build up a nation; you cannot build up a morality; anything that you will build on the foundation of caste will crack and will never be a whole'* (Ambedkar, 2002:102). In the long run, only a democratic society can have a democratic system. India has yet to adopt a democracy 'as a way of life' only after a long and gradual process involving generation. Caste as a social institution, it is strongly entrenched and in spite of the modernisation trends in India (as a result of urbanisation, improved means of communication and development of secular education) the caste factor persists. Democracy is not a form of Government, but a form of social organisation. Ambedkar observed that "Caste system is a grave impediment in the path of democracy." The old 'Laws' of Manu have been replaced by a secular Constitution. Constitution created rights but could not eradicate caste from the hearts of citizens. Constitution abolished untouchability, the need today is to abolish the material base of the system that sustained untouchability, now spawning newer forms of discrimination and violence. Caste has psychological connotations as it gets expressed more in psychological than material terms. It manifests more in terms of the exploitative behaviour and body language adopted by one group towards the other, than in the distinctions of colour, sex and ethnicity. In order to provide fair chance to all, the Government enacted reservation policy for Backward and Deprived Castes. Reservations came as an exceptional policy for the selected social groups to overcome the exceptional social handicap obtaining in India. Dalits and tribals needed reservation because otherwise the Indian society, with its deep-drawn social prejudices, would never grant them their dues. If we wish to preserve the Constitution in which we have sought to enshrine the principle of Government of the people, for the people and by the people, let us resolve not to be tardy in the recognition of the evils that lie across our path and which induce people to prefer Government for the people to Government by the people, nor to be weak in our initiative to remove them. That is the only way to serve the country. I know of no better (Ambedkar, 2017: 9).

It was in the nature of a countervailing force of the State against the inherent discriminating attitude of the society with implicit objective of removing this societal disability within a specified time frame. But the manner in which it was formulated missed out these important premises. Politically, it was instituted as some kind of insurance for the State against the risk of leaving huge masses of the proletariat without any structural stakes in the system. Despite initial grudges against the policy, it was largely reconciled with, by people. But as the politics turned competitive, the ruling classes picked it up as a weapon to manipulate masses. Ambedkar expressed hope that the prejudice of caste would disappear. Yet the upper caste has proved him wrong. Reservation given to SCs is laid down in the Constitution. But this was despite his opposition. He was against reservation which he compared with crutches. Ambedkar realised at that time the political parties on the one hand and vested interests among Dalits particularly the creamy layer on the other would go on prolonging the reservation for electoral advantage.

It was in this context that V.P. Singh decided to implement the Mandal Commission Report in 1990, which made provision for an extension of the reservation policy. Caste question became more complex than the binary of SCs and General categories. This shift in State policy created new competition among those located in "middle" of the presumed caste hierarchy. The growth and expansion of new middle class, attendant on demographic, technological and economic changes is altering the operation of caste. The dynamics of change unleashed by neo-liberal economic policy over the past quarter of a century and growing aspirations for mobility out of village and agrarian economy among a wide range of communities has only made this competition more intense.

At another level, the Mandal Commission also fundamentally changed the discourse on caste–from being an aspect of traditional culture to an active and alive institution still shaping social and economic life. However, approaching caste as social and economic reality will also require us to recognise its dynamic character. Unlike ritual status, social and economic realities are fluid and keep changing. This opens up a new domain of State policy where communities are recognised as bearers of deprivation demanding development and inclusion, for constant tracking of which we need data. Hence, there is a demand and need for a socio-economic survey of caste communities. But what we need is a more comprehensive presentation on variations across caste communities and sub-sections within them (Jodhka, 2015: 9).

Caste politics all over India during the 1990s has been dominated by the OBCs' phenomenon; these aggregates–the OBC and India–have gradually lost their relevance, with individual *jatis* and States becoming the real units of analysis. Many of the regional parties, which now represent half of the Indian voters, are associated with a single caste and/or religious community–and this is also true of some State units of national parties. Such a development is largely due to the fact that the States themselves are often identified with a few jatis. As a result of the redrawing of the Indian map, the Marathas, for instance, became the dominant caste of Maharashtra.[1] However, in most States; there were usually two or more dominant castes. In Andhra Pradesh, Kammas and Reddys were locked in some rivalry. Similarly, in Karnataka, was the case of the Vokkaligas and the Lingayats, who opposed each other. But the two-party system constituted by the Reddy-supported the Congress and the Kamma-supported the Telugu Desam Party (TDP) was disturbed by the emergence of a newcomer in 2008, the Praja Rajyam Party, in turn supported by a caste benefiting from rapid upward social mobility, the Kapus.

The logic of exceptionality was disbanded and backwardness got associated with reservation. It opened the floodgates for infinite politicking with promises of reservations for all and sundry. Every conceivable social group today wants reservation claiming backwardness for itself. Gujarat's economically and politically Powerful patel community is demanding reservation in Government jobs and education. The Jat reservation agitation was a next series of protest in Februray 2016 by Jat people of North India, especially those in the State of Haryana. The protesters sought inclusion of their caste in the OBC category. It has shaped and continues to shape regimes of opportunities. The ground realities of caste are constantly changing and evolving. As per the Constitution and judgment of Supreme Court, the State cannot make any change in the structure of reservation for SCs, STs and OBCs, nor it can give reservation beyond 50 per cent. Various States' Government at different points of time give reservation by going against the Constitution and judgment.

State and its Will of an Egalitarian Society

In India, majority of Dalits demanded increasing intervention from the State, which they see as a more reliable option as far as their welfare is concerned. The relationship between Dalits and the State becomes one of the mere patronages and is so oppressive in the sense that Dalits tend to internalise their inferiority vis-à-vis the State. The misdoings of Dalits should be attributable to the State. Reservation is unsatisfactorily implemented, have benefited the beneficiaries in the SC and ST communities. If caste-based reservation is still existed, it is due to the failure of the Indian State to implement land reforms and give land to the landless; to provide quality education equitably to all children as per its commitment to the nation. It has dynamically divided the entire Dalit population into two categories of families: those that have availed of reservation and those that have not benefited from it so far. Affirmative action has only created a creamy layer sub-class and the benefits are still being denied to the vast, submerged poor in the Backward Classes, and the poor in all the castes. If there is no reservation, the entire argument for categorisation falls flat. The storm raised however still serves the purpose of politicians as it does in any other reservation discourse. A reservation on economic bases is understoodable but it's hard to comprehend why a well off family needs it. Unfortunately, so far, caste is an identity and pride issue rather than something being out of control. According to Andre Beteille, it is because of electoral politics and the media which keep caste alive.

The colonial State employed diverse strategies like Census, enumeration, classification, codification and documentation to reinvent and substantiate caste. Castes were the building blocks of social structure in the pre-colonial India. The caste-based enumeration was a colonial design aiming at disintegrating the unity of Indian society. Here, it is naively assumed that nation is not an imagined community and a homogeneous society existed in India before the colonial invasion. If counting caste was necessary for its perpetuation, it is equally necessary for its eradication. As Ghanshyam Shah (2012) has argued, there is no grand path to attend the objective of the annihilation of caste. The annihilation of caste calls for a systematically and impartially generated empirical data of all the castes and tribes–without justifying or glorifying them, it would be too naive to assume that the inclusion of caste as an essential criterion of Census would increase casteism. This reminds us of the popular logical fallacy that the removal of mention of caste from the caste certificate will curb casteism. The casteism has continued to haunt the Indian polity and civil society despite the fact that nearly eight decades have passed since the caste-based Census was suspended. Moreover, can we afford to assume that sex-based Census enhances gender discrimination and language as a parameter adds to linguistic strife? Media always criticises casteism in TV and conferences, but has been collecting the caste-based data in their organisation. Thus, we are in the bend: we must do away with caste system to create equalitarian society and our caste ethos and caste culture requires that we count caste to do justice to them in terms of Government jobs, reducing economic gaps and fulfilling aspiration of lower castes. Caste continues to play a contradictory role in our society both regressively and progressively. Enumeration of caste was also seen as undesirable because the modernist political and bureaucratic elite class feared that its enumeration would keep caste sentiments alive and may even strengthen.

Unlike perceptible identities like colour or race–caste is a product of self-categorisation and depends largely on people's perception of themselves. The caste-based classification is enshrined in the Constitution and has been institutionalised in the current system of reservations. If however, we are committed to a casteless society, this move will only perpetuate it. It will cement a caste-based political agenda for at least the next two decade. This opens up a new domain of State policy where communities are recognised as bearers of deprivation demanding development and inclusion. The experience of internal classification of the SC population is certainly much more than instance of competitive vote bank politics. The Government of Andhra Pradesh decided in June 1997 to classify its SC population into A, B, C and D categories and fixed a specific quota of seats against each of the caste categories. This was done in response to the powerful Dandora movement. But much before the question of "quotas within quotas" for the SCs became a controversial subject in Andhra Pradesh. The Government of Punjab had introduced two-fold classification of its SC population. The Government of Haryana too decided in 1994 to divide its SC population in two blocks, A and B.

Even conversion has not helped Dalits. They are treated in Christianity or Sikhism in the same way as in Hindu society. Sachar Committee has pointed out the inhuman treatment meted out to them when they have embraced Islam. Dalit practicing Christian faith are excluded from the SC category. In other words, the Indian State seems to be telling Dalits if they want to derive SC benefits, they should strengthen the Hindu caste order by remaining in it. It is irony that just practicing their faith of choice; Christians are excluded from all the benefits that they originally enjoyed as Dalits in a democratic and secular country. These benefits however, have not accrued to all their constituent castes tribes equitably. The Ranganath Mishra Commission Report was tabled in December 2009 in Parliament. The report recommends 10 per cent to Muslims and remaining 5 per cent to minorities. It also recommends the inclusion of Dalit Christians and Dalit Muslims in the list of SCs. At present all minorities, including the so-called Dalit Muslims and Dalit Christians, are entitled to reservation of 8.4 per cent out of the 27 per cent reservation meant for the OBCs. This percentage has been hiked and religion has been kept out of reservation for the SCs in the Report. The report has said that the SC status should be de-linked from religion and the SC net should be made "religion neutral". While exercising the right to the choice of religion, they would like to remain as Dalits and strengthen their unity.

Class relationship has been implanted on caste relationship and hence there is a kind of parallelism between the erstwhile caste order and the present-day caste-class order. The divisive prowess of castes was recognised and deftly used by the ruling classes but Dalits, whose movement appeared to echo the Ambedkar's call for annihilation of castes, have also rushed forth strangely asserting their caste identities. As we do not support poverty or economic inequality by enumerating people according to their income, and gender discrimination by enumerating them according to their sex, we do not help to increase casteism by merely counting caste. Instead, by not counting them, we will be depriving the victims of caste from assessing their own deprivation and underdevelopment. In the absence of caste as a parameter, financial income remains the only significant criterion of gauging the individual's position in society. What lies behind such a take is that it is class and not caste that is the basis of Indian backwardness.

Caste, as a system, has continued to reproduce itself through endogamy. There is hardly any change in the practice of caste endogamy, particularly in rural areas, endogamy being the core of the caste system. The main challenge before social scientists is to develop an understanding of the dynamic of caste relations, the factors that induce or prohibit change. They also need to work on developing policies to promote forces and factors that induce positive change. The commonly accepted view that inter-caste marriages are widespread in India is hardly sustainable. At present, we do not have any authentic data to substantiate such a claim. Such a belief obscures the fact that intra-caste marriages are the rule and inter-caste marriages are only the exception. In the long run, only a democratic society can have a democratic system. Today, we need a more comprehensive presentation on variations across caste communities and sub-sections within them.

Caste had entered the political arena even before independence, particularly in peninsular India. But the adoption of universal adult franchise after independence altered the charter and scope of the involvement of caste in the political process. But outside policies the consciousness of caste has been dying down, though not very rapidly or dramatically. The mobilisation of electoral support on the basis of caste is a complex phenomenon where outcome gives scope for endless speculation. It will be a pity if the State allows what goes on in the media to reinforce the consciousness of caste and to persuade us that caste is India's destiny. In dealing with the relationship between caste and politics, however, the tendency is to start at the wrong end of the question: is caste disappearing? The caste structure provides one of the most important organisational clusters in which the population is found to live, politics must strive to organise through structure. Politicians mobilise caste groupings and identities in order to organise their power. Caste itself becomes a political category, it is futile to argue as to whether caste uses politics or politics uses caste (Kothari, 1994:1589). The components itself undergoes a major organisational transformation and is subjected to new symbols of affiliation and identity. A sustained effort to change the mindset and remove the clogs of superstition can make a dent into this widely prevailing caste. But no political party is interested in doing so.

As a matter of fact, caste system came into being long after different races of India had commingled in blood and culture. To hold that distinctions of castes are really distinctions of race and to treat different castes as though they were so many different races as a gross perversion of fact. What racial affinity is there between the Brahmins of Punjab and the Brahmins of Madras? What racial difference is there between the Brahmins of Punjab and Chamars of Punjab? The Brahmin of Punjab is racially of the same stock as the Chamar of Punjab. Caste system does not demarcate racial divisions. Caste system is a social division of people of the same race (Ambedkar, 1987b: 38).

The World Conference against Racism, Racial Discrimination, Xenophobia and related intolerance (WCAR), was held in Durban, South Africa in 2001. However, it brought the issues from the close-door discussion in international bodies into public domain in India. Dalits could make use of limited space in this conference to raise the issue of discrimination based on caste. The UN treaty bodies examined the problems effecting India–including illiteracy, wretched poverty, bonded labour, child labour, religious discrimination, human rights violations, gender discrimination–without realising that caste discrimination is a major factor contributing to these problems and that the majority of people who suffer from these problems are Dalits.[2] The Government of India argues to the UN human rights bodies, including the WCAR, that caste discrimination is not an issue relevant to the evaluation of its performance vis-à-vis the human rights conventions to which it is a party. This argument is based on three main premises: (a) Caste is not race: The term 'caste' does not denote race or racial grouping and even the term 'descent' in Article 1 of the International Convention on the Elimination of all forms of Racial Discrimination (CERD) refers solely to racial descent; (b) Use of internal mechanisms, nor external ones: Numerous laws and Government schemes exist already within the country to promote the welfare, rights and socio-economic condition of the SCs; (c) Change takes time: Change is a slow process and respective countries are doing all they can to solve the problem (Paul and Ajai, 2004: 16-17). The word 'Dalit' is no more a stigmatised subject; rather it represents a genealogy of the Indian political system. Discursive mechanism through which the word 'Dalit' transcended the apparently negative connotations which might have been associated with the past, possibly in favour of a recent confrontational identity seeking to displace the terms of exclusion with radical demands for inclusion (Rao, 2009: 1).

Theology of Caste System

In the Indian society, caste is the most powerful factor in determining a person's dignity. The caste system is the result of the Hindu belief in reincarnation and Karma. The four castes eventually developed into a social mosaic of 3000 sub-castes, with the untouchables at the bottom of the list. The practice of caste system and untouchability was the corner-stone of the Hindu society. The period from 500 B.C. (the time coinciding with the rise of Buddhism) to the fourth and fifth centuries A.D. (the Gupta Age) is widely regarded by historians as the period of formation of the Indian caste system and its supporting ideology (Habib, 2000: 169). The first most intricate theoretical exposition of the Brahminical societal structuring is found in Manusmriti. By the early centuries of the Common Era, Manu had become the standard source of authority in the Hindu orthodox tradition. There is a hierarchy other than that of the pure and the impure, namely, the traditional hierarchy of the four *Varnas*. The set of the four *Varnas* divides into two: the last category, that of the Shudras, is opposed to the block of the first three, whose members are 'twice born' in the sense that they participate in initiation, second birth, and in religious life in general (Dumont, 2002: 162). Brahmins introduced an elaborate system to preserve their purity. In order to maintain purity, all relations with lower castes were prescribed. Those who opposed the Brahmin religion were branded as untouchables and thrown out of the society. The caste system cannot be said to have grown as a means of preventing the admixture of the races or as a means of maintaining purity of blood. By any standard, *Varna*, caste and untouchability made Hindu society one of the most oppressive, exploitative and less productive social system in the world.

There is a presence of Brahmins and Dalits in every geographical area in the country but we will not find the Kshatriya and Vaishya of the North in the other region. That is why Vincent Smith has argued:

> The Hindu theory that mankind is divided into four *Varnas*, or groups of castes– Brahman, Kshatriya, Vaishya and Sudra– was wholly foreign to the southerners. To this day Kshatriya and Vaishya do not exist among them (Smith and Spear, 1986: 42-43).

That means the Hindu social structure with four-fold *Varna* hierarchy as taught in classrooms is more of a North Indian Phenomenon than pan-Indian.The caste system legitimates and perpetuates hierarchy and inequality based on birth. We have a society which is highly stratified, multi-layered and multi-cultural. On the social plane, we have a society based on the principles of graded inequality which means elevation for some and degradation for others. On the economic plane, we have a society in which there are some who have immense wealth as against many who live in abject poverty. "Reason and Morality," Ambedkar wrote in his *Annihilation of Caste,* "are the two most powerful weapons in the armoury of a reformer. To deprive him of the use of these weapons is to disable him from action" (Nanda, 2016: 43).

In the existing practice, Dalits do not have the freedom of faith as given to all citizens of the country; they continue to be the SCs if they remain untouchables, impure and polluted or if they convert to Buddhism or Sikhism. Whereby four categories are distinguished, the highest is that of the Brahmins or priests, below them the Kshatriyas or warriors, then the Vaishyas, in modern usage mainly merchants and finally the Shudras, the servants or have-nots...... there is in actual fact a fifth category, the untouchables, who are left outside the classification (Dumont, 1998: 66-67). M.N. Srinivas argues that in the Rigvedic hymn *Purusukata,* the four *Varnas* formed the limbs of primeval man:— the Brahmins emerged from his mouth; the Kshatriyas from his arms; Vaishyas from his thighs and Shudras from the feet. The untouchable castes find no mention in the hymn (Karanth, 2004: 161).

M.N. Srinivas argued that the sources of *sanskritisation* could be *Varna* based on land ownership and local dominance or based on political power (Kannabira, 2009: 37). Louis Dumont attempts to construct a textually informed interpretation of caste. Dumont proposed his formulation as nothing less than a synopsis of Hindu civilisation itself, which he saw a being animated by a unique and coherent structure of core values (Bayly, 1999: 14). Within this century, those people in India formerly known as "untouchables" have protested the indignity of their social and economic condition through a variety of organised movements. The objective of Dalit movement was, obviously, to liberate the historically known untouchable classes from the most oppressive practice of untouchability observed unscrupulously by the caste-Hindus, and to bring the former on par with a socio-cultural level of the privileged classes, so that they could be brought to the national mainstream.

It is against this background that the newly exploding caste identity and consciousness needs to be viewed. Those, who should seek obliteration of the division and disparities that characterise the deeply hierarchical native of the caste system, are found to use it the most, still hoping to undermine it by undertaking basic transformation in the social order. There is no clear and well thought-out ideological framework that is relevant to undertaking these new struggles. We are nowhere near the end or even the glimpses of an end to iniquity and exploitation. But it appears from a variety of indications that the process has started and there is need to provide fresh impetus and intellectual understanding backed by political action based on new models of coalition making that cut across the wide array of deprived and oppressed social stratas and the victimised sections of society.

Caste and Democracy

The creations of caste have never simply been aspects of ritual status and religious beliefs. These have actively interacted and intersected with other aspects of social and economic realities as with the regimes of powers. The contemporary assertion of caste that has increasingly come from below, thanks to the explaining process of democratic polity, is primarily for leveling the sphere of citizenship, not for resurrecting hierarchies of caste. The caste which is the most powerful institution of the Hindus is a dead or dying institution would be an unwarranted exaggeration. Caste system is the dominating influence in her social life, the tidal wave of democracy is sweeping the political life of India. The problem which India has to face is whether caste and democracy are incompatible forces, utterly opposed to and completely destructive of each other, whether a democratic State can co-exist with a society based on caste; whether the direct effects or even the implications of democracy are not irreconcilable with caste as a social force. Caste is an institution peculiar to India. Racial, social and occupational divisions of classes exist elsewhere, but they differ fundamentally from the peculiar social structure of India. Caste is not merely a principle of social division, but a comprehensive system of life, dealing with food, marriage, education, association and worship. It is a religion rather than a changing social order. Its non-observance is met with condign punishment and the rigidity with its rules are enforced could put to shame even the Grand inquisition (Panikkar, 2007: 4).

Both in its principles and in its tendencies, democracy presents a striking contrast to caste. Before examining the differences in the ideals of the two systems, their methods and their effects on social life, it is necessary to define clearly what democracy means. It needs, perhaps, to be emphasised at the very outset that what we are concerned with here are the ideals and principles on which the democratic conception of society is based, and not the institutions, whether parliamentary, fascist or sovietic, by which different nations have tried to effects to them. The danger now in India is not the resulting from the threatened destruction of caste, but from a possible resistance to such a movement. Democracy and caste are totally opposed. One is based on equality, and the other on inequality of birth. The one is actuated by the principle of social inclusion, the other by the principle of social exclusion. Democracy tries to break down the barriers of class, caste seeks to perpetuate them. Democracy imparts universal education in order that class consciousness might vanish; caste refuses education except to the governing classes. In all matters that are of importance, caste and democracy are fundamentally opposed, they are at their very bases, incompatible.

The first postulate of democracy, therefore, is that the State represents, not symbolically, but in reality, the organised energy of the whole community–the people. Political power as well as social authority rest not in individuals, families or groups, but in the community as a whole. Democracy, then, would mean a State of society, an organisation of Government, a system of social relationship in which no single individual has inherent authority over his fellow creatures. It would be clear then that the definition of democracy as 'the Government of the People' is only partially true. It is more than that. Democracy is the realisation of the unquestionable and fundamental doctrine that man is an end in himself (*Ibid.*: 18).

However, caste turned out to be more than mere sentiments or cultural reality. It shaped social and economic life and activity intersected with new nation's political life. It was able to survive the assault of modern democracy and shape its contours. Democracy gave voice to groups and communities traditionally located on the margins of caste society through growing participation in electoral system and political mobilisation. The new political elite that emerged from these margins spoke the language of caste but articulated it differently. They foregrounded the questions of deprivation, inequalities and exclusions and asked for participation, citizenship and entitlements (Jodhka, 2015. *Op. cit.*: 9).

Democracy in India has become internal to the common people's consciousness; it is a model of society approved by the people. It has given them a space to fight for their dignity, rights, and entitlements. The right to vote, in a sense, flattens hierarchies and equalises people; it enables the unprivileged to transcend their social location; it gives them a sense of power that they never experience in social life. Democracy could not develop without the emancipation of the individual from the constraints of the community. As has been argued by some scholars, 'caste' is increasingly becoming a 'difference' rather than 'hierarchy' (Manor, 2012). As Ambedkar has argued, the caste system is not based on inequality alone, but on graded inequality (you may call it hierarchical inequality). Except the Brahmins, every caste suffers from denial of equal rights, but suffers unequally, to the extent that the entitlement or assignment of rights reduces as one moves down in caste hierarchy from Brahmin to untouchable. All, except Brahmin, lose rights, but some lose more than others. Today, legally speaking, every individual has equal rights. However, in practice different castes face denial of equal rights to different degrees in different spheres (Thorat, 2012).

Dalits and lower castes no longer accept their birth or past *karma* as a reason for their poverty and deprivation. They squarely blame upper or middle castes for their exploitation. However, the situation is complicated. Those who defy ritual hierarchy also invoke myths and symbols, and reconstruct their caste history in terms of their real or imagined upper caste status. While doing this, they invariably have in mind some other social groups that are socially and ritually 'lower' than them. On the other hand, the traditionally upper castes project their upper caste status because of their imagined ritual status. Ritual hierarchy has become almost irrelevant. Today, we talk about caste mostly in the context of assertion by 'Backward Castes' and Dalits against deprivation and social injustice. We could say that the present moment of caste denotes social identity in terms of power relationships than ritual hierarchy. Even the 'village studies' carried out by social anthropologists during the 1950s observed a great deal of variation in social ranking of local social groups and their socio-political relationship. The empirical situation was at variance from the textbook Hindu social order. It was (is) essentially power relationships, often expressed in terms of socially 'high' and 'low' status with a purity-pollution nuance (Shah, 2012. *Op. cit.*). Today, Caste is not just something in people's minds–it is not just an idea or an imagining. It concretely affects the lives of people. It can help people to gain tangible advantages, and equally, can prevent that. So it is not just 'false consciousness'. Caste as a social institution (if by 'caste' we mean jati) remains quite strong, despite the declining power of hierarchical thinking. So it continues to affect the opportunities and capabilities that people have–for good, and for ill. As we discuss change and continuity, we need to keep the materiality of caste in mind (Manor, 2012: *Op. cit.*).

The caste system has essentially always been a power relationship where besides the economic power, ascribed status, and internalised value system of high and low; continue to influence our behaviour and interpersonal relationships. However, it is not meaningless to talk about caste as a 'Hindu tradition' despite the increasing irrelevance of ritual ranking. For example, the SCs continue to suffer discrimination, open or subtle, and often become victims of violence when they violate traditional caste rules. There is a need to re-interrogate 'Hindu tradition' with reference to the caste system. If India is to become progressive and effective in this world, she has to become an organised community, with conscious purpose and high social ideals. That such a consummation is impossible, as long as the iron-grip of caste remains unshattered, on the vast majority of Indians. Since caste and democracy are opposed in ideals, contrary in method and fundamentally different in results, they cannot co-exist in any conceivable set of circumstances.

Democracy is a quite different from a Republic as well as from parliamentary Government. The roots of democracy lie not in the form of Government, Parliamentary or otherwise. A democracy is more than a form of Government. It is primarily a mode of associated living. In India, system of inequality–based on caste gives rise to inflexible deficiencies. It is not just based on economic differences. It is rigidly hereditary, life chances are based on hierarchy, where, for the governed, food entitlement is completely based on the position occupied in the specialisation within the production process. It generates gradations of ritual impurity among those who do manual work, and these hierarchies are just based on age-old (feudal) practice, but on the sacrality of sanctions from scriptures. These inherited hierarchies and inequalities defy every norm of democratic justice, even of decency. Democracy in India is, therefore, not just a case of dispersal and sharing, or mode of power. It is also a means of social and cultural recognition, and the use of power to attack those norms that stand in the way (Alam, 2012: 17). Equality in India today means struggles for inclusion, because the exclusions in India were based on multiple sources and were differently graded. Creation of equality therefore became the founding principle of democracy in India. And the quest for it remains, in diverse ways, the driving force in the survival of democracy.

Caste and Untouchability

Dalits are those who are traditionally known as the Chandalas, the untouchables. According to the *Manusmriti*, they are the offspring of the union of Brahmin female and Shudra male. They are the most deprived section. Their interaction with other caste groups was prohibited. Manu declares the Chandalas and others like them to be worthy of being settled outside the town limits. The Brahmin is the Lord of all *Varnas* because of his superiority of birth and observation of rituals and sacraments (Michael, 1999: 64). The ideas of purity, whether occupational or ceremonial, are found to have been a factor in the genesis of caste, are at the very soul of the idea and practice of untouchability. G.S. Ghurye has remarked six classical features of Indian caste system, viz. segmental division of society based on birth, a definite scheme of social hierarchy, restriction of feeding and social intercourse, civil and religion disabilities, lack of unrestricted choice of occupation and restriction on marriages (Ghurye, 1979: 38).

On the social plane, Ambedkar launched several struggles to counteract the unequal treatment meted out to untouchables by caste

Hindu. He was against the Hindu caste structure as he felt that this structure has been primarily responsible for committing all sorts of atrocities on various sections of the society, particularly the SCs and STs. He studied the Hindu social order. He knew that Hindu as a way of life is based on high ideals of non-violence, tolerance. But the gap between theoretical views and practical life in Hindu society was the main cause of its weakness. The Hindus were never a society as an organised system of individuals with a common purpose. There were always a system of castes with different rights and purposes. According to him, *Hindu society as such does not exist. It is a collection of castes, each caste is conscious of its existence.* The most unfortunate characteristic of Hindu society was that classes developed into castes and Hindu society gave sanction to the division of labour and such type of society did not recognise the individual as a centre of social purpose. This society is based on birth, occupation, caste, class and with sanction of religion. Hindu religion treats some people as untouchable and denies them equal rights in society. Ambedkar said that *Manusmriti* is responsible to create a division in society. He also expressed that: "*Manusmriti* gives a blank cheque to the Brahmin to commit all sorts of atrocities on Dalits".

Division was created between touchable and untouchable. Untouchables were given only duties with no rights. The higher castes in Hindu society enjoyed all rights and privileges. Ambedkar was of the opinion that Hindu society failed to unite and it was unfortunate that religion was a rock on which Hindus built their houses. The Hindu will never give up untouchability because for him it is a gold mine. Isolation and exclusion of untouchables is a unique feature of Hindu Social Order. One of the reasons that caste has excited sociology imagination because it is seen as a representation of pure status, based on religious and ideological grounds with class inequalities. The two aspects of caste inequalities which deserve our attention are (a) inequality of opportunity and inequality of outcome. However, caste-based inequalities are not simply limited to inequality of opportunity. It has also been argued that even highly qualified members of lower caste face social and economic discrimination resulting in inequality of outcomes.

The principle of graded inequality has been carried into the economic field. "From each according to his ability, to each according his need" is not the principle of the Hindu social order. The principle of the Hindu social order is: From each according to his need to each according to his nobility (The illustrations given above are merely drawn from imagination). They are facts of the history. Through *sanskritisation* movement, a section of untouchables could improve their economic condition, either by abandoning or continuing their traditional occupations. A low caste was able, in a generation or two, to rise to a higher position in the hierarchy by adopting vegetarianism or teetotalism, and by Sanskritising its rituals and pantheon (Srinivas, 1972: 32). They tried to justify their claims to a higher social status in caste hierarchy by inventing suitable mythologies.

Indian sociologists have used the suggestive terminology like 'untouchables', 'lower castes', Harijans, etc. for Dalits, these terms coined by intellectuals and the elites of society, are not objective categories. The objective situation is that Dalits were/are known either by their regional names or by a term equivalent to 'untouchables'. The emerging Dalit identity has been compelling the social scientists for an in-depth analysis of various issues that go to constitute Dalit identity. But the main line social scientists had concentrated their effort to examine caste as a social reality, kinship and village as sociological category to comprehend the Indian social reality. For centuries untouchability was being practiced in the Hindu society. The main causes were the observation of the Brahmins to maintain purity and to avoid pollution. Endogamy is the essence of the caste system.

The term 'Scheduled Caste' is an administrative coinage and terms such as 'Chandala[3], exterior caste Harijan, purity in order to maintain Dalit[4], etc. have been in currency, each of which had a different origin. The breed of the Chandala is a degraded one and is ranked with that of dog and pig. The contention here is that the Hindu doctrine of creation refers only to four *Varnas* and if so, how does one court of Panchamas, those of the fifth? The fact that even Gandhi was not prepared to support Ambedkar's fight against untouchability is a reflection of his deep attachment to a form of social organicism (Jaffrelot, 2017: 10). Gandhi adopted the use of the term "*Harijan*" in place of 'untouchable'. He insisted that caste (*Varna*) system was essential to Harizans. Ghurye divided untouchables into two: 'pure' and 'impure'. The untouchables become pure through abjuring 'beef and such other anathematic diet, this is precisely what M.S. Srinivas christened as *sanskritisation*[5]. However, *sanskritisation* is scarcely functional for achieving higher ritual status for the untouchables (Oommen, 2008: 60-81). It is tribute to the subtle dynamics of Hindu society that in spite of this psychological cost, the adjustments of *sanskritisation* go on all the time; and one of the many reasons is that the structural distance that is sought to be jumped can often be related to the achievement of other indices of power and position in the modernist segments of society (as perceived both by the striving group as well as by a majority of the other groups) (Kothari, 2008: 13).

Caste System and Social Justice in India

Caste is, undoubtedly, an all-India phenomenon in the sense that they are hereditary, endogamous groups which form a hierarchy, and that each of these groups has a traditional association with one or two occupations. In 1935, at Yeola in Nashik district of Maharashtra, B.R. Ambedkar had declared his firm resolve to change his religion. He said that "To reform the Hindu society is neither our aim nor our field of action. Our aim is to gain freedom. We have nothing to do with anything else". The struggle for the emancipation of the Depressed Classes from the thralldom of untouchability and casteism has been in continuation for a pretty long time. However, Dalit liberation movement got an impetus during the British period. With the dawn of democratic institution in India, Dalit liberation movement steadily became more vocal, assertive and effective. Mahatma Jyotirao Phule could properly realise the importance of education in improving the lot of the untouchables and BCs. He stated very categorically that "for want of education intellect deteriorated; for want of intellect morality decayed; for want of morality progress slopped; for want of progress wealth vanished; for want of wealth the Shudras perished. All these sorrows sprang from illiteracy (Phule, 1980: 189).

Phule strongly attacked the exploitation of peasants by the bureaucracy. Ambedkar and Periyar both supported and helped the organised movements of peasants against landlords. The denial of temple entry to Dalits by status quo and conservative caste Hindu is seen as a part of the social oppression that is still intertwined with class oppression as most of Dalits are poor farm workers. Dalits have been denied entry into temples. Ambedkar's scathing comment on

Hindu scripture culminated in a public burning of *Manusmriti* in 1927 and in 1935. Ambedkar announced his vow to leave Hinduism entirely and to convert to some other religion. Mehar Satyagraha and Kalaram Satyagraha were also an attempt to gain entry in the temples. The main figures of this larger anti-caste movement, Jyotirao Phule, B.R. Ambedkar, and E.V. Ramaswami 'Periyar' with many others throughout India attacked the system of exploitation at all levels, culturally, economically and politically. They asserted that Hinduism had not been the religion and culture of the majority but rather it was an imposed religion. Phule tried to formulate a new theistic religion, Periyar promoted atheism, Ambedkar turned to Buddhism.

Through conversion movement, Dalits offered a new alternative religion, Buddhism, in negation of Hindusim. It started with Ambedkar's personal conversion announcement in 1935 which was followed by a Mahar conference in 1936 where Ambedkar declared, if you want to make the world in which you live, happy, change your religion; if you want independence, change your religion. The conversion movements made an immense appeal to Dalits, though its benefits are mostly limited to mental relax but other size impact is remarkable (Ambedkar, 1987 b. *Op. cit.*: 192). If Dalit question could be answered by religion, i.e., if the problem is somehow the bane of Hinduism alone, non-Hindu religion should have solved the problem a long time ago. What is the condition of Dalits, for example, in a State like Punjab where Sikhism, as egalitarian and non-Hindu religion has had to sway for three centuries? The charge is equally placed at the doorstep of Christianity. Ambedkar asked that: Can a leopard change its spots? No, Never. "Hinduism is like the leopard there can be no "Hindu" without a caste...... untouchability is a part and parcel of Hinduism. If you become a Muslim, you will get the political rights as Muslims; if you become a Christian, you will get the political rights as Christians; if you become a Sikh, you will have your political safeguards as Sikhs. In short, our political rights will accompany us. Ambedkar had famously declared that the untouchables had two enemies: Brahminism and capitalism.

Ambedkar's first political party, the Independent Labour Party (ILP), was fashioned on the lines of the British Labour Party, which followed the Fabian line of peaceful transition to socialism but abhorred capitalism. Ambedkar's ILP was then the true leftist party of India, with the communities then going the Congress party. Moreover, the Communist Party of India (CPI) had borrowed its method of class analysis from the Comintern, which left caste, the pervasive reality of Indian life, out of the realm of investigation. The ILP, on the other hand, demonstrated in practice how to embed caste and class in the struggle for social justice.

Gandhi's solicitous attitude towards the upper castes is revealed time and again. Untouchables were not allowed to enter the temple until 1936. Travancore became one of the places to enact a law opening its State temple to untouchables. At the time of the Yeravada fast Gandhi asked Kelappan to call off his fast for opening up the Guruvayar Temple in Malabar on the specious ground that not enough notice had been given. Gandhi frequently contained that "there should not be coercion. We must, by patient toil and self-suffering, convert the ignorant and superstitious but never seek to compel them by force". At this time, Ambedkar spoke against conversion to another religion as a means of removing disabilities, and he stressed self-improvement, unity, and organisation as the paths to a better life for the untouchables. He used the Vaikam Satyagrah with its high caste participants as an example, not of caste Hindu sympathies, but of the political importance of the untouchables.

Although Ambedkar did not completely reject Gandhi's support until their political battle over Depressed Class political rights in 1931, two remarks in the 1925 address portend his later action. Ambedkar's complaint that Gandhi had not required an oath of disbelief in untouchability as a precondition for membership in the Congress later turned to a wholesale condemnation of the Congress resolutions on the subject as hypocrisy.

At the 1930 Round Table Conference, Ambedkar explained why the untouchables needed a Swaraj Government. As per Ambedkar's proposal put before the Round Table Conference in 1931 and again in 1932, separate electorate means a territorial constituency comprising exclusively of untouchables only in which they alone will vote for their hand-picked candidates. Gandhi's real objection to separate seats for the Depressed Classes was not that it gave too little to the Depressed

Classes but it would "destroy Hinduism", as Gandhi stated in his letter to Ramsay MacDonald before beginning the Yeravada fast.

At the Second Round Table Conference, Ambedkar confronted Gandhi, who not only refused to consider separate electorates for the Depressed Classes but also opposed any form of social representation involving reserved seats. After the Third Round Table Conference, during which Gandhi was in jail, the British Government announced a decision regarding representation which it was hoped would affect a compromise between the Congress and Ambedkar. Communal Award of 1932 gave the Depressed Classes a double vote, one in special constituency for a modest number of reserved seats, and one in a special electorate. Gandhi's response to the Communal Award was to enter a "fast unto death" on 20 September, 1932.

The British Government's response to Gandhi's fast was to declare that a solution to the representation of the Depressed Classes had to be settled within the Hindu community. Consequently, the man whose leadership of the Depressed Classes was challenged by Gandhi in London became the arbiter of Gandhi's fate. The struggle between Gandhi and Ambedkar, a struggle in which Gandhi used a fast unto death pressurised Ambedkar into accepting his terms. This fast unto death, it should be remembered, was not against the British, the enemy, but against a component of the national struggle, the fledging Dalit movement led by Ambedkar. Ambedkar succumbed under this pressure. Perhaps it was the effect not so much of the moral pressure as much as of the real threat that, were Gandhi to die for the cause of Hindu unity, Dalit would be attacked by upper caste Hindu in innumerable places. This patient toil and self-suffering in the struggle against untouchability did not include a fast unto death, weapon he was willing to wield against Ambedkar and the demand for separate electorates for the untouchables, but not against the upper castes to demand an end to untouchability. No wonder Ambedkar was compelled to ask, "Why did he not undertake a fast unto death against untouchability? Kancha Ilaiah writes, "The fundamental difference between Ambedkar and Gandhi lies in positioning themselves from their own communities." He adds further that "Ambedkar was not only born in an untouchable Mahar family but all through his life stood for the suppressed, oppressed and exploited masses. Gandhi on the other hand, was born in a Baniya family and stood for the oppressor and exploiting upper castes" (Ilaiah, 2001: 126).

Prime Minister Ramsay MacDonald, in a letter dated September 6, 1932 tried his best to assure Gandhi and through him the Hindus that this Award would not take away the untouchables from Hinduism. In all general constituencies, he said the untouchables will vote with Hindu electorate on equal footing. Ambedkar submitted a memorandum on behalf of the "Bahiskrit Hitakarini Sabha" which argued for an untouchable seat quota rather than for separate electorates. It demanded 22 seats in the 140 seats of Bombay Assembly and for the electoral franchise to be extended to all untouchables (Ambedkar, 1987b. *Op. cit.*: 338). "Poona Pact" has converted the untouchable's representation in Parliament and State Legislature into careerist. The term *"Harijan"* (untouchable) is a part of Hindu society. Besides, they have been the obedient and free servants and slaves of the Hindus. "Poona Pact" did give more seats to the untouchables. But what is the use of these additional seats? Those elected under reserved seats will be mostly slaves. The Communal Award was intended to free the untouchables from the thralldom of the Hindus. Politically, untouchability would weaken the numerical strength of the Hindus by forcing the untouchables to break their connections with Hinduism. Ambedkar made it clear that if universal suffrage were not granted, he would campaign for separate electorates (Jaffrelot, 2005: 55).

Some of Dalit writers with a Marxist orientation, who addressed themselves to the cause of wider category of Dalits, including industrial workers, landless labourers, etc. argued that Ambedkar was not only against casteism but also against capitalism. Dalit literature is sometimes called "Samantar Sahitya" in order to identify it closely with international communist literature. And also limiting the movement to Neo-Buddhists would have defeated on the principle of equality and justice. Thus, this type of literature is concerned with both those who are socially Dalit and economically Dalit. The other group refutes this by saying that all those who are economically Dalits necessarily socially Dalits. But those who are socially Dalits are invariably the victims of economic inequality.

Ambedkar argued that political democracy cannot last unless there lies at the base of it social democracy; we must begin by acknowledging the fact that there is a complete absence of two things in Indian society. Social justice as a form of justice means what is socially just; and what is socially just varies with time and space. The term 'justice' has a very vast canvass; and it is very difficult to give a very precise but comprehensive definition. Traditionally, justice means "the virtue by which we give to every man what is his due, opposed to injury or wrong". Plato defined social justice as, "the principle of a society consisting of different types of men... who have combined the impulse of their need for one another and their concentration on their combination in one society and their concentration on their separate functions, have made a whole which is perfect because it is the product of image of the whole of the human mind. Justice is bond which holds a society together, a harmonious union of individual each of whom has found his life work in accordance his natural fitness and his training. This is Plato's elaboration of prima facie definition of justice as "giving to every man his due." For what is due to him is that he should be treated as what he is in the light of his capacity and his training, while what is due from him is the honest performance of these tasks which the place accorded him requires (Sabine, 1975: 64-65).

John Rawls (1971: 65-66) believed that his theory of justice is an improvement over utilitarian accounts of justice as maximum welfare. He developed the following principles of justice: (a) each person is to have an equal right to most extensive basic liberty compatible with similar liberty for others, (b) social and economic inequities are arbitrary unless they are reasonably expected to be the advantage of the representative man in each income class, (c) inequalities are to attach to positions and offices equally open to all. Rawls interprets the system of natural liberty, liberal equality, and democratic equality. Similarly, taking a leaf from Rawls' theory of social justice, the fundamental issue in distributive justice is equality; a more equal or at least a less unequal distribution of the benefits and of social co-operation. In India, division was created between touchable and untouchable.

Plato and Rawls' concept of social justice would mean giving every man his due. The basic aim of social justice is to remove the imbalances in the social, political and economic life of the people to create a just society. In terms of culture-specificity, the term social justice has a different meaning in Indian society. It means dispensing justice to those to whom it has been systematically denied in the past because of an established social structure. Ambedkar's quest for social justice can be visualised in the philosophy, policy and ideals of the Constitution of India. It is a fact that Ambedkar did not propound any specific definition or theory of social justice. His thoughts are eloquently portrayed in his writings and speeches published posthumously. On the basis of these, it can easily be argued that Ambedkar has mentioned multiple principles for the establishment of an open and just social order in general and Indian society in particular. Ambedkar was of the opinion that social justice can be dispensed in a free social order in which an individual is end in itself. Similarly, the term of associated life between members of society must be regarded by consideration founded on liberty, equality and fraternity. In a way, these principles of social justice are similar to those of social justice as mentioned in Rawls' theory.

Ambedkar's philosophy of Hinduism analyses the worth of Hinduism "as a way of life" and summarily trashes it as antithetical to Liberty, equality, fraternity and on both, justice as well as unity. This has to be for every individual and that social justice can be delivered to the members of society only if the society is based on these principles. However, one can argue that this can happen only when there is fraternity in society. In this context, let us see what Ambedkar says. According to him, "Ideal would be a society based on liberty, equality and fraternity…" After India's independence for dispensing social justice in the wake of emerging democracy in a hierarchically arranged society, Ambedkar discussed the operationalisation of principles of equality, liberty and fraternity, which were considered to be cardinal principles of any democracy. For social justice, he tried to find a creative combination of democracy and modernity. He looked at democracy as an initial condition or the sphere which could be used for converting opportunity into an asset. For him, conversion could be achieved only through modernity. Ambedkar tends to treat democracy as an initial condition of social justice both as consciousness and also as a material possibility. He does not take the position that social backwardness or historical discrimination is the final conditions within a claim to social justice can be established without moral justification. For Ambedkar, moral justification needs to be internal to social justice implicating the most marginalised section of society. Moral justification is internal to the *Bahujan* or orthodox concept of social justice, as the most marginalised cannot afford to either rubbish or trivialise such institutions; claims meet just the partial conditions when understood from the point of view of subaltern universe of justice.

The tragic part was that the Mahomedans, Parsis and Christians shunned and avoided the untouchables as well as the Hindus. Ambedkar acknowledged that the caste system was not universally absolute in his time; it was true, he wrote that some untouchables had risen in Indian society above their usually low status, but the majority had limited mobility, or none, during Britain's colonial rule. According to Ambedkar, the caste system was irrational. Ambedkar listed these evils of the caste system: it isolated people, infused a sense of inferiority into lower-caste individuals, and divided humanity. The caste system was not merely a social problem, he argued: it traumatised India's people, its economy, and the discourse between its people, preventing India from developing and sharing knowledge, and wrecking its ability to create and enjoy the fruits of freedom. The philosophy supporting the social stratification system in India had discouraged critical thinking and cooperative effort, encouraging instead treatises that were full of absurd conceits, quaint fancies, and chaotic speculations. The lack of social mobility, notes Ambedkar, had prevented India from developing technology which can aid man in his effort to make a bare living, and a life better than that of the brute. Ambedkar stated that the resultant absence of scientific and technical progress, combined with all the transcendentalism and submission to one's fate, perpetrated famines, desolated the land, and degraded the consciousness from respecting the civic rights of every fellow human being.

Ambedkar began investing the origin of the caste system more than a decade before Govind Sadashiv Ghurye–the first Indian anthropologist to do so. Yet his contribution was overlooked for many years, Oliver Herrenschmidt emphasises as a prelude to his own efforts to redress this imbalance. The core of Ambedkar political strategy remained constant: Brahmins and Capitalism were the main enemies. Dalits, as the super-oppressed and exploited, must maintain their autonomy. It was Ambedkar who felt for the untouchables to come forward and play a pioneering role in the eradication of caste destruction of the Brahminical system. The process of change was to involve a rejection of slavery by the slave, social struggles and political movements. The Indian anthropologists such as M. N. Srinivas and Louis Dumont have ignored Ambedkar, even though he anticipated many of their arguments.

Ambedkar insisted against Gandhi, that a partial attack on untouchability would not do and that it was the caste system as such which needed to be overthrown. He proposed that Hindu society needed to reorganise on the basis of the principles of "Liberty, Equality and Fraternity"; that for this the sense of religious sanctity behind caste and *"Varna"* must be destroyed only by discarding the divine authority of the Shastras (Ambedkar, 1987b. *Op. cit.*: 86). Ambedkar said that there can be no "Hindu" without a caste. "Hinduism", said Dr Ambedkar "is the other name for caste system which is the bed-rock on which Hinduism is built. Untouchabilility is a part and parcel of Hinduism". As long as caste system exists, untouchability will not go. All these Hindu reformers are complaining only of untouchability but have no programme to abolish caste. Dalits should know that the Constitution of India had gone much forward than what the State system is trying to do (Ambedkar, 1987a: 14).

According to Ambedkar, caste is religion and religion is anything but an institution. It may be institutionalised by it is not the same as the institution in which it is embedded. Religion is an influence or force suffused through the life of each individual moulding his character determining his actions and reactions, his likes and dislikes. These likes and dislikes, actions and reactions are not institution, which can be lopped off. They are forces and influences, which can be dealt with by counteraction or controlling them. If social forces are to be prevented from contaminating politics and perverting it to the aggrandisement of the few and the degradation of the many then it follows that it will contain mechanism, which will bottle the prejudices and nullity and injustice, which the social forces are likely to cause if they were let loose.

Ambedkar described the untouchables as belonging to the same religion and culture, yet shunned and ostracised by the community they lived in. The untouchables, observed Ambedkar, recognised the sacred as well as the secular laws of India, but they derived no benefit from this. They lived on the outskirts of a village. Segregated from the rest, bound down to a code of behaviour, they lived a life appropriate to a servile State. According to the code, an untouchable could not do anything that raised him or her above his or her appointed station in life. The caste system stamped an individual as untouchable from birth. Thereafter, observed Ambedkar, his social status was fixed, and his economic condition was permanently set.

Ambedkar's notion of social justice is based on equal rights and human dignity through legal framework. As the result of his thought, Indian Constitution guarantees equal rights to all. He was the first person to demand separate electorates and reservation system in favour of Dalits in Round Table Conferences. Ambedkar realised that affirmative action is the only way to improvement of Dalit communities which safeguard through legal institutions. Ambedkar did not encourage the aspiration of caste system within India as it generates inhuman practice among the communities. Ambedkar believed that economically Dalits are very poor. They lack access to political, social and economic power. Ambedkar did consider Dalit representation into mainstream political arena which generated Dalit movement in various Indian States for freedom and justice. He also believed that law is an important powerful weapon to fight against discrimination.

The relevant provisions in the Constitution of India for the upliftment and welfare of Depressed Classes are included under the Articles (12, 13,14,15,16, 17, 23, 25, 29, 35, 38, 41,124, 164, 244A, 275, 330, 332, 335, 337, 338, 342, 371, 371A, 371B, 371C). These are aimed at preventing discrimination and promoting social justice. The Fundamental Rights guarantee equality before the law and equal protection of law (Article 14), prohibition of discrimination on the grounds of religion, race, caste, sex or place of birth (Article 15). Though untouchability has been abolished under Article 17 of the Constitution, yet it continues to prevail in different forms. SCs and STs are treated like animals with no human rights and as worse than slaves. The preamble to the Constitution outlines the objectives to be achieved, and indicates basic guiding principles as foundation of Constitution. The constitutional commitment of the creation of a classless society by promoting equality and human dignity is sheltered by the rampant practice of untouchability and of bonded labour system.

Ambedkar believed in the political process and was only anxious that the Depressed Classes' share in it according to their number and needs (Zelliot, 1992: 97). Ambedkar did not waver in his belief. Through a sustained process of political mobilisation on the one hand and hard political bargaining on the other, he is in fact succeeding in establishing the SCs as to politically relevant category, to themselves and to others. In political terms, he brought them from invisibility to visibility, from silence to articulate to protest.

The Indian State need to be reformed and reinvented is manifestly clear. The question is: do we have the State which can finally redeem the pledges made by the framers of the Constitution which can make India, in Ambedkar terms, a social democracy rather than a mere political democracy? There are many benefits that accrue to particular castes based on their treatment by the State. Reservation programmes in India provide benefits based on caste identity. These have the effect of exaggerating the difference between a favoured and an unfavoured caste, though they may be economically the same. It is trivial that data collected from the Census will form the basis for formulation and modification of existing State policy relating to caste-based programmes. Absence of a corresponding threat of a sanction and given the huge institutional advantage in distorting the Census figures, there is a big incentive to cheat. Official classification does not merely reflect social identities but has a role in transforming them. A process of categorisation necessitates a definition. It also entails order and rigidity. Individuals find themselves firmly fixed as members in various groups of a particular dimension and substance–as defined by the State.

Need for Restructuring the Indian Society

"The Dalit question" and "the caste question" are not identical. While the former deals with the aspiration, assertion, mobility and emancipation of Dalit community, the latter deals with the domination, discrimination, exclusion, humiliation and violence that are embedded in the caste system as perpetuated by the Hindu social order. Ambedkar was never satisfied with the prevailing Hindu social system. Therefore, he felt a need of restructuring the Indian society. He expressed: *They took birth as untouchables, they lived as untouchables and they died as untouchables.* In 1913, Ambedkar got an opportunity to go to USA for higher education. He was the first from the community of Mahar to study in a foreign university. At Columbia University, USA he explored as widely as possible the economic and social aspects of American development. It is not surprising that a person deeply affected by the social and economic system. He tried to understand the ways in which social and economic system functions. The place where he explored the principles of social service is not common. It was in Columbia University, almost literally under the shadow of the statue of liberty. He enlarged his mental vision and horizon. Against the background of bitter experience of humiliation due to untouchability, the exposure to Western values and ways of life was a wonderful and moving experience for Ambedkar. Then he determined to diagnose the ills of Indian society. The academic degree not only enriched him in ideas but also made him conscious of his social obligations towards Dalit community, and he organised Dalits and founded the *Bahiskrit Hitkaraini Sabha* (outcaste's welfare association). The aim of the Sabha was to uplift the downtrodden people socially and politically.

In 1918, the first All-India Depressed Classes Conference was held at Bombay. In it, Ambedkar along with others raised his voice for social reforms to uplift the Depressed Classes. He stressed the need for a separate electorate system. This demand irritated the Hindus as well as the Congress party. But he got immense response from the untouchable community. In 1920, he started a fortnightly paper titled, "*Mook Nayak*". He wrote on inequality and discrimination. According to him, the backwardness of non-Brahamins was due to lack of education and power. He was nominated a member of Legislative Council in 1927 and made a speech on *Jahgirdari* or *Inamdri* System in India. On 2 March 1930, Dr Ambedkar started temple entry movement at Kalaram Temple in Nashik. The agitation continued up to the end of October 1935. Dr Amebdkar declared a revolutionary statement: *"I solemnly assure you that I will not die a Hindu"*. Since Ambedkar himself had experienced most of the ignominies and socio-religious disabilities, he internalised fully the multiple deprivation and disabilities of Dalits as a whole (Ram, 1995: 89). In so far as the legacy of Ambedkar is concerned, it was two-fold: Buddhism and Republican Party of India (RPI). Omvedt (1994: 149) notes: "two institutions that Ambedkar saw necessary for the liberation of Dalits and the welfare of country, Buddhism and RPI, a spiritual force and a platform". Ambedkar was also at the forefront of political parties whose aim was to organise the most deprived sections of society and to influence the process. He wavered between efforts to widen his social base to all workers: as manifested in the ILP in 1937 and a desire to focus only on Dalits, as borne out by the Scheduled Castes' Federation of India (Jaffrelot, 2005. *Op. cit.*: 55). Ambedkar rejected the 'left bloc' forming within the Congress party during 1930s under Nehru's leadership just as strongly as he rejected Gandhism. He accused Indian socialists of being unfaithful to their ideals due to their upper caste base; he warned that no socialist movement in India could ignore this issue. The fact was that the Nehruvite left was even more reluctant to give attention to caste than Gandhi was, the mass of youth who thronged the Congress campaign at the time were still very largely high caste, and the notion of Dalit or low caste empowerment, which was so central to their movement for liberation, did not even have a hearing (Omvedt, 1994. *Op. cit.*: 252).

The independent Labour Party won 15 seats in the 1937 election to the Central Legislative Assembly. The party focused on the needs and grievances of the landless poor, tenants and workers. Being a member of Assembly, he introduced a number of Bills like *"A Bill to Abolish Khoti System, Mahar Vatan"*. He was the first legislator in India to introduce a bill for the abolition of the Serfdom of agricultural tenants. In 1942, he founded All India Scheduled Castes' Federation (AISCF). The organisation was representing Dalit classes. He attempted to explain the formation of the Shudras, i.e., the lowest caste in hierarchy of Hindu caste system.

Dr Ambedkar contributed a lot towards the nation. The Indian Constitution drafted by him is the first and foremost social document. Majority of India's constitutional provisions either directly further the aim of revolution or attempt to faster this revolution by establishing conditions necessary for its achievement. The text prepared by him provided constitutional guarantees and protections for a wide range of civil liberties for individual citizens. One of the greatest contributions of Ambedkar was in respect of Fundamental Rights and Directive Principles of State Policy enshrined in the Constitution of India. The primary instrument for ensuring political participation of Dalits in Part IV of the Constitution provides them reservation. Directive Principles of State Policy also categorically express the idea of social justice by introducing economic democracy. He believed that political democracy and economic democracy lie at the base of social democracy. He also emphasised the idea of including specific economic rights like right to work, right to adequate wages and better standard of living in the best of fundamental rights. However, he could not incorporate his total vision of economic structure. The Directive Principles are designed to secure social justice. Article 39(A) has been introduced to impart free legal aid to the poorer sections of society and with no fees from SCs and STs, irrespective of their income. A very few advocates are prepared to accept the nominal fees to be paid by the Government for pleading their cases.

The Constitution recognised the evil of caste and provided for affirmative action with a view to ultimately eliminate it from our social structure but unfortunately, it remains stronger even today. These have only created a creamy layer and subclass and benefits are still being denied to the vast submerged poor in the Backward Classes and poor in all castes. Dalit is now a widely used category in social science as well as in popular discourse. Politicians use the category in an undifferentiated manner on account of their vested interest. Casteism in politics is politicisation of caste, which in turn, leads to a transformation of the caste system. Dalits are equally entrenched and a victim of the ideology of caste system, their own acceptance of caste system prevents them from articulating an alternative ideology. Dalits also practice the principle of exclusion of relation to each other. As the Ad-Dharm movement in Punjab had to project Dalits as a separate *quam* out of *Varna* system. Some castes within the SCs in Punjab have progressed more than the others. They try to keep a distance from the search for a different cultural space to overcome humiliation is reflected in their large-scale movement towards *deras*, which have become a centre of their separate culture (Ram, 2010: 236-239).

The Constitutional Order 1950, paragraph 3, unfortunately defined a SC in terms of religion and not in terms of social and educational backwardness. Dalits practicing Christian faith are excluded from the SC category. If we look at the living conditions of all Dalit Christians, there is no difference in their economic or social condition than other Dalits. Those Dalits, who profess Christianity or

Islam, should also be treated as Dalit with full of benefits that come under SC category.

Recent studies on emerging Dalit identities show that a new identity is rising, one that determines that Dalits will not acquiesce for ever with their subordinate position. Today, the subaltern communities that have been discriminated against for centuries identify themselves as Dalits. They find a new identity by coming together with the perspective 'Dalit is dignified' thereby rejecting the sub-human status imposed on them by the Hindu social order, (Bharati, 2002: 4339). In more recent years, it has become a nation-wide phenomenon and is widely used by all untouchables irrespective of tradition and parochial caste distinctions, also becoming a symbol of their identity. Dalits' disappointment with the Indian State on which they had relied so much for ending their State of oppression and discrimination–and still do–the poorer and socially marginalised sections including the ethnic and religious minorities, have started seeking out their own futures on the basis of their identities and numbers. This has led to the mobilisation based on caste, sub-caste, tribe ethno-regional identities.

In this upsurge, the struggle for social justice is found beyond the logic of class or of socialism, and thus, also constitutes a major challenge to both the politics of left and politics of what are known as the new social movements. It is against this growing irrelevance of various grass root movements that the new Dalit movement in India is emerging or seems like emerging. Dalit consciousness is by no means limited to the SCs. It has begun to symbolise a much broader spectre of the oppressed and hitherto excluded social strata. It is based on an attempted though by no means still realised solidarity of the poor and the discriminated classes of the people, long held back and frustrated its leadership divided and brought over, distanced from the masses and co-opted within the mainstream and in establishment structure and positions. It may be time to look for new models of social stratification in India. One possibility would be to argue that caste relations, just as the Western sociological literature has argued that industrialisation was associated with a movement from hereditary privilege associated with the concept of estate held by nobility to an open society in which the bourgeoisie could gain status through their achievements in the marketplace.

Caste system prevalent from ages till today is a major example of social evils that hinders the revolution of any society or country but also degrades it totally. Moreover, the brutal caste laws practiced till today by higher caste people not only make the life of the lower caste people hell but also sow the seeds of hatred, enmity and distrust in each other's heart. Hence, makes it hard for the society to march on the path of progress and overall development. Brahmins are descendent of Aryans; came to India as conquerors; subjugated the aborigines of India and with their power they supported the original inhabitants and gave to them the term "Shudras". Utilising their powers they laid out various rules and regulations based on caste, creed and colour. According to these baseless laws, the Shudras cannot go to temples; they cannot sit with the Brahmins, etc. These laws are being practiced even today. In order to provide fair chance to all, the Government enacted reservation policy for Backward and Deprived Castes. Ghanshyam Shah (2001: 396) examines the politics of reservation. Reservation is one of the methods of State to provide a helping hand to those who have been traditionally deprived in the caste structure thesis but it is not enough; it has to be accompanied with the support of other socio-economic forces. Reservations are now being treated as a panacea for the problem of backwardness of the people.

Caste is now established as perhaps the most important identity for securing State benefits. Further amends to existing systems are very likely to be based on the data collected through the Census (and if not, then this dilutes the argument for carrying out this exercise in the first place). There is a perverse incentive for groups to en masse misreport their social and economic status in a way which would further enhance their own interests.[6] The question on Caste, Tribe or Race was asked from each individual right from 1872, though the type of information collected was different in different Censuses. In 1881, caste if Hindu sect; if of other religion, were recorded. In 1891 main caste and sub-division of caste or race was recorded. In 1901 and 1911 Censuses, the caste of Hindus and Jains; tribe or race of those of other religions were recorded. In 1921, 1931 and 1941 Censuses, caste, tribe or race of all the individuals enumerated was recorded. In the 1931 Census, tabulation of figures for individual castes was limited to: (i) Exterior castes; (ii) Primitive castes; and (iii) All other castes with the exception of: (a) those whose members fell short of four per thousand of the total population; and (b) those for which separate figures were deemed to be unnecessary by the local Government. The 1941 Census, the last to be conducted by the British, was constrained by the War-time economies, and did not tabulate any data except the basic population totals and community totals. Pursuant to the policy of Government of India is to discourage community distinction based on caste, the 1951 Census marked a complete departure from the traditional recording of Race, Tribe or Caste and the only relevant question on caste or tribe incorporated in the Census schedule was to enquire of the person enumerated was a member of any 'SC', or any 'ST' or any other 'Backward Class' or if he was an 'Anglo Indian'. In 1961 and 1971 Censuses, the information was collected only for each SC and ST.

In 1931 Census, the word 'caste' was mentioned but in 1951, 1961, 1971, 1981, 1991 and 2001 Censuses, the word 'caste' has been omitted. The caste has become a big factor in 2011 Census. India is gearing up its decennial Census now. The present opposition to the caste-based Census has a long lineage. G.S. Ghurye, one of the pioneers of Indian sociology, had, way back in 1932, criticised the colonial practice of the caste-based Census and the consequent politicisation of caste. He also attributed the origin of caste-based reservation to this politicisation and recorded his disapproval to the idea of caste-based reservation. The caste-based reservation in the present form is bound to produce inequality, not only across but within castes. The basic fallacy is that while the beneficiary is an individual or a family, the attribution is to the caste to which he or she belongs. Those who argue for categorisation should also see that the degree of inequality may be far greater within the most beneficiary caste than between it and others or within the less beneficiary castes. This understanding should make one at least sceptical about the categorisation solution. The roots of democracy are to be searched in the social relationship, in terms of associated life between the people who form a society (Ambedkar, 2002: 28). Caste was an obvious suspect even though, through the efforts of B. R. Ambedkar and other anti-caste movements of India introduced quotas or reservation at different levels of the State system, the idea of planning for development was otherwise caste blind. Poverty and deprivation were recognised and enumerated but treated as 'secular' phenomena.

Can the categorisation really constitute the solution to the problem of iniquitous distribution of reservation benefits? Those who think it can, confuse people with castes. For instance, one easily sees social democracy in providing "opportunities for each caste, both big and small". Leave apart caste categories, even if reservation is appointed to each caste, the problem would not be solved. If it succeeded in equalising distribution of prospective benefits across castes by this way, it would create inequality within the castes. Ambedkar has always been for establishment of a society based on the principles of liberty, equality and fraternity. This has to be for every individual and that social justice can be delivered to the members of society only if the society is based on equality, liberty and fraternity.

The above analysis provides an understanding about the nature of caste system in India. Caste system should neither be identified merely as ideological or superstructure, nor should it be identified simply as a cluster of concrete and interacting jatis. Caste system is set of kinship like social practices and the rules that surround them; the former are material, the later are ideological but in the sense of unconscious rules of behaviour as contrasted with a conscious system of ideology. The caste assumption of caste being an entity specific to Hinduism, which shaped the concept of Depressed Classes in the colonial India, and is implicit in the category of SCs in Independent India, is widely shared in contemporary academic writings and beyond. Whether it is a project of tracing the origin of caste from the *Purusha Sukta of Rig Veda,* or that of proposing its annihilation through the delegitimisation and disfiguration of *Manusmiriti*, Hinduism has been central to the institution of caste (Samarendra, 2016: 47). This politicisation of caste is found to be even more disconcerting with the changed focus of claims and demands on the part of those who press their caste identities from economic advancement to social status and political power. The pluralism that has all along been there and has been accepted as inherent to Indian social terrain is now being expressed in an upsurge of equity and social justice, not as a result of State policy but as a matter of right, hence, sought to be acquired through access to State power.

Notes

1. Something Dr Ambedkar had anticipated and feared.

2. Dr Ambedkar highlighted the proportional relationship between caste status of Dalits and their socio-economic condition in South Asia before the Round Table Conference in 1930: "The helpless, hopless and sapless condition of the Depressed Classes must be entirely attributed to the dogged and determined opposition of the whole mass of orthodox population which will not allow the Depressed Classes to have equality of status or equality of treatment. It is enough to say of their economic condition that they are poverty-stricken or that they are a class of landless labourers, although both these statements are the statements of facts. It has to be noted that the poverty of the Depressed Classes is due largely to the social prejudices in consequence of which many an occupation for earning a living is closed to them. This is a fact, which differentiates the position of the Depressed Classes from that of the ordinary caste labourers and is often a source of trouble between the two. "A Scheme of the political safeguards for the protection of the Depressed Classes in the future Constitution of a self-governing India", a memorandum submitted by Dr B.R. Ambedkar and Rao Bahadur R. Srinivasan to the Round Table Conference, Sub Committee No. III (Minorities), 31-12-1930).
3. The term 'Chandala' was of Hindu textual origin, exterior caste had been introduced by the British officials, and the term 'Harijan' was coined by Narsinh Mehta and propagated by M. K. Gandhi. However the term 'Dalit' was coined by activists of SC background and has gained wide acceptance.
4. The term 'Dalit' literally grounded, oppressed or broken includes SCs, STs and other Backwards Classes, however, in current political discourse; the term Dalit is mainly confined to SCs.
5. Sanskritisation can be defined as a process by which a low caste or tribe takes over the customs, ritual, belief and style of life of a high and in particular a twice-born caste. For more details see: M.S. Srinivas (1952:88).
6. For long, consciousness of caste was the preserve of the Brahminic upper caste. Today, something quite different is happening: the very suffers from the system (including caste system) are invoking caste identity and claims. For more details see Rajni Kothari (1994).

References

- Alam, Javeed. 2012. *Who Wants Democracy?* New Delhi: Orient BlackSwan.
- Ambedkar, B.R. 1987a. *Why Go For Conversion?* Banglore: Dalit Sahitya Akademy.
- ———. 1987b. *Writing and Speeches.* Bombay: Education Department, Government of Maharashtra, Vol. III.
- ———. 2002. 'Caste in India.' In *Caste and Democratic Politics in India,* edited by Ghanshyam Shah, 83-107. New Delhi: Permanent Black.
- ———. 2017. 'Ambedkar's last Words of Wishdom.' *The Tribune*: 14 April.

- Bayly, Susan. 1999. *Caste and Politics in India.* New Delhi: Cambridge University Press.
- Bharati, S.R. 2002. 'Dalit, a Term Asserting Unity.' *Economic and Political Weekly* XXXVII (42): 4339-40.
- Dumont, Louis. 1998. *Homo Hierarchicus: The Caste System and its Implications.* Delhi: Oxford University Press.
- ———. 2002. 'Hierarchy: The theory of the Varna.' In *Caste and Democratic Politics in India,* edited by Ghanshyam Shah, 60-79. New Delhi: Permanent Black.
- Ghurye, G.S. 1979. *Caste and Race in India.* Bombay: Popular Prakashan.
- Habib, Irfan. 2000. *Essays in Indian History, Towards a Marxist Perception.* New Delhi: Tulika.
- Ilaiah, Kancha. 2001. 'Dalitism vs Brahmanism: The Epistemological Conflict in History.' In *Dalit Identity and Politics: Cultural Subordination and the Dalit Challenge,* edited by Ghanshyam Shah, 108-128. New Delhi: Sage Publications.
- Jaffrelot, Christophe. 2005. *Dr Ambedkar and Untouchability, Analyzing and Fighting Caste.* Delhi: Permanent Black.
- ———. 2017. 'Defenders of Varna.' *The Indian Express*: 4 August.
- Jodhka, Surinder S. 2015. 'Lift the Veil off Caste-blind Approach.' *The Tribune*: 15 July.
- Kannabira, Kalpana. 2009. 'Sociology of Caste and the Crooked Mirror: Recovering B.R. Ambedkar Legacy.' *Economic and Political Weekly* XLIV (1): 35-40.
- Karanth, G.K. 2004. 'Replication or Dissent? Culture and Institutions among 'Untouchable' Scheduled Castes in Karnataka.' *Contributions to Indian Sociology* 38 (1 and 2): 137-165.
- Kaviraj, Sudipta, ed. 1997. *Politics in India.* New Delhi: Oxford University Press.
- Kothari, Rajni. 1994. 'Rise of Dalits and the Renewed Debate on Caste.' *Economic and Political Weekly* 29 (26): 1589-99.
- ———. 2008. *Caste in Indian Politics.* New Delhi: Orient BlackSwan.
- Manor, James. 2012. '*Conversation on Caste Today*' invited by Surinder S. Jodhka, seminar on 'Caste Matters.' New Delhi: 6 May.
- Michael, S.M. 1999. *Dalits in Modern India: Vision and Value.* New Delhi: Vistaar Publications.
- Nanda, Meera. 2016. 'Ambedkar's Gita.' *Economic and Political Weekly* LI (49): 38-45.
- Nehru, Jawaharlal. 1992. *The Discovery of India.* New Delhi: Oxford University Press.

- Omvedt, Gail. 1994. *Dalits and the Democratic Revolution*. New Delhi: Sage Publications.
- Oommen, T.K. 2008. 'Disjunction between Field, Method and Concept: An Appraisal of M.N. Srinivas.' *Sociological Bulletin* 57 (1): 60-81.
- Panikkar, K.M. 2007. *Caste and Democracy*. New Delhi: Critical Quest.
- Paul, N. Divakar and Ajai M. 2004. 'UN Bodies and Dalits, a Historical Review of Interventions', In *Caste, Race and Discrimination, Discourses in International Context* edited by Sukhadeo Thorat and Umakant, 16-17. New Delhi: Rawat Publications.
- Phule, Jotirao. 1991. *Slavery: Collected Works of Mahatma Jotirao Phule*. Vol. 1, Bombay: Government of Maharashtra.
- Phule, Mahatma. 1980. *Samagra Vigmaya.* Bombay: Maharashtra Rajya Sahitya and Sanskriti Mandal.
- Ram, Nandu. 1995. *Beyond Ambedkar: Essays on Dalits in India.* New Delhi: Har Anand Publications.
- Ram, Ronki. 2010. *Dalit Chetna: Sarot ate Sarup*. Chandigarh: Lokgeet Parkashan.
- Rao, Anupama. 2009. *The Caste Question: Dalits and the Politics of Modern India*. Berkeley: University of California Press.
- Rawls, John. 1971. *A Theory of Justice*. London: Oxford University Press.
- Sabine, George H. 1975. *A History of Political Theory.* New Delhi: Oxford and IBH Publishing Co.
- Samarendra, Padmanabh. 2016. 'Religion, Caste and Conversion, Membership of a Scheduled Caste and Judicial Deliberation.' *Economic and Political Weekly* LI (4): 38-48.
- Shah, Ghanshayam. 2001. *Dalit Identity and Politics.* New Delhi: Sage Publications.
- ———. 2012. '*Conversation on Caste Today.*' invited by Surinder S. Jodhka, Seminar on 'Caste Matters.' New Delhi: 6 May.
- Smith, Vincent A. and Percival Spear, ed. 1986. *The Oxford History of India.* New Delhi: Oxford University Press.
- Srinivas, M.N. 1952. *Religion and Society among Coorgs of South India*. Delhi: Oxford University Press.
- ———. 1972. *Social Change in Modern India.* Delhi: Orient Longman.
- Thorat, Sukhadeo. 2012. '*Conversation on Caste Today.*' invited by Surinder S. Jodhka, Seminar on 'Caste Matters.' New Delhi: 6 May.
- Zelliot, Eleanor. 1992. *From Untouchable to Dalit: Essays on Ambedkar Movement.* Delhi: Manohar Publishers and Distributors.

Chapter - 2

Dalit Assertion in India: Crossing the Threshold of Indian Politics

Dalit as a socio-political concept appears frequently in the contemporary discussion on Indian politics. It has become a form of academic violence which promotes casteist myths. Thus, Dalits become a static community. The great Dalit and Bahujan intellectual tradition, beginning the nineteenth century, from Phule, Iyothee Thass, Aiyappan, Acchutanand and many others leading to Ambedkar and Periyar, embodied an all-around political, economic, and cultural perspective dedicated to this. Such a Dalit perspective has been slow to develop in post-independence India for many reasons. Part of the problem has been the slow development of mass education, one of the most important unachieved aspects of the anti-caste programme and continued upper-caste monopoly of communication and culture (Omvedt, 2011: 506).

The term 'Dalit' is referred to broken, ground downtrodden people who become subject to deliberate act of exploitation by those above them in a hierarchical social system. The term 'Depressed Classes' was mentioned in the Census report 1921, but since the enactment of the Government of India Act 1935, Dalits are consistently referred to as "SCs". The term 'Dalits' is supposed to have been used first by Jyotirao Phule (1827-90) in his attempt to work for "Dalituthan", that is, upliftment of Dalits. Though Ambedkar did not popularise the word "Dalit" for untouchables, his philosophy has remained a key source in the emergence and popularity of the term 'Dalit'. Dalit category was used by Ambedkar in his fortnightly *Bahishkrit Bharat.* He defined it comprehensively: Dalithood is a kind of life condition which characterises the exploitation, suppression and marginalisation of Dalits by the social, economic, culture and political domination of the upper caste Brahminical order (Ambedkar, 1990: 194). Ambedkar, however, did not use this category often, preferring to deploy different terms depending upon the changing context, for example, when dealing with the imperial State, he used the category of Depressed Classes (Louis, 2003: 146).

The term 'SCs' appeared for the first time in the Government of India Act, 1935. The word "Harijan" which means "children of God"– a term coined by Narasimha Mehta and adopted by Mahatma Gandhi in 1933 (Tripathy, 1994: 2). None of the common words, SCs, Depressed Classes, and Gandhi's euphemism, Harijan had the same connotation. Dalit implies those who have been broken, ground down by those above them in a deliberate and active way. There is in the word itself an inherent denial of pollution, Karma and justified caste hierarchy (Zelliot, 1992: 267). In recent years, the term 'Dalit' has been discarded as a socially reactionary category by a section of the community who prefer "Bahujan" over both the Buddhist as well as Dalit categories.[1] The construction of the identity of Dalit, in place of the patronising identity of Harijan, is strident critique of the Hindu social order and the present political system, and promise of an alternative social justice have raised Dalit consciousness and expectations (Pai, 2002: 223).

Dalit Movements and Party Politics

Dalit movements in India are not homogeneous and exhibit many regional specificities. These movements are beset with an assortment of challenges and have to grapple with the complex problem of rising belligerency of rightwing political and cultural mobilisation. Dalit movements have potential versatility and are conspicuously distinct enough to chart an autonomous course in India's somewhat democratically-nurtured syncretism, without being carried away in the strong saffron current. Dalit activists are foot soldiers of India's secular democracy and it is erroneous to construe it otherwise.

The Indian Government is not ready to acknowledge that caste is one of the fundamental causes of deprivation, atrocities, and honour killings in most parts of India. The Dalit movements traversed a path which is independent and unusual to mainstream imagination to secure a society based on liberty, equality, justice and compassion. It is different matter that the sacrifices of many have not been effective to remove everyday sufferings of countless and uproots the institutionalised social and structural constraints. Caste places structural obstacles in the way of exercising full human rights in the broadest social and political sense. It forcefully denies most rudimentary rights which are basically a blatant disrespect of equality, social justice and human dignity. Strong demands currently emanate from the real-life experiences of lower caste groups. Dalit right movements are vociferously emerging in different States of India. They claim that Dalits are synonymous with human rights. The internationalisation of the violation of Dalit human rights is underway, demanding international consensus that caste is a problem. India denied the role of caste in gender inequality and changed the word caste to "social origin", drawing passionate and critical reaction from civil society groups.

Many scholars regard Dalit movement as the most influential social movement in Independent India. In the wider sense of lower caste struggle against Brahminical hegemony, the 'Dalit movement' has coexisted with the idea of caste itself. The British colonisation with its bourgeois liberal ethos coupled with the imperatives of their ruling strategy created space for the working up of subaltern identities, mainly in terms of caste and religion. The changes during colonial rule–the institutional, social, economic and cultural–gave an added impetus to the aspirations of the lower castes and created the environment for the emergence of an opposition to Brahminical hegemony on the basis of strong modern values of liberty, equality and fraternity; while the strategic compulsions of the British allowed an opportunity for deft political maneuvering within electoral and representational quotas.

In the pre-Independence period, the anti-caste movement comprised strong non-Brahmin movements in Maharashtra and Tamil Nadu as well as Dalit movements in Punjab, Western UP, Bengal, Kerala, coastal Andhra and Hyderabad. Independent India saw two decades of silence through the Nehru era, before the issue of caste once again burst into the national consciousness with the founding of

Dalit Panther in 1972 and the emergence of Dalits as a major electoral force through the 1980s and 90s.

B.R. Ambedkar was the sole national voice of Dalits in the first 30 years of the movement, provided with its ideological framework which demarcates the general rubric for Dalit resistance even today. Ambedkar's resistance drew on the ideas of the nineteenth century Dalit reformer Jyotirao Phule. Ambedkar like Phule attacked Hindu society from a metaphysical perspective and shared his stand on the complete dismantling of an innately anti-democratic and anti-modern Hindu as the only way to do away with entrenched hierarchies of domination and subjugation. Both propagated the idea of an egalitarian society with decidedly modern ideals. Phule, influenced by the European 'Aryan theory of race' and the doctrines of the 'Right of Man' proposed that Dalits and the Shudras were the original inhabitants conquered by the invading Aryans. In this, violence and ideology were the driving forces of history. Phule propagated the replacement of Hinduism with a more universalistic, egalitarian and rationalistic religion which he called the 'sarvajanik satya dharma'. Ambedkar, on the other hand, rejected the overbearing racial element in Phule, believing the caste system to have come into being through practices of excommunication long after the intermingling of Aryan and indigenous races. Ambedkar chose to look at the caste system as a construct of power relations, as more of a social phenomenon. Moreover, while Phule's criticism is directed more at the oppressiveness of Hinduism and calls on a discourse of benevolence and compassion. Ambedkar's focus is on the irrationality and superstition of the religion, and he felt comfortable only with an alternative like Buddhism which had effectively rationalised God–that would allow him recourse to the call of 'reason'.

The 1920s and 30s saw Ambedkar's increasing radicalism, and it is in these years that a number of his most crucial ideas were put into practice, like the right of untouchables to public utilities with the Mahar Satyagraha in 1927 and the entry of untouchables into temples in Nashik in 1930. Through the '30s, Ambedkar became an increasingly controversial character in the Indian political scene for his dogged insistence on holding to communitarian identities amidst a strengthening nationalist freedom movement built on modern, secular ideals. Ambedkar, like Phule, was willing to appreciate the positive aspects of British imperialism, in that they were harbingers of modernity in feudal India and had been instrumental in alleviating the conditions of Dalits, in whatever small measure. While he declared categorically his opposition to any form of imperialist hegemony, his primary concerns lay with his own Mahar community's plight, as was clear in his advocacy for reservations for Dalits in jobs and electorate in British India. The movement's first attempt at formal political organisation stuck not only to Ambedkar's Dalit agenda but also broadened the scope and support for the movement by taking up peasants and workers issues which ran closely with those of caste discrimination. As a result, in 1937, ILP pushed for legislation on the abolishment of the oppressive *khoti* landlord system prevalent in many parts of the country at the time. As the agitation reached its climax in 1938, Ambedkar was able to conduct a successful one-day general strike of Bombay textile workers in support of the peasants. In 1938, ILP joined the one-day general strike against the Bombay Industrial Dispute Bill, with its Dalit cadres fully in support of the workers.

In his attempt to weld together the caste and class movements, it would seem that Ambedkar would have a natural affinity to the Marxist movement which was also gathering strength at the time. But this was not to be, for a number of reasons. The main disagreement between Ambedkar and the Marxists was on the centrality of the caste question. For the Marxists, with their mechanical understanding of class, caste was a comparatively irrelevant category as it was only an outcrop of feudalism that would disappear with a successful class revolution. For Ambedkar, on the other hand, India could be mobilised to revolution only once its intense caste consciousness has been dismantled, which meant that caste was the bigger problem. For the Marxists, the main enemy was the imperialist, while for Ambedkar; it was upper-caste hegemony. Moreover, Ambedkar alleged casteism even within the ranks of the Communist movement, which drew its members primarily amongst the educated, upper-caste, university-educated bourgeoisie.

On similar grounds, he laid out his opposition to the Congress party, which he labelled as also being a preserve of Brahminical hegemony. He accused the Congress of creating the delusion of a unified India, calling it an artifice to maintain the status quo in a country where caste forms the primary identity. He took particular exception to Gandhi's ascriptive and patronising use of the word 'harijan' and denounced Gandhism as unscientific, traditionalist and as still being within the clutches of Hinduism's oppressive spiritual doctrines. Dalits, Ambedkar claimed could never be represented by the Congress. Thus, Ambedkar's radicalism set him at loggerheads with the two strongest political forces of the time, thus, foreclosing any possibility of support from them.

The 1940s saw the escalation of Hindu-Muslim tensions and increased political manoeuvering in the run-up to Independence. In 1942, Ambedkar formed the AISCF which remained mainly as a pressure group to secure better conditions and legislation for Dalits in the soon to be independent India. This party, after Ambedkar's ambitious effort at a radical fusion of caste and class resistance, seemed lukewarm in comparison. But it was him only trying to make the best of his tactical position to strengthen the community in terms of both social standing and political representation.

As India entered the 1950s with a new Constitution framed by Ambedkar's Drafting Committee, Ambedkar began to look towards a spiritual resistance to the hegemony of Brahminism. Months before his death in December 1956, Ambedkar along with thousands of his supporters, converted to Buddhism as the ultimate sign of protest. In Buddhism, Ambedkar found a rational, equalitarian philosophy which he found in agreement with his political principles. Through his conversion to Buddhism, it can be said that Ambedkar intersected the ideas of both Phule and Periyar in that all three believed in the need for a weapon at the metaphysical level to combat Hinduism in all its claustrophobic irrationality. After the death of Ambedkar, however, Dalit movement began to lose its vitality. The RPI was again an attempt to convert the AISCF's narrow caste agenda into a broad-based movement against inequality, discrimination and injustice. The party, however, proved to be only a name-change and in the post-Independence Nehruvian utopia of industrialisation and secular modernity, the call of Dalits was either ignored or pacified.

But by the 1970s, as promises of development grew stale and the old resentment began to resurface, Dalit movement returned in a decisively more militant mode. In 1972, Dalit Panthers came to the fore with the stated intention: "We don't want a little place in Brahmin *galli*; we want the rule of the whole country" (Rajkhowa, 2008). Strongly influenced by the Naxalite movement, Dalit Panthers, in an attempt similar to what Ambedkar tried in the '30s, welded together disparate issues of land reform, untouchability and communalism. Like Ambedkar, the Panthers also stood as a critique of both the Congress Government and the facile, sold-out left, and tried to bring together the most diverse groups as a viable political alternative. The group was active through the 1970s but by the 1980s, it was rife with internal splits that rendered it ineffective.

With an apparent exhausting of the militant solution, Dalit movement began to become politically more assertive as caste-based parties like the BSP started to gain political weightage. The 1990s had come to be defined by caste politics, particularly with controversy on the Mandal Commission report on reservations in Government jobs at the start of the decade becoming a high point of Dalit struggle. In the new decade of coalition politics, as caste-based regional parties gain prominence, a few questions were still casting a shadow of doubt. Throughout Dalit movement, its response has always been tactical in nature, depending upon the incumbent circumstances. Consequently, one may at times find the movement's political positions to be in apparent contradiction – their use of caste identity in an attempt to fight caste inequality; their seemingly favourable stance towards British imperialism in India as against their opposition to globalisation.

Dalit Movements in UP

There are a good number of studies on the neo-Buddhists, the dominant SC in Maharashtra. However, there are very few studies on other SCs like *Mang, Chamar, Dhor, Mochi, Bhangi*, etc. Moreover, most of the studies are based on single or two variables like caste or/ and class. It is to be remembered that in a complex society like India, single factor analysis gives one-sided picture, which is far away from reality. It is, therefore, necessary to study the nature and impact of SCs movement, impact of Government policies, also the impact of the efforts of the voluntary agencies and most importantly the impact of the political process during the last sixty years. Owing to the democratic process since independence, increasing means of communication and the spread of education, there is increasing awareness among all the sections of society and the SCs are not exception to it. The Constitution has released the forces of liberalism. Because of these forces, an era of politicisation has started in all walks of life and traditional gap between politics and society has come to an end. Now politics has become a new instrument for achieving socio-economic development. Socio-economic development of the SCs would be the precondition for their integration in the mainstream of society, which the Constitution has visualised. Much has been done by way of constitutional provisions, administrative efforts and proper response from a larger section of the upper castes. However, whatever is done is not enough to match the rising expectations of the weaker sections including the SCs. Still they are unorganised and constitute the larger chunk of the population. On the other hand, the organised sections even in SCs have grabbed the benefits of socio-economic development. If we want to analyse this reality, the study should be interdisciplinary and based on variables–caste, class, religion, region, ideology, gender, identity, etc. The problem of the SCs is dynamic in nature.

UP had not responded much to Dalit movement in the pre- and early post-independence periods. However, during the late seventies and eighties, things changed dramatically and the State witnessed a resurgence of Dalit Movement with a clear political agenda for social change. The movement had a leading objective to capture State power for Dalits. This objective was equipped with the expectation that once Dalits get enough economic and political benefits using State power, it would automatically improve their social status. By giving voice to the voiceless and instilling self-respect and confidence in Dalits, Mayawati's rule in UP has brought about some concrete changes. The BSP sought to change the nature of the State Government by transferring Dalits into key positions in the bureaucracy and by expanding Dalit presence in the police force. In the six months that the BSP's Mayawati was chief minister in 1997, she transferred 1,350 civil and police officers (Jaffrelot, 2003: 419), made a concerted effort to recruit Dalits to the police force, and made existing reserved seats in Government training and professional training more accessible to Dalits. Jaffrelot (2007: 262) noted that the Mayawati's Ambedkar Village Scheme set aside funds for the socio-economic development of the 25,434 villages where at least half of the residents belonged to the SCs. Enhanced economic and political status has continuously provided enormous power to the upper castes and ensured them a dominant social position. To make this happen, Dalit political party, the BSP is the chief political party in UP politics.

Even if Dalit movement of Northern India puts its political project as a top priority, the ideological concepts, such as 'social mobility', 'relative deprivation' and 'reference group', remain central to Dalits' social, economic and political status. Orthodox Hindu culture and traditions are recognised by Dalit leaders as the factors responsible for the marginalisation of Dalits. This ideological stand of Dalit movement has influenced its developmental and political priorities. The formation of the BSP as a political party was a strategic part of Dalit movement and was expected to continue to be the spearhead of the movement. But on the contrary, the BSP is being seen as a harbinger of major changes in the fundamental ideological propositions of Dalit movement which was supposed to be espoused by the protagonists of the movement.

In the mid-1990s and the first decade of twenty-first century, the BSP brought major changes in the nature and ideology of Dalit movement in UP in terms of setting up political coalitions first with Hindu-minded political parties like the BJP and the Congress, and later it formed a coalition with its all time opponents, the Brahmins through 'social engineering'. This relationship was looked at from two levels – firstly, the BSP's ability to fulfill the goals of Dalit Movement through its political and developmental agenda while it had been in power, especially, after the introduction of its 'social engineering' project, and secondly, the perception of the BSP cadres at the local level about considering the BSP as a part of Dalit Movement. The latter was being posed by the BSP as a social coalition rather a political tie. This development brought about vivid changes in the BSP with major changes in the social development policies of the BSP Government (2007 onwards).

Dalit Movements in Maharashtra

The political dimension of the cultural contradiction in India in general and Maharashtra in particular has always occupied an important position in academic debates. It is true that the cultural tradition of Dalits in Maharashtra did not receive due recognition from the Maharashtra upper-caste society. The study of the interface between Ambedkar and Dalits' cultural movement in Maharashtra is warranted due to the more serious development in the realm of Dalit culture. The Dalit cultural movement can be very broadly defined in term of its constituent components like literature, both oral and written, different popular musical traditions among Dalits and the various forms of theatre activities. It has been argued that the Dalits of Maharashtra have created a rich history of cultural traditions of their own. Among the different Dalit castes with the necessary cultural and musical background, it is only Mahars who could relate their musical and cultural tradition to the ideology and politics of Ambedkar (Guru, 2001:191).

The *non-Brahmin* movement generated in Bombay province (now Maharashtra) had its effect in Kolhapur–a small Maratha State–under the control of Bombay Government by Maharaja Chatrapati Shahu. The Maharaja, displeased with the Brahmins, devoted much of his time to the non-Brahmin movement. He declared in 1902 that he would reserve at least half the posts in the State for qualified men of *non-Brahmin* communities. To give fair opportunities to all communities, the Prince started a hostel in Kolhapur city for *non-Brahmin* youths. Kolhapur may be set to be the first State to adopt the reservation policy, though there had been some ineffective attempts earlier by the British Government to break the monopoly of one community. Kolhapur, therefore, has been a landmark in the Backward Class movement towards equality. The Backward Classes' movement in India originated in Maharashtra and Tamil Nadu. Gail Omvedt considers that the deficiencies shown by the SCs had been imposed upon them by servitude under the traditional social order and could be removed by the contemporary policies of the modern State.

The OBCs of Maharashtra, whose number grew from 125 castes in 1953 to 160 castes in 1967, also mobilised themselves as social groups. But the Government policy was to move from caste to income criterion. In November 1961, the State Government appointed a Backward Classes Committee (headed by B.D. Deshmukh). The Committee in its report of January 1964 grouped Backward Classes into four categories; and recommended that reservations for Backward Classes should be related to the percentage of their population in the State. The Government broadly accepted the above recommendations and made the following reservations in the State services and educational institutions for Backward Classes: SCs and STs converted to Buddhism 13 per cent; STs, Denotified Tribes and Nomadic Tribes 4 per cent; and Other Backward Communities 10 per cent.

Self-respect Movement in Tamil Nadu

In the process of struggling against iniquitous social order and for reservations in the Government services, the Backward Classes acquired the State power in Tamil Nadu. The social movement of the Backward Classes for reservation was started during the colonial period itself, but the social character of the movement was subjected to a lot of changes. In the changing process of the reservation category, the advanced castes were excluded from the Backward Classes list and most Deprived Castes were included in the list.

The *non-Brahmin* movements of the 1910s and 1920s and much more violent 'radical' *Dravidian* or anti-Aryan movement launched by E.V. Ramaswami Naicker in the 1930s are the important phases in the history of Tamil Nadu BCs movement. One of Naicker's main targets was the temple and he mobilised a militantly anti-Hindu campaign, ostensibly in the name of atheism, to smash the temples and destroy the Gods. The important factor, which created the strain for the origin of the *non-Brahmin* movement, is the domination of *Brahmins* in education and Government employment. The Mandal Commission comes to a conclusion that the *non-Brahmin* movement was started when the runaway lead taken by the *Tamil* and *Telugu Brahmins* in the field of education in the erstwhile Madras Presidency and it is well documented. By the turn of the century, the male literacy rate among the *Tamil Brahmins* was 73.6 per cent as against a similar rate among the *Vellalas* of 6.9 per cent. Whereas the male literacy in English was 17.9 per cent among the *Tamil Brahmins;* it was only 0.19 per cent among the *Vellalas.* The *Brahmins* had established a near monopoly of the Government services and the professions. As far back as 1851, the Madras Revenue Board had instructed the District Collectors to restrict the number of *Brahmin* entrants into the services. In spite of this, the *Brahmin* domination of the Government services and the professions went on unabated. The caste's domination in the Provincial Congress Committee had been well established. Alerted by the advent of the Montague-Chelmsford reforms and diarchy, the *non-Brahmin* elite castes took the lead in establishing first the South Indian Liberal Federation, and then, the Justice Party in 1916.

Tamil Nadu Backward Classes Commission has missed the opportunity to revisit the State's reservation policy in a way that could have stopped affluent castes from cornering quotas. In the land of Periyar, E.V. Ramasamy, founder of the Self-respect Movement and the Dravida Kazhagam through which he worked for the eradication of the caste system, caste is still the worst scourge. If caste still persists as a pervasive social evil in a society which had militant anti-caste movements, and a minuscule group of the affluent castes have been cornering the State's patronage and access to its opportunity structure, it is because of the vested interest in caste of the SC-called Dravidian parties which have been ruling Tamil Nadu since 1967. This vested interest is most viciously promoted by the State's aggressive reservation politics since the 1970s. The State's overall reservation shot up from 41 per cent during the period 1954-1970 to 49 per cent in 1971, to 68 per cent in 1985 and to 69 per cent in 1990. The number of castes included in the Backward Classes' list, not counting SCs and STs, rose from about 181 in 1970 to 222 in 1980, and to 251 in 2011 (the clubbing together of several cognate castes makes the actual number much higher). The State's population included in the Backward Classes' list (including the Most Backward Classes) is now 67 per cent, besides 19 per cent SCs and 1 per cent STs.

This treatment of 87 per cent population as BCs is egregious, particularly when seen in the context of the argument by majority of the judges (of the nine-judge Bench) in the Mandal rulings (Indra Sawhney v. Union of India) of November 16, 1992 that reservation for all is reservation to none. But in Tamil Nadu, politicians have scant respect for such arguments and scant concern for phasing out reservation and ushering in a casteless egalitarian society. Even as politicians need caste the most to stay in politics, production of the certificate for claiming any BC, MBC, SC, ST benefit is a sad and stark reminder of the caste of the claimant as the certificate invariably contains the caste name of the person. This has driven the State to a vicious circle of forcing the majority of its people to relieve caste through the very policy which is intended to erase it from their minds; and to an irrational dead end of political diatribes and policy distortions as evident from the 2011 report of the Tamil Nadu Backward Classes Commission prepared at the instance of the Supreme Court. Even as the judicial delay of 17 years in deciding on the validity of the Tamil Nadu Reservation Act 45 of 1994– which for political expediency was included in the Ninth Schedule under Article 31B by the P.V. Narasimha Rao led the Congress Ministry at the Centre– enabled the Tamil Nadu Government to persist with its specious quota law, the Supreme Court did not express any opinion on the validity of the Act while disposing of on July 13, 2010 the long pending writ petitions against this law.

The report 'Justification of Reservation under the Tamil Nadu Act 45 of 1994 on Quantifiable Data' by the Tamil Nadu Backward Classes Commission, headed by retired High Court judge, M.S. Janarthanam, was in response to the court's direction to the State Government to place all quantifiable data before the Commission and, on the basis of such data the Commission would decide the quantum of reservation in the light of the parameter laid down by the Court that if a State wants to exceed 50 per cent reservation, it was required to base its decision on quantifiable data. But the report was not based on any quantifiable data; it was verbal jugglery, full of frills and dubious information. Justice Janarthanam's predilection as a staunch supporter of reservation had set the tone of the report as evident from the Foreword to it.

The Foreword was followed by 13 chapters in 188 pages. These chapters clearly showed that the report has hardly any bearing on the Commission's mandate. Among other things, it questions the judiciary for its Mandal rulings, portrays it as an interloper in State policy, and overturns its mandate to the Commission. A case in point is paragraph 5.9: "The function of the judiciary is to adjudicate and not to legislate. The addition of the concept of creamy layer in either Article 15(4) or Article 16(4) by the Supreme Court can, by no stretch of imagination, be construed as an act of adjudication but that will tantamount to an act of legislation, that too not an ordinary legislation, but a constitutional amendment." The Commission had a rare opportunity of revisiting the reservation site by comparing the employment and educational status of the BCs in 1980-81 as available in the Tamil Nadu Second Backward Classes (Ambasankar) Commission report with corresponding data after about three decades. The Commission did not use this opportunity.

There is no exclusive model available for the development of Dalits. The development of Dalits has historically been articulated in emancipatory terms: emancipation from caste oppression, bondage, social exclusion, humiliation and so on. It is true that caste is an anathema in a secular democracy and must be abolished and our Constitution rightly abolished it. But it is important to know the reality. Dalits bear a disproportionate share of its socio-economic burdens. Not only do they usually fare the worst according to almost all indices of economic well-being or quality of life, but among all the underprivileged groups in India, only Dalits are marked by a legacy of the deepest social detraction in the form of a centuries-old tradition of "Untouchability". The untouchables or Dalits, as they are presently known, have been one of the most vulnerable sections of society. They have been subjected to multiple oppression and subjugation for centuries and had lived a miserable life (Sharma, 2006: 5). Untouchability forms part of a complex of discriminatory practices that impose social disabilities on persons by reasons of their birth in certain castes (Shah, Mander, Thorat, Deshpande and Bhaviskar, 2006: 13).

Note

1. The term *"Bahujan"* was floated by Kanshi Ram and also Prakash Ambedkar and Makharam Pawar from Maharashtra.

References

- Ambedkar, Dr Babasaheb. 1990. *Yanche Bahishkruit Bharat ani Muknayak (Marathi) (translated to mean the Depressed India or Frontrunner).* Education Department, Government of Maharashtra.
- Guru, Gopal. 2001. 'The interface between Ambedkar and the Dalit Cultural Movement in Mharashtra.' In *Dalit Identity and Politics,* edited by Ghanshyam Shah, 160-194. New Delhi: Sage Publications.
- Jaffrelot, Christophe. 2003. *India's Silent Revolution: The Rise of the Lower Castes in North India.* New Delhi: Orient Blackswan.
- ______. 2007. 'The BSP in Uttar Pradesh: Whose Party is it?' In *Dalits in Modern India: Vision and Values*, edited by S.M. Michael, 262-263. New Delhi; Sage Publications.
- Louis, Prakash. 2003. *The Political Sociology of Dalit Assertion.* New Delhi: Gyan Publishing House.

- Omvedt, Gail. 2011. 'The Anti-caste Movement and Discourse of Power.' In *Democracy in India*, edited by Niraja Gopal Jayal, 481-508. New Delhi: Oxford University Press.
- Pai, Sudha. 2002. *Dalit Assertion and the Unfinished Democratic Revolution, the Bahujan Samaj Party in Uttar Pradesh.* New Delhi: Sage Publications.
- Rajkhowa Gaurav. 2008. Dalit Movement: From Where, Where to. Access at *www.out-caste.blogspot/2008),* March 7.
- Shah, Ghanshyam, Harsh Mander, Sukhadeo Thorat, Satish Deshpande, Amita. Bhaviskar. 2006. *Untouchability in Rural India.* New Delhi: Sage Publications.
- Sharma, Pradeep K. 2006. *Dalit Politics and Literature.* New Delhi: Shipra Publications.
- Tripathy, Rebati Ballav. 1994. *Dalit: A Sub-Human Society*. Delhi: Ashish Publishing House.
- Zelliot, Eleanor. 1992. *From Untouchable to Dalit: Essays on Ambedkar Movement*. Delhi: Manohar Publishers and Distributors.

Chapter - 3

Emergence of Dalit Political Parties: An Analytical Study

Democracy not only accepts the multiplicity of interests in society, it also considers this fact to constitute its necessary condition. The democratic process in India has deepened with new social groups entering the ambit of political system presented by new parties like the BSP embodying the interests of Dalits. Yet in recent years, political parties are in a state of disarray, intra- and inter-party conflicts have eroded the legitimacy and reputation of both parties and leaders. The recent astonishing emergence of the 'Aam Aadmi Party' (AAP) in Indian politics has, undoubtedly, shuddered the political considerations of many after a long time; at least to the extent of reimagining an alternative politics. Dalit political parties in North and Central India have overwhelmingly pursued an agenda of recognition, calling for equal respect, rather than one of redistribution. While this has improved the social and economic standing of Dalits better situated in terms of class, it has failed to substantively improve the lives of the majority of Dalits. Ultimately, Dalits' quest for equal treatment will be limited so long as it lacks a redistributive politics that addresses exploitative economic relations (Sarkar and Sarkar, 2016: 14).

Theoretical Framework of the Political Parties

Parties are instrument of collective human action. In one sense, parties are an outgrowth of the modernisation process, for with modernisation individuals begin to participate in public life and the entire pattern of Government-citizen relations changes. Regional political parties, as a field of study, have too far been neglected in India. An indirect reference of regional parties, however, is found in Maurice Duverger's (1951) concept of "minor party" which is basically minority minded. The theory of minor parties is primarily based on the distinction between major and minor parties reflecting the difference in mentality.

Duverger believes that "a party is not a community, but a collection of the communities, a union of small groups dispersed throughout the country (branches, caucuses, lacal associations, etc)" (Duverger, 1962: 17). The present day parties are distinguished far less by their programme or class of their member than by the nature of their organisation. Parties can be usefully divided into interior and exterior parties on the basis of their parliamentary majority together. Outside the parliament, the party has a marginal existence. Duverger further notes that the parties are related to the evolution of national Parliament and the growth in the size of electoral parties. Duverger postulates some stages in party development: first, the creation of Parliamentary group; their organisation of electoral committees; and finally, the establishment of permanent connection. The most interesting in Duverger analysis is the classification of party structure. The four types of structure suggested by him are: The caucus, the branch, the cell and the militia (*Ibid.*: 17-40).

A definition of party might as well begin with its simple word derivation. Every party in its very essence signifies partnership in a particular organisation and separation from other by a specific programme. Hume accepted parties as unpleasant consequences badly as a condition of free Government. And there is, undoubtedly, a world of difference between viewing parties as de facto inevitable and the Burkeian view that parties are both respectable and an instrument of free Government. The most commonly accepted definition of a political party is the one given by Burke. According to him, "Party is a body of men united for promoting by their joint endeavours the national interests, upon some particular principle in which they are all agreed" (Sartori, 1976: 9).

The Indian National Congress Party is the oldest political party in Asia and one of the oldest and largest non-Communists Party in the world. It was founded in 1885, only three decades after the founding of Republican Party in the United States and in the same decade in which the British Labour Party was organised. Since Independence, the Congress has won every one of the four elections to the national parliament; and until February 1967 election, almost every election for State Legislature Assemblies. Though the Congress party has a number of important defections, no Congress Government in the State or New Delhi has ever collapsed, because the party was unable to command the loyalty of its members. The party's electoral success over the years has been attributed to its ability to represent and more importantly, to contain the various social divisions that pervade Indian society. The most of the explanations of party's decline has focused on why the Congress could no longer contain within its fold the various social divisions that characterise Indian society. Sission, in his study in Rajasthan, provides a theoretically interesting case for the study of political institutionalisation. The creation of the Congress in Rajasthan was a contract between collegial leaders of the regional organisation and this fact has inhibited the rise of single dominant and cohesive political elite within the Congress party. The organisation of power within the Congress party organisation has been pyramidal and segmentary. Factions at each level of political organisation have tended to stay relatively autonomous (Sission, 1972: 313). Significant feature of party system in India has been the dominance of the Congress party. The studies undertaken by various authors such as Richard Sission, Rajni Kothari, Morris Jones, Gopal Krishna, etc. have illuminated the main features of one party dominance in India. But more than the inauguration of the second dominant-party system in terms of structure of competition, it is the ideological terrain this development needs careful scrutiny. In true with the true implication of the idea of a dominant party system, the rise of BJP as the dominant force also underscores emergence of a new politics that brings to the second critical aspect of current political scene.

In a free society or a totalitarian regime, the organisation called the party is expected to organise public opinion and to communicate demands to the centre of Government power and decision. The organisation means of assuring stable conformance and control. Very Analysts have concentrated instead on the party strategies, its discourse, and its social base share of votes in various elections. Few studies have been undertaken on the organisation of political parties especially the BSP which has been emerged as a representative of Dalits in recent years. The breaking of party organisation that is the process by which a party's members are induced to defect to other parties–has been a significant theme in recent years in several States. Lack of organisation means lack of reliable instrument for reaching more votes.

Caste and the Political Parties

Parties, in general, have played a critical role in the democratic process, especially in drawing historically disadvantaged sections of society into the political system (Hasan, 2002: 1-2). One important issue which pertains to the role of social cleavages, more precisely, is the relationship between social cleavages and political mobilisation. Equally important is the democratic upsurge amongst the hitherto underprivileged sections of society and their perceptible influence on the working of democracy and political institutions.

The study of interaction between caste and politics is a result of the new emphasis in the political science of analysing the political process in terms of the determining social institutions. It was in fact middle class, educated or semi-educated Dalit youths who provided impetus to most of the militant organisations that arose from the late 1960s, Dalit Panthers in Maharashtra, Bheem Sena and Dalit Sangarsh Samiti in Karnataka. By the middle of 1960s India was enveloped in all around economic and political crisis. Strikes and all forms of political agitations took place in the 1967 elections. The Congress lost heavily in several Northern States as disaffected peasants and middle castes turned to the opposition. Disaffection hit every political party including the Communists as the apparently revolutionary message of Mao helped to spark the "Naxalite" revolt (Omvedt, 2001a: 152, 153). The Congress's decline has complex causes. The most striking feature is the inability for the party to maintain the political bases of its coalition, especially the loyalty of the socially disadvantaged groups. It is true that the Congress party continues to secure support across the social spectrum. Middle class Dalits were in an equally tension ridden and in a more ambivalent position. They had more economic security than their lower-class brethrens, and hence, could aspire for considerable upward mobility.

Indian society is composed of various castes, none of which by itself has the numerical strength to determine electoral outcomes in most election constituencies. Caste-based parties were the key element of the 1996 United Front Government. For the first time since independence in 1947, the Indian party system, which had been dominated by the catch-all Congress party, is fractured along regional caste and religious lines. The emergence of caste-based party system is described in the inherent conflict between backward and forward castes, a conflict whose roots lie in the different positions occupied by the castes in an economic and social hierarchy. The BSP since the mid-1990s has no longer been described as an exclusively Dalit party (Jaffrelot, 1998: 35). The party's decision to form an alliance with the Congress party in the 1996 Assembly elections in UP and two coalition Governments with the BJP invited criticism and has been characterised as technocratic rationally. There is a strong Dalit assertion, but they don't have sense of direction and agenda for change. The movement needs to develop a new ideological perspective based upon the needs of the disadvantaged sections to carry forward its project of social transformation (Pai, 2002: 244).

However, the experience suggests that powerful leadership, efficient organisation and sustained mobilisation over a period of time leading to high levels of social awareness and politicisation, are required to create strong Dalit parties. Ambedkar followed the normative aspects of political power throughout his life. To capture this redeeming aspect of political power, Ambedkar imagined or positively identified comprehensive ideal like freedom, justice and equality with institutional arrangement like representative democracy with majority vote. He advised Dalits to organise themselves into a "third force" he thought that it was necessary to hold the balance of power between rival political parties (Guru, 2007: 157). In 1937, Ambedkar's newly formed the ILP backed 14 SC candidates for reserved seats and four Hindus for general seats in the Bombay Legislature Assembly. The party won 11 reserved and 3 general seats. The RPI was not intended to be confined to untouchables. As party president, Ambedkar tried to set himself as a leader of the "labouring masses". This step was largely due to his need for an electoral strategy, as he had become aware that he had to widen his social base of support. Questioned on the name of his party, he replied that the word "Labour" was used instead of the word "Depressed Classes" because labour includes Depressed Classes as well. Ambedkar considered that Indian workers were victims of both Brahminism and capitalism, the two systems being dominated by the same social groups (Gokhale, 1993: 132).

Ambedkar acquired national prominence since the Round Table Conference and clash with Gandhi, had wished to establish his party beyond the Bombay presidency in 1932. But in the central province and in Bihar the ILP gained only 3 out of 20 seats reserved for untouchables. These results clearly indicate that in spite of his efforts, the ILP remained a party of untouchables centered in Maharashtra. With 10 seats in the Legislative Councils of the Bombay presidency, the ILP became the second party of opposition to the Congress in the province, behind the Muslim League, Ambedkar was naturally one of ten elected members. The ILP gradually established itself as a full-fledged organisation. In 1940, Ambedkar embossed it with a red flag, in the upper left corner of which were eleven stars symbolising the eleven provinces of British India, a sign of the party's pan-Indian ambitions. In fact, the ILP remained confined to the Bombay presidency.

The Samata Sainik Dal ("the party of the fighters for equality") formed by Ambedkar, provided the ILP activists for street or door to door agitation as well as muscle men to maintain order during demonstrations. The Dal's uniform included *khaki* shorts and a red shirt but its flag was blue, the traditional colour of Dalit politics since then (Moon, 2001: 66). Ambedkar formed "The Scheduled Castes' Federation" (SCF) (or Dalit Federation in Maharashtra) in July, 1942, which was a shift in political strategy: the emphasis was again on caste. The SCF was a step backwards from the 1930s radicalism. Its very formation meant giving of the effort to form a broad radical party of Dalits and caste Hindu workers and peasants for the different goal of uniting Dalits on all-India level (Omvedt, 1994: 217). The immediate reason for this decision was the Cripps Mission formula, which was submitted in March 1942 to resolve India's constitutional impasse. It proposed the election of a Constituent Assembly without taking into account any of the demands of untouchables, whereas Muslims were virtually guaranteed the prospect of a separate State. In reaction to the

Cripps's proposal, the All India Depressed Classes Conference met in Nagpur. It brought together 70,000 delegates from Punjab, Bengal, Madras and Bombay presidency. The first resolution voted on this occasion demanded a separate electorate for untouchables, the second sought the establishment of separate villages for untouchables at a distance the Hindu villages, and the third announced the creation of the SC Federation (Zelliot, 2008: 52-53).

Ambedkar formed the SCF in the hope of uniting all untouchables in a new battle for political power (Zelliot, 2008: 207). Ambedkar was fundamentally opposed to the political domination of one community over another, and therefore, wanted to maintain a balance of political forces in Indian politics. He advised Dalits to organise themselves into a third force. Only through this force, Dalits would be able to acquire effective bargaining power. Ambedkar also suggested broad political unity of the SCs, STs and the OBCs in the country. In trying to create a common force of the Bahujan, Ambedkar was willing to change the name of Scheduled Caste Federation to Backward Class Federation.

The creation of the SCF, therefore, reflected a new mood, a new sense of identity among untouchables. In the elections of 1945-46, the SCF gained only two seats in the provincial assemblies, one in Bengal, and the other in the central province. This setback partly reflected the voting system. In the primaries in which, only untouchables voted, the SCF gained more votes than the Congress in the presidencies of Madras and Bombay and in the Central Provinces. But these results could not translate into commensurate number of seats because of the electoral system. The situation in the United Provinces was specially revealing of the distortion inherent in the electoral system. There twenty seats were reserved for SCs, including urban constituencies, which were the only ones the SCF contested. In the primaries, nine of the party's candidates were successful as against four for the Congress–but in the second round, the latter won all the seats, thanks to the support of non-Dalit voters (Reeves, Graham and Goodman, 1975: 316). Ambedkar considered that the failure of the SCF in the elections of 1945-46 did not endow it with the status of an important player, or even merit a particular role in the constituent Assembly.

The very modest rise in the influence of the SCF gradually encouraged Ambedkar to revisit the ILP's strategy in order to win support beyond untouchables. Indeed, the elections of 1951-52 delivered no better results than those of 1946. The SCF won only 2.31 per cent of the valid votes and two seats in the Lok Sabha, one in Hyderabad and the other in Bombay presidency where Ambedkar was defeated and where the performance of the party was far weaker than expected. On the other hand, the SCF for the first time won representation in the assemblies of Madras, Hyderabad, and State of Mysore, PEPSU (Patiala and East Punjab States Union). In the elections of February 1957, the SCF won 4 seats (two of which were reserved for untouchables) in the Lok Sabha in Bombay province and 15 in the Legislative Assembly of the province–most of them in Bombay.

Under the impact of the ideas and activities of Ambedkar, SC leaders formed "United Provinces Scheduled Castes' Federation" (UPSCF) in 1944. It was a branch of AISCF formed by Ambedkar. The UPSCF contested the 1945-46 elections and led a movement in 1946-47 in the United Provinces that was both anti-colonial and anti-Congress (Shah, 2001: 35). The RPI was to be the end-product of these cogitations, although it was formally established in October, 1957. The RPI was conceived by Ambedkar a short while before his death in 1956, when he was concerned with the need to forge an alternative to Communist Party. The RPI, in fact, projected a programme in which the notion of caste faded away behind that of class, but with the aim of appearing as a federation of oppressed population because of their ascribed status, be they Dalits, OBCs or tribal in the manifests that the SCF produced before the February, 1957 elections. The party had already indicated that it was prepared to change the name and call itself the Backward Classes Federation so as to include both sections (OBCs and tribal in addition to the SCs) in common organisation. The RPI contested in the third general elections held in 1962. It contested 68 Parliamentary and 301 Assembly seats all over the country, winning only 3 in the former, all in UP, and 11 in the latter, 3 in Maharashtra and 8 in UP. Thus, RPI performed better in UP than in Maharashtra (Pai, 2001: 263).

The RPI was a victim of factionalism and crisis of leadership that followed Ambedkar's death. In 1967, the two RPIs won only 2.48 per cent of valid votes at the national level and only 5 MLA seats, all located in Maharashtra. In 1971, the four factions gained one seat in the Lok Sabha but managed to get elected only three MLAs in Maharashtra (Jaffrelot, 2005: 153). The claim of the RPI, and its various factions, to be the exclusive legatee of the Ambedkarite tradition was challenged in the early 1970s by the rise of Dalit Panthers. The Panthers were heavily critical of the record of the RPI, which they saw as an organisation that had lost its roots among the mass of its supporters. The future of the Panthers and the continued disarray in the ranks of the various factions of the RPI led to repeated attempts to bring Dalit movements together through the late 1970s and 1980s.

Emergence of Dalit Political Parties after Dr Ambedkar

The building of a pan-Indian Dalit party had been the goal of Ambedkar for twenty years. He successively initiated the ILP (1936), the SCF (1942) and the RPI (1956). But none of them could make an impact, largely because individual Dalit jatis were not prepared to join hands and together support the same party. In fact, the Mahars–Ambedkar's caste fellows–were the only ones who tended to support his party. The BSP has gradually overcome this handicap. The BSP was in a position to cash in on the development of a Dalit counter-culture (including a poignant literature) and programmes of positive discrimination which have given birth to a Dalit middle class whose dedicated members were keen to organise themselves and their caste fellows. Dalit consciousness arose very late in India, due to the absence of a large-scale and sustained Dalit movement until the last decade of the colonial period. In contrast, in Western and Southern India, early awakening among Dalit and the 'reformist impulse', particularly in Maharashtra and to a lesser extent in Madras, were conducive to change (Pai, 2002. *Op. cit.*: 221).

In its stronghold in UP, where the BSP could rely on the All India Backword (SC, ST, OBC) and Minority Communities Employees Federation (BAMCEF), a movement of mostly Dalit public sector employees that Kanshi Ram had organised from the 1970s onwards, the BSP became the third largest party in 1989. It then benefited from being a coalition partner of the Samajwadi Party at the helm of the Government of UP in 1993-95. In this capacity, it advocated policies intended to promote the interests of Dalits at large, including the Ambedkar Village Scheme (Jaffrelot, 2007:10). Mayawati, the BSP leader, repeated the same strategy when she became chief minister of UP with the support of the BJP in 1996-97 and 2003. Eventually, the BSP won a majority of the seats in the State Assembly in 2007.

Kanshi Ram inaugurated a new type of movement when he founded, on October 14, 1971, "The SCs, STs, OBCs and Minority Communities Employees Association". This association was limited to the district of Poona but prefigured Kanshi Ram's future organisation since he already endeavoured to federate employees of Dalit, tribal, low caste and religious minority background. On December 6, 1978, he officially formed the BAMCEF whose aim was to organise the elites of the *Bahujan Samaj*, essentially wage earners with intellectual qualifications, who had benefited from quotas. BAMCEF could make rapid headway and reach a kind of critical mass because of the growing number of SCs' members in the administration. In UP, for instance, the literacy rate among the SCs increased from 7.1 per cent in 1961 to 10.2 per cent in 1971, which partly explains the growing number of SCs' members in the administration, even if the quotas are only filled in the lower rungs of the bureaucracy. Kanshi Ram travelled all over India to convince the *Bahujan Samaj* to get organised within the BAMCEF. Gradually, he built a network of activities that carried this message in the country side. In early 1990s, BAMCEF had almost 200,000 members, amongst whom 15,000 were scientists and 3,000 MBBS graduates (Jaffrelot, 1998. *Op. cit.*: 35-52).

It remains true that all public functions of BAMCEF have sought to include leaders of various Backward and Minority Communities. Kanshi Ram's major organisational and rhetorical thrust was, in fact, to develop BAMCEF as the major support organisation for a later, if indefinite, political thrust (Omvedt, 1994. *Op. cit.*: 163). While BAMCEF endowed Kanshi Ram with a core group of followers, he did not really regret its official dissolution since he no longer regarded it as his priority to do social work among the employees. Kanshi Ram started with the idea of social transformation and economic emancipation. He said, "I still want my people to advance socially and economically. But I have realised that unless we have political clout, we cannot advance much on those sides". Kanshi Ram formed "Dalit Soshit Samaj Sangarsh Samiti" (DS-4) (Committee to fight for the community of the exploited and the oppressed) on December 16, 1981. This organisation dispensed with the official euphemisms (Backward Classes, SCs) preferring instead the word Dalit and that politicised untouchables use more frequently to designate themselves. However, Dalit does not refer here to the untouchables only, as it is often the case, especially in Maharashtra (Jaffrelot, 2007. *Op. cit.*: 11). Along with the untouchables, the lower and BCs of Hindu society, Kanshi Ram also included the various religious minorities as a part of the *Bahujan Samaj*. His view of Indian society, later expounded with a sketch in his book *The Chamcha Age* that shows Brahmins, Kshatriyas and Vaishyas constituting 10 to 15 per cent of the population at the top of the social structure built out of various castes. On the eve of the 50th anniversary of 1932 Poona Pact the Congress was preparing to celebrate with great pomp, Kanshi Ram in his book *The Chamcha Age*, denounced this agreement as sealing the alienation of the untouchables. He argued that the system of reserved seats that had been forced on Ambedkar, who favoured a system of separate electorates, had helped the high castes dominated the Congress; co-opt Dalit candidates who were mere sycophants (*Chamchas*) of the Congress, the SCs were not in a majority in any single reserved constituency. Facing such a situation, the DS-4 had to act as a political party and contest elections. It was the only way out since, "a tool, an agent, a stooge or a *Chamcha*, is created to oppose the real, the genuine fighter. The DS-4 presented 46 candidates for the Assembly elections of Haryana in 1982, without making much of an impact (Ram, 1982: 90).

The BSP, officially formed on April 14, 1984, being Ambedkar's birth day, took over from the DS-4, it did not imply much more than a change of name but by rechristening his organisation that way, Kanshi Ram consummated his shift from social work to party politics. The BSP has made rapid progress on the electoral front. During the General election of 1984, it received more than one million votes. This number multiplied six-fold in 1989 when the party got 6,21,5093 votes, 2.07 per cent of the recorded votes and obtained three seats in the

Lok Sabha. In 1991, it won only two seats and 1.61 per cent of the votes but five years later it gained 11 seats with 3.64 per cent of the votes. The BSP has done increasingly well at the polls; it rose from 3.64 per cent to 4.2 per cent in 1999 and 5.3 per cent in 2004. Its geographical heartland is in UP, where it grew from 12 MLA seats in 1989 to 66 in 1993 (Jaffrelot, 2005. *Op. cit.*: 156). The 1996, all India election figures show that the BSP contested 201 seats, won 11 seats and was able to get 3.8 per cent of the total valid votes of the 11 seats; the BSP won six in UP, three in Punjab and two in MP (Pushpendra, 2001: 35).

The Assembly elections of November-December 2008 in several States, the BSP contested all the seats in Delhi, Rajasthan, Madhya Pradesh, and Chhattisgarh, that proved the desire of the party to become a truly national party eventually achieved due to the fact that in all States, the party got more than six per cent of valid votes–a requirement fixed by the Election Commission of India (ECI) for a party to be classified as a national party. In 2008 Assembly elections, the BSP fared poorly in all the four States. Out of 590 seats, it could win only 17 seats, 7 in MP, 6 in Rajasthan, two in Delhi and two in Chhattisgarh.

The formation of the BSP gave a new impetus to the movement and succeeded in breaking down the vertical patron-client relationship with the upper castes and accompanying political mobilisation pattern of the vote banks which was characteristic of one of the largest States with substantial proportion of Dalit population (Sharma, 2006: 145). The BSP not only raced ahead of its political opponents winning 206 of the 402 seats in 2007 but also was the first party since 1991 to come to power on its own in UP (Ramakrishnan, 2007: 10).

Until the BSP became a force to reckon with in UP politics in the early 1990s, the received wisdom was that such a development would take place either in Maharashtra or in the South, given their legacy of lower caste/Dalit movements for over a century (Babu and Bhan, 2009: 22). The problem of Dalits will never be solved unless they got political power in their own hands. If this is true, then (the) problem of Dalits is as Ambedkar argues eminently a political problem and must be treated as such' (Statement by Ambedkar at the first Round Table Conference, London, 1930) (Jaffrelot, 2007. *Op. cit.*: 74).

The BSP: its Organisational Strategy

The Election Commission recognised the BSP as a national political party on 25th November, 1997. Ms. Mayawati is the president of the party. Election Commission provided 'Elephant' as election symbol to the party. The party can use it in all States except Assam, Sikkim and Pondicherry. The Flag of the party is made of blue cloth with the symbol of Elephant embossed over it.

Policies and Programme of the BSP

Policies and programmes of the BSP can be divided into the following headings:

(a) Social Programme

- The party is totally against discrimination on the basis of caste, colour, creed and sex in the social sphere.
- Untouchability shall be opposed.
- Social and economic exploitation of Dalits should be abolished.
- Commissions shall be appointed for the progress and development of the SCs and STs.
- Carrying of human waste on the head and bonded labour shall be stopped.
- Protection and recognition to be given to the separate culture of Adivasis.
- To make sure that proper representation is being given to Dalits in the administration.
- Liberal policies to be adopted for the reservation of Dalits in the Government jobs and Legislative Assemblies.
- Special attention is to be given for the education of the children of downtrodden.
- To bring improvement in the condition of Dalit women.
- To establish educational institutions and universities on Dr Ambedkar's name.
- To make special arrangements for the professional and technical education of Dalit students.

- The party believes in implementing the plans of converting *Kuccha* houses into *Pucca* houses of Dalits in the rural and urban areas (Interview of the workers in the BSP office, Jalandhar, 25 September, 2014).

(b) Economic Programme

In economic field, the party believes reducing economic inequalities and making just distribution of wealth; establishment of economic system free from exploitation; establishing control of Dalits on the means of production; the physical resources of the nation should be distributed in such a way that these should not be centralised in few hands only. Economic policies and programmes of the BSP can be divided into the following headings:

- To make the common people free from the exploitation and hold of money lenders, zamindars and feudal.
- To bring improvement in the condition of landless and small farmers.
- To make plans and implement them to improve the economic life of Dalits living in rural areas and to encourage cottage industries.
- To establish industries, to provide maximum employment, to restart the sick units, to provide special assistance to the traditional industry of jute, leather and coconut.
- To make the public sector strong, opposition of liberalisation and privatisation.
- To abolish child labour and encourage the formation of special programmes for the protection of interests of labour class (*Ibid.*).

(c) Miscellaneous Policies

The BSP believes in:-

- Rooting out administrative and political corruption.
- Making the bureaucracy more answerable.
- Reconsidering of Centre-State relations.
- To solve the interstate disputes by mutual discussion.
- To control the increasing violence in the day-to-day life.

- To take strong action against the intimidation of voters of weaker classes.
- To strengthen the democratic system.
- To provide maximum autonomy to the local and regional institutions of rural and urban areas (Interview with the key functionaries of the BSP, 22 October, 2014).

(d) Foreign Policy

The party is the supporter of India's policy on Non-Alignment. The party is also in favour of getting permanent seat in Security Council, to promote friendly relations with neighbours and for India to play an important role in the maintenance of international peace.

Objectives of the BSP

The objectives of the BSP:

- To continue the struggle initiated by B.R. Ambedkar for abolishing the economic, social and political inequalities.
- To encourage Dalits to have self-confidence and to enlighten them for their rights.
- Political power is main objective of the party without which the condition of the *Bahujan Samaj* cannot be improved.
- To abolish social order based on Manuism and Brahminism.
- To provide security to the depressed and exploited people, to provide more opportunities to help their skill and to provide employment to all.
- The party has faith in the present democratic system and is in the favour of bringing about a change through democratic means (Interview with the BSP leaders, 22 March: 2014).

The BSP's only emphasis was on Dalit being a political category. In the ultimate, all questions of identities tend to be political question, and the BSP is, therefore, not to be blamed for this short-cut method. This amply explains the lack of any long-term social programme in the BSP's agenda (Kumar, 1999: 19). The BSP embodies the interests of Dalits.[1] Ambedkar statues have played an instrumental role in the BSPs successful mobilisation, confirming the popular appeal of symbolic politics (Jaoul, 2006: 178). The socio-cultural movements and mobilisation by Dalit based (the BSP) thrown off by increasing democratisation of the polity (Pai, 2000: 189). The phenomenon of fragmented and divided leadership has retarded the development and amelioration of Dalit community. The leadership of the RPI, Dalit Panthers, BAMCEF, and recently of the BSP to quote just a few, are the glaring examples of the fragmentation (Kumar, 2002: 17). In the past, Dalit leadership mainly faced the crisis of unity of inter-caste alliances, particularly alliance with OBC and minorities in crying out agitation or movement or capturing political power, and bringing out social change and transformation in the society. The constructive effort of BAMCEF can strengthen the non-political roots of the oppressed and the exploited society.

The BSP claimed its roots in Ambedkarism which acquired considerable influence in Northern India in the 1990s. The electoral symbol of the party of Ambedkar, being the elephant on a blue base, and its activities greet each other with "Jai Bhim" (victory of Bhim-Ambedkar's first name). One of its slogans proclaims plainly *"Baba (Saheb Ambedkar) Tera Mission Adhura, Kanshi Ram Karega Pura"* (Baba, your mission remains unfulfilled; Kanshi Ram, the founder of the party, will complete it). The issue was that the Ambedkar's political parties had always relied on the support of a particular caste groups rather than on Dalits as a whole. The *Mahars* in Maharashtra and the *Chamars* (or *Jatavs*) in North India, particularly UP, formed the backbone of the party. This produced suspicion and distrust among the other sections of Dalit population who felt both excluded and neglected. The BSP's main weakness also reminds Ambedkar's political parties, namely, mediocre grasp of organisation, which goes with a disturbing personalisation of power. Kanshi Ram had been continuing to appoint district heads and even party functionaries in charge at the tehsil and block level. Hence, the slogan of the BSP is: "the BSP is Kanshi Ram, and Kanshi Ram is the BSP". This peculiar feature threatened to affect it permanently, just as Ambedkar Parties were debilitated by poor organisation.

The Pali word "*Bahujan*" is popularly found in the literature of Buddhism. Lord Buddha used this word to guide his disciples to work for the *"Bahujan Hitay Bahujan Sukhay"* (Meaning: Benefit and prosperity of majority people). The meaning of the word *"Bahujan"* is people in majority. The term *"Bahujan"* is like the plebeians in the Roman sense, the second estate, in opposition to the patricians. However, in the Indian context, the *Bahujan* hardly form a "Samaj", i.e., a "community" because of caste and class division as well as ethnic, religion and language based cleavages. The term "*Bahujan*" entered political discourse around the turn of the century through the *Satyashodhak Samaj*, a lower-caste social and religious reform movement in Maharashtra that attacked Brahminic Hinduism. *"Bahujan"* literally means "majority" in Marathi, its language of origin and in Hindi, the language in which Kanshi Ram popularised it (Omvedt, 1996: 4). In Kanshi Ram's words, *"Bahujan Samaj*" is comprised of SCs, STs, OBCs and Converted Minorities. Kanshi Ram introduced the category *"Bahujan"* which he defined as an ascriptive category consisting of a collection of subordinate ethnic categories, hitherto considered separate, that constitute a majority of the Indian population. The BSP organised Dalit movement in UP by mobilising on the basis of identity and created a strong Dalit based party. These developments gave Dalit politics a seminal position both in UP and national politics. Bahujanwad, based on caste identities, might have seemed to work–as in the case of the BSP– in strategising electoral wins (Sebastian, 2009: 33).

The term "*Bahujan*" symbolises not a majority as perceived by Buddha and Phule, but an ideological category that can create the base of empowerment. Kanshi Ram continued to engage himself blissfully in playing with *"guru killi"*, the Punjabi synonym for the "*master key*", the Ambedkar definition of political power, by which he intends to open every lock whether social, political, economic or cultural (Dubey, 2001: 289). The BSP claimed to represent the exploited 85 per cent of Backward Classes including Dalits, Adivasis, OBCs and Minorities, its most significant slogan in many ways was *"Jati Jodo, Samaj Jodo*". The BSP and DS-4 were organising increasingly huge rallies, and in the process increasing their hold over SCs ans BCs Government employess. (Omvedt, 2001b: 164). The issue of Backward-Dalit relationship in politics is very important as it is often mentioned that Dalit Bahujan alone can fight the monopoly and control of the upper castes. Many left historians have particularly referred to this possibility of a Dalit-Bahujan alliance while numerically this alliance is more than workable.

Kanshi Ram further reiterated the fact that there are two ways by which the political position of Dalit-Bahujan can undergo transformation. The first is capturing power through mobilisation and electoral victory from the Brahmins. He consistently pointed out that since the Brahmins comprise only 10 to 12 per cent of the population, if the more numerous Dalit Bahujan votes for the BSP, they can seize the system from within that is capture of State power without social revolution. At the second stage, with the use of State power the revolution can, under the leadership of the BSP, penetrate deep into society, transforming it. As a political party, its goal is to capture the State power in order to undertake social engineering from above; the BSP believes in entering into electoral alliances and coalition with conservative mainstream parties representing the upper castes, which can put it in danger of losing its carefully constructed identity.

It is important to understand that the BSP is not an anti-systemic party or movement, which has challenged and sought to transform the basic structure of the Indian social system, replacing caste and the accompanying social system, economic exploitation and political domination by an egalitarian society (Omvedt, 1994. *Op. cit.*: 224). Rather it is a party that wants to work within the system, reforming it in the light of its own ideology and philosophy. A central characteristic of the BSP is its exclusivism, i.e., its ideology and goal appeal to only some segments of the population. The BSP is not a revolutionary party of change for the lower orders, as Dalit Panthers professed to be its inception. In contrast, it is a reformist party that has adopted the political path of gradual social transformation. The BSP played power politics at the formal level, and it was remained the party of Dalits with the objective of capturing formal power at the State and national level. The BSP, in contrast to the RPI brought a paradigmatic shift in the orientation of Dalit assertion, whereas the former approached the issue in terms of social equality for Dalits, the latter has been playing the game of power similar to the other political parties. The ideology of the BSP is "social transformation and economic emancipation" of the *Bahujan Samaj*, which comprises of the SCs, the STs, OBCs and Religious Minorities such as Sikhs, Muslims, Christians, Parsis and Buddhists, which account for over 85 per cent of the country's total population. The people belonging to all these classes have been the victims of the *"Manuwadi"* system in the country for thousands of years, under which they have been vanquished, trampled upon and forced to languish in all spheres of life. In other words, these people were deprived even of all those human rights, which had been secured for the upper caste Hindus under the age-old "Manuwadi Social System".

Withering BSP: UP Assembly Election, 2017

In 2017 UP Assembly election, the phenomenal scale of the victory of the BJP and its allies, 325 seats out of 403, of which the BJP accounted for 312, the Apna Dal (Soneylal) for nine and the Suheldev Bhartiya Samaj Party four, was also in keeping with the retention of vote share. In 2014, when the BJP won 71 of the 80 Lok Sabha seats in the State, it had led in 328 Assembly segments. On the other hand, the Samajwadi Party-Congress combine, could rustle up only 28 per cent of the vote share–the SP got 21.8 per cent; could win 47 seats and the Congress 6.2 per cent, could win 7 seats–which, incidentally, was less than what they had obtained in the 2014 Lok Sabha elections, when they had fought separately and the SP obtained 22.20 per cent and Congress 7.50 per cent. Interestingly, the third major force in the State, the Dalit-oriented BSP, actually increased its vote share from what it had in 2014, but still ended up losing big time. Its vote share rose to 22.2 per cent from 19.6 per cent in 2014. Still, the party could only win 19 seats, its second-lowest tally in UP. Its lowest tally was in 1991 when it won 12 seats, at a time when the party was still considered to be building up its mass base. In 2012, the BSP secured 25.91 per cent vote share and could win 80 seats. Just 3.22 per cent difference of vote share deprived BSP to win 144 seats.

The result could, in the medium term, pose challenges to the BSP's ability to hold on to its core Dalit vote base. Although it boosted its overall vote share, the party could win only two out of 84 seats reserved for Dalits. It was also trounced in most of its traditional seats. It could not win even a single seat of the nine in Agra, considered to be the Dalit capital of UP. This traditional BSP bastion had given the party six seats even in 2012, when it was voted out of power. Dalit-dominated districts such as Sitapur, Sonbhadra, Auraiya, Jalaun, Barabanki, Chitrakoot and Kaushambi also signaled a move away from the BSP. More importantly, only five of its 100 Muslim candidates won, raising questions about the Dalit-Muslim brotherhood that the party was actively promoting during campaign.

In fact, Kanshi Ram chose the name *"Bahujan"*, or "Majority". For his new party, not only because of its association with non-Brahmin social movements but also because the name signaled that this party had the numbers to be a viable winner. The arithmetic was backed by an ideological and organisational infrastructure. Over the years, the BSP stopped investing in this infrastructure, relying on the promise of power to compensate. But a party that depends only on winning cannot withstand repeated losses and that is why the party is now in such dire straits. It was not magic but just micro planning of caste combinations that allowed the BJP to repeat its 2014 performance. In the process, the Congress party and regional heavyweights like the BSP and the SP were largely wiped out from the political scene. The BJP bitterly trampled down the showcase of hollow development model displayed by Congress-Samajwadi alliance and slogan of *"Sarvajan Hitaye, Sarvjan Sukhaye*" led by the BSP. This long standing project, which sought to forge a social and political alliance against the Yadavs, who form the core support base of the SP, the Jatav Dalits, the core support base of the BSP and Muslims, attained concrete and massive dimensions in the 2014 Lok Sabha elections. It was with that election that the BJP was able to do away with the image of being an upper-caste Brahmin-Bania-Rajput party.

The BJP built up this OBC-MBC-Dalit coalition as a sort of Hindutva force opposed to the Yadav, Jatav and Muslim communities. The strategy of reverse social engineering that BJP scripted was clearly aimed at mobilising the most BCs, notably non-Yadav and non-Jatav Dalits, to capture the heartland State. In pursuit of this agenda, it distributed tickets copiously to non-Yadav OBCs and to non-Jatav in reserved seats. The traction for this campaign came essentially from the Hindutva-oriented social engineering that the BJP had built up among the non-Yadav OBCs and Most Backward Castes (MBCs) communities and the non-Jatav Dalit communities.

The most ambitious, but less known, is the BJP's division of caste strategy. It was designed to fragment the non-Jatav Dalit voters from the fold of the BSP. In a shrewd political exercise to dismantle Dalit consolidation under the BSP fold, the BJP gave 65 tickets to non-Jatav Dalit community out of 87 reserved constituencies. It worked and it won 68 seats from the reserved constituencies. Out of around 25 per cent Dalit votes in UP, non-Jatavs make around 14 per cent vote share. Jatavs among Dalits continue to be firmly behind the BSP. Similarly, Yadavs, more or less, continue to be with the SP. Hence the BJP had formulated a clear strategy to target remaining Dalits and BCs. The target area for the BJP among Dalits was to placard the support from the Pasi, Dhobi and Khatik castes. These three castes together were given 39 tickets. The party had also given representation to around 11 other non-Jatav Dalit castes in ticket distribution. On the other side out of the 403 seats up for grabs, the BSP had distributed 97 Muslim candidates (12 more than 2012), 87 Dalits and 106 OBCs, besides earmarking 113 seats for upper castes—Brahmins 66, Kshatriyas 36 and others 11.

The communities include OBCs such as Kurmis, Lodhs and Pals, MBC castes such as Maurya, Nishads and Rajbhars, and Dalit communities such as Sansiyas and Valmiki's informal estimates state that these communities account nearly 25 per cent of total UP population across 38 caste blocks, with over 200 sub-castes and groups. Economically, these communities are classified as landless labour class. The landowning OBC Yadav community accounts for approximately 9 per cent and the economically upwardly mobile Dalit Jatav community for approximately 10 per cent of the population. While both the SP and the BSP have conventionally sought to supplement their core vote base with the Muslims.

In India, where the BSP chief Mayawati is a contemporary Dalit icon, this method of "integrating" Dalits into the Sangh Parivar is not just out of sync with the times; it is within a Hindutva framework that is unacceptable to assertive Dalits, such as those, who believe that traditional Hinduism is the reason for their low social status. They see its limitations and are suspicious of the Rashtriya Swayamsevak Sangh (RSS), an organisation that, they believe, has an essentially upper-caste mindset. However, beyond this sense of befuddlement and anger, there are several tangible factors that led to the BJP's comprehensive victory. Three key factors among these were the ability to retain a Hindutva communal narrative throughout the campaign, the supplementation of this through the advancement of post-truth pronouncements and exercise from the party machinery, including top leaders, and finally, the deployment of superior organisational machinery. Communal narratives were advanced at different levels, starting with grassroots door-to-door campaigns and building up to communally charged exhortations and utterances from the top BJP and Sangh Parivar leadership. Leading all this was the BJP leaderships through its multifaceted rhetoric, touching upon the issues like "Kabaristan versus shamshanghat" and also the creation of acronyms like "Kasab" to curb the Congress, the SP and the BSP.

For the BSP, the winning of elections has always depended on what its workers call the "plus" factor. In every constituency, it counted on the votes of Dalits plus some section of others (Backwards Castes and Muslims initially and upper castes eventually). For the BJP, it has depended on what it could be called the "minus" factor. The BJP aimed to build a winning vote by cobbling together the support of Hindu upper castes, BCs and Dalits–everyone but the Muslims. This is an old strategy of the BJP, taken to new, more systematic, level in 2017. Electoral arithmetic–alliances and tickets–was always an important part of this effort.

The plunge in seats is not accompanied by a similar plunge in votes, but in a 'first past the post' electoral system, minor shifts in seats. The BSP's survival crisis is not about something more than the party: it is about the nature of identity-based politics that the BSP represents. To understand why, consider the way in which the two main alternatives, the Congress and the BJP, appeal to Dalits. The Congress appeals to Dalits by promising assimilation into a national mainstream. The BJP appeals to Dalits by promising immersion in a Hindu mainstream. The BSP's form of identity-based assertion, by contrast, is based on pride in Dalit-identity as it exists in the present, not on the promise of assimilation or transformation in the future. It believes that the Dalits did not have to become someone else in order to take pride in them. So why did the BSP lose, especially when its healthy vote share suggests that it is likely to retained much of its core, predominantly Dalit, vote base? The answer lies in its failure and the BJP's success, in crafting the right caste-based combinations.

The BJP and the Sangh Parivar, by contrast, back their appeal to Dalits and BCs by a strong ideological and organisational infrastructure. The Sangh Parivar has also begun to redefine the model Hindu in a way that incorporates Dalit and BCs' cultural symbols. In 1983, the RSS chose April 14, B.R. Ambedkar's birth anniversary, to establish the Samajik Samrasta Manch, or social harmony platform, that would celebrate Ambedkar Jayanti every year. It created the Samajik Samrasta Manch (Social Assimilation Platform), with the goal of harmonising "the Phule-Ambedkar thought with the Hindutva Philosophy". In 1989, the Vishva Hindu Parishad (VHP) ensured that it was a Dalit who laid the first brick for the Ram Temple at Ayodhya. PM claims his BC identity proudly. "The next decade", he has said repeatedly, "will belong to the Dalits and the backwards." This is a remarkable statement for the leader of India's largest upper caste party to make. The objective was aimed at ending untouchability and "integrating" Dalits into Hindu society, a necessary precondition for Hindu consolidation. For the BJP, in particular, "Hindu unity" was of paramount importance to enlarge its support base. But the unstated part of the RSS agenda was that Dalits should be integrated into Hindu society without upsetting the hierarchy of the caste system, a far cry from Ambedkar's call for annihilation of caste.

BSP chose to ignore the fact that the BSP was skating on thin ice for some years; its inability to widen the social base would eventually lead to party's decimation. The BSP's base seems destined to slowly wither away unless something dramatic happens. The party could not evolve a structure which can sustain political attacks at different levels. The party has only one leader and she responds to everything coming before the party. It also failed to mobilise non-Jatav Dalits and extremely BCs which the party had effectively done during early years.

Discussions within the SP-Congress combine as well as section of the BSP are increasingly revolving around the absence of a Bihar-style grand alliance (*Mahagathbandhan*) as a key factor in the phenomenal triumph of the BJP. The SP-Congress combine has 28 per cent of the vote share, the BSP 22.2 per cent. Put together, it is massive 50.2 per cent. In the first-past-the-post electoral system, a *mahagathbandhan* could result in the mother of all electoral sweeps. The BJP leadership is of the view that such a grand alliance will never happen in UP, essentially because of Mayawati's inability to fit into coalition politics. The simple arithmetic shows that the BSP and the SP could have made a winning combination. The coming together on broader alliance would have made smaller castes vote for such an alliance. The BSP supremo should accept the electoral-decision of electorates by healthy political mindset.

The result upset the perceptions that dominated the election scene throughout the long-out process. However, this was in contrast to the doubts over the result expressed rather angrily by the BSP's supreme leader Mayawati, who said the electronic voting machines had been tempered with and that contributed to the BJP's huge success. Mayawati, meanwhile, could not relish the unprecedented reversals of her party and even before the final outcome of elections. Mayawati alleged that BJP manipulated and rigged the polls and dishonestly obtained mandate in the State, thereby, "killing democracy".

Note

1. Former untouchable caste groups describe themselves as Dalit in preference to Harijan or SC.

References

- Babu, D. Shyam and Chandra Bhan Prasad. 2009. 'Six Dalit Paradoxes.' *Economic and Political Weekly* XLIV (23): 22-25.
- Chandra, Kanchan. 2004. *Why Ethnic Parties Succeed: Patronage and Ethnic Head Counts in India.* New Delhi: Cambridge University Press.
- Dubey, Abhay Kumar. 2001. 'Anatomy of a Dalit Power Player: A Study of Kanshi Ram.' In *Dalit Identity and Politics*, edited by Ghanshyam Shah, 288-310. New Delhi: Sage Publications.
- Duverger, Maurice. 1962. *Political Parties*. London: Methuen & Co. Ltd.
- Gokhale, J. 1993. *From Concession to Confrontation*: *The Politics of an Indian Untouchable Community.* Bombay: Popular Prakashan.
- Guru, Gopal. 2007. 'Concept of Power.' In *Ambedkar in Retrospect,* edited by Sukhadeo Thorat and Aryama, 155-63. New Delhi: Rawat Publications.
- Hasan, Zoya. 2002. 'Introduction: Conflict, Pluralism and the Competitive Party System in India.' In *Parties and Party Politics in India*, edited by Zoya Hasan, 1-2. New Delhi: Oxford University Press.
- Jaffrelot, Christophe. 1998. 'The Bahujan Samaj Party in North India: No Longer Just a Dalit Party.' *Comparative Studies of South Asia, Africa and the Middle East* 18 (1): 35-52.
- ———. 2005. *Dr Ambedkar and Untouchability*. New Delhi: Permanent Black.

- ———. 2007. The Strategy Pays off. *Tehelka* 4 (20): 26 May.
- Jaoul, Nicolas. 2006. 'Learning the Use of Symbolic Means: Dalits, Ambedkar Statues and the State in Uttar Pradesh.' *Contributions to Indian Sociology* 40 (2): 176-202.
- Kumar, Pradeep. 1999. 'Bahujan Samaj Party.' *Mainstream* 1 (25): 19.
- Kumar, Vivek. 2002. *Dalit Leadership in India.* Delhi: Kalpaz Publications.
- Moon, Vasant. 2001. *Growing up Untouchables in India: A Dalit Autobiography.* London: Rowman and Littlefield.
- Omvedt, Gail. 1994. *Dalits and the Democratic Revolution, Dr Ambedkar and Dalit Movement in Colonial India.* New Delhi: Sage Publications.
- ———. 1996. *Cultural Revolt in a Colonial Society*. Mumbai: Scientific Socialist Education Trust.
- ———. 2001a. 'Ambedkar and After: Dalit Movement in India.' In *Dalit Identity and Politics*, edited by Ghanshayam Shah, 143-59. New Delhi: Sage Publications.
- ———. 2001b. 'Kanshi Ram and the Bahujan Samaj Party.' In *Caste and Class in India,* edited by K.L. Sharma, 153-69. Jaipur: Rawat Publications.
- Pai, Sudha. 2000. 'New Social and Political Movements of Dalits: A Study of Meerut District.' *Contributions to Indian Sociology* 34 (2): 189-90.
- ———. 2001. 'From Harijan to Dalits: Identity Formation, Political Consciousness and Electoral Mobilisation of Scheduled Castes in Uttar Pradesh.' In *Dalit Identity and Politics, Cultural Subordination and Dalit Change*, edited by Ghanshyam Shah, 258-287. New Delhi; Sage Publications.
- ———. 2002. *Dalit Assertion and the Unfinished Democratic Revolution, the Bahujan Samaj Party in Uttar Pradesh.* New Delhi: Sage Publications.
- Pushpendra. 2001. 'Dalit Assertion through Electoral Politics.' In *Dalit Identity and Politics,* edited by Ghanshyam Shah, 311-339. New Delhi: Sage Publications.
- Ram, Kanshi. 1982. *The Chamcha Age: An Era of the Stooges*. Delhi: Privately printed.
- Ramakrishnan, Venkitesh. 2007. 'Focus on Sarva Samaj.' *Frontline* 24 (10): 19 May.
- Reeves, P.D., B.D. Graham, and J.M. Goodman. 1975. *Elections in UP, 1921-51.* New Delhi: Manohar Publishers and Distributors.
- Sarkar, Radha and Amar Sarkar. 2016. Dalit Politics in India, Recognition without Destribution.' *Economic and Political Weekly* LI (24): 14-16.
- Sartori, Giovanni. 1976. *Parties and Party Systems*. London: Cambridge University Press.
- Sebastian, P.A. 2009. 'Dalit in Indian Soceity.' *Economic and Political Weekly* XLIV (4): 33.

- Shah, Ghanshyam. 2001. 'Introduction: Dalit Politics.' In *Dalit Identity and Politics*, edited by Ghanshyam Shah, 35-37. New Delhi: Sage Publications.
- Sharma, Pradeep K. 2006. *Dalit Politics and Literature*. Delhi: Shipra Publications.
- Sisson, Richard. 1972. *The Congress Party in Rajasthan.* Delhi: Oxford University Press.
- Verma, A.K. 2009. Bahujan Samaj Party: Beyond Uttar Pradesh. *Economic and Political Weekly* XLIV (7): 22-26.
- Zelliot, Eleanor. 2008. 'Gandhi and Ambedkar, A Study of Leadership.' In *Caste in History*, edited by Ishita Banerjee, 207-15. New Delhi: Oxford University Press.
- ———. 2008. 'Learning the Use of Political Means: The Mahars of Maharashtra.' In *Caste in Indian Politics*, edited by Rajni Kothari, 27-65. New Delhi: Orient BlackSwan.

Chapter - 4

Dalits in the State of Punjab: An Analysis of their Assertion

It is truism that the nature and content of politics undergo transformation from one territory to another. What is less obvious is that the caste system also evinces several level of differentiation. These levels require to be specified before a proper understanding can be achieved of the transformation in the relation between caste and politics from one level of organisation to another (Beteille, 2008: 245). The uniqueness of Punjab lies in the historical evolution of its social structure and culture amidst an atmosphere of interactions among people of diverse cultures. Amidst such a changing social, cultural, economic and political scenario and the emerging contradictions within the entire sphere of life in Punjab, there has been a collective concern to resolve opposition of all kinds at different stages of history through the synthesis of various cultures. An understanding of the distinctive pattern of caste hierarchy in Sikhism which points to a new pattern of competing parallel to that of Hindus, calls for deeper insight into the dynamic of political power and economic relations both at the local and regional levels. There is certainly a complex mix of socio-religious tension at the root. The contemporary Indian Punjab has been a rather fluid region. It has seen many changes in its social and political geography over the last sixty years or so. The region has been quite fluid socially and culturally. Despite the popular image of Punjab being a Sikh State, it was only in 1966, after its reorganisation on linguistic basis, that the Sikhs became a majority in the State. Though, the Sikh leadership in Punjab has always recognised the fact of caste.

Even the Sikh reformers during the last early twentieth century attacked caste, the Sikh leadership, having become aware of the significance of numbers, did not deny the existence of caste among the Sikhs or that Dalits among the Sikhs did not face any disabilities due to their birth.

Dalit Movements in Punjab

Dalit movement is the result of the constant hatred being generated from centuries from the barbaric activities of the Hindu upper castes of India. The main issues around which most of Dalits have been centred in the colonial and post-colonial periods are confined to the problem of untouchability. The Kuka movement which was founded by Bhagat Jawar Mal, generally known as *"Sian Sahib"* in the 1840s, tried to purify Sikhism by removing certain abuses and superstitions that crept into from Hinduism. The movement became popular among the Namdhari Sikhs. Both the Singh Sabha and Arya Samaj launched a campaign of *shuddhi* (purification and conversion ceremonies). After 1890, Aryas openly converted Sikhs and cut their hairs in public (Gerald, 2000: 72). The founder of Arya Samaj, Swami Dayanand called upon all the Hindus to adopt Vedic Hinduism. His slogan was "Back to Vedas". By this, he meant a Hindu society for the Hindus (Sharma, 2000: 97). Initially, Shuddhis were performed on those untouchables who had embraced Islam and Christianity.

The Christian movement in Punjab was gaining strength and assertiveness in the years following 1857. By 1857, the European missionaries had established mission stations at Ambala, Amritsar, Delhi, Jalandhar, Kangra, Kotgarh, Lahore, Ludhiana, Multan, Peshawar, Rawalpindi, Sabathu and Sialkot. The mission in Jalandhar was run by the American Presbyterian Mission. The Mission School offered Western education which included instruction in both the English language and the Christian religion, became throughout most of the nineteenth century, the major sign of the Christian presence in Punjab (Webster, 2000: 115).

The greatest response to Christian evangelistic work, however, did not come from the educated urban elites or from their children in the mission school, but from rural *Chuhras* (Balmikis) primarily in the central Punjab. *Chuhras* were considered to be at the bottom of the caste hierarchy. Previously, many had converted to Islam and Sikh religion (Musallis and Mazhabis) in their search for dignity and respect. The conversion movement started in several unconnected villages at about the same time. From those individuals who had taken the lead in seeking baptism, it spread through kinship, village and even business connections in the Sialkot, Gujranwala, Gurdaspur, Lahore, Amritsar and Ferozepur districts.

According to Juergensmeyer, the Christian missionaries had not really intentionally targeted the low castes for conversion. Apparently, these were the untouchables who came out seeking conversions to Christianity (Juergensmeyer, 1988:189). They would have obviously seen a potential for social mobility in conversions. Emanual Nahar's study pointed out that untouchability, lower status, and social economic problems compelled Dalits to adopt new religion, i.e., Christianity (Nahar, 2007: 76-77). The socio-economic condition of the community is the main obstacle in the way of various political activities in Punjab. The majority of Christians belong to agricultural labour. They are neither organised nor members of any workers or Labour Party in Punjab. The 1911 Census reported 1,63,994 Indian Christians in Punjab. These gains were due almost entirely to *Chuhras* conversion. The conversion movement made the plight of Dalits in Punjab, as elsewhere in India.

Similarly, a large number of Chuhras (who are called Mazhabis) and Chamars from other parts of Punjab (who are called Ramdasis) converted to the Sikh faith in order to distance themselves from Brahminical Hinduism. Sikhism seems to have worked as an important alternative source of religious symbol for Dalits of Punjab. In Punjab, Christian Dalits live in the same kind of villages (Bastis or Thathi), are dependent on the same kind of land-owners, suffer the same kind of disparities and atrocities, are subject to the same social and economic pressure, and face equally limited opportunities as do other rural Dalits *Ibid.*: 237-238).

Buddhist revolution was revolutionary in denying caste and gender inferiority (Ambedkar, 1989: 41). Judge and Bal (2005: 108) mentioned in their book that Dalits of Punjab did not follow Ambedkar as no mass conversion to Buddhism took place. A few conversions to Buddhism in recent years indicate the changing orientation of the Punjabi Dalits to Buddhism though it is largely confined to the intelligentsia. S.L. Virdi (2000) mentions that in a function organised by Punjab Buddha Mahasabha, 3500 people converted to Buddhism in 1991 (Virdi, 2000: 225). "Buddh Vihars" have been constructed in Hoshiarpur, Jalandhar, and Kapurthala districts. Except Buddhist revolution, Ad-Dharm movement proponents advocated that the untouchables were a separate *quam.*

The Ad-Dharm movement was born out of a volatile social and political background in the early twentieth century in the Doaba region of Punjab which brought together all the SCs (then known as Depressed Class) on a single platform to fight against the system of social oppression, economic deprivation and political indifference. The Ad-Dharm movement saw itself as a religious movement. Its proponents advocated that the "untouchables" were a separate *quam*, a distinct religious community similar to the Muslims, Hindus, and Sikhs, and should be treated as such by the rulers (Jodhka, 2009: 81). Despite stiff opposition from the local Hindu leadership, the colonial Census of 1931 listed the Ad-Dharmis as a separate religious community. The emphasis of Ad-Dharmis being a separate religion, a *quam* was to undermine the identity of caste. As a separate *quam*, Ad-Dharmis were equal to other *quams* recognised by the colonial State, the Hindus, Muslims and Sikhs. Mangoo Ram also expected to bring other untouchable communities into the fold of Ad-Dharmis and emerge as a viable community at the regional level. A total of 4,18,789 persons reported themselves as Ad-Dharmis in the 1931 Punjab Census, almost equal to the Christian population of the province. They accounted for about 1.5 per cent of the total population of Punjab and around a tenth of the total low-caste population of the province. Nearly 80 per cent of the low castes of Jalandhar and Hoshiarpur districts reported themselves as Ad-Dharmis (*Ibid.*: 81-82).

However, despite its success, the movement could not maintain its momentum for very long and began to dissipate soon after its grand success in 1931. According to the popular understanding, the causes of the decline of Ad-Dharm movement lay in its success. Its leaders joined mainstream politics. Mangoo Ram himself, along with some of his close comrades, became members of the Punjab Legislative Assembly. The caste issue was gradually taken over by the emerging pan-Indian movement of Dalits and it finally merged with it. The Ad-Dharm Mandal began to see itself as a social and religious organisation and in 1946 decided to change its name to Ravi Dass Mandal, "entrusting the political work to All India Scheduled Castes' Federation in conformity with rest of India" (Juergensmeyer, 1988. *Op. cit.*: 153). After having changed its name to Ravi Dass Mandal in 1946, the movement activists shifted their focus to social and religious matters. They had realised long ago that in order to consolidate themselves as a separate *quam*, they needed a religious system of their own, which was different from the Hindus and Sikhs. However, in order to do that they chose a caste-based religious identity: Chamar = Ad-Dharmi = Ravidassi.

During its early days, the Ad-Dharm movement had aspired to bring all the "ex-untouchable" communities together into the same faith. Their appeal had remained confined mostly to the Chamars of Doaba. Guru Ravidass appeared to be an obvious choice for the Ad-Dharmis as a religious symbol for the community. Thus, the Ad-Dharm movement played a very important role in developing an autonomous political identity and consciousness among the Chamar Dalits of Punjab. Ad-Dharm flourished from 1925 to 1935 in the central Punjab districts of Jalandhar and Hoshiarpur, claiming perhaps a million adherents. The name of the movement "Ad-Dharm" signified the central concept: that the SCs (the untouchables) were not members of Hinduism, Islam, Sikhism or any other upper caste religion. Rather, they were members of a distinctly separate religious community (Dhami, 1988: 382).

Sant Ravidass was projected a spiritual preceptor and Guru Bhagwan, Satguru Namdev, Mahajan Kabir and Rishi Valmiki were also included in the theology of Ad-Dharm. The construction of a Ravidass Temple in Benares and the expansion of the Ravidass dera (Temple) in village Ballan, near Bhogapur town of Jalandhar were focal points of the new Ad-Dharm movement, designed to highlight the significance of saint Ravidass for the cause of Dalit consciousness. The revived Ad-Dharm movement attempted to widen the scope of the Ad-Dharm religion by including in its fold the *Chuhras* (Sweeper Caste), *Mazhabi Sikhs*, *Ramdasias,* and Ambedkar Buddhists (Ram, 2004b: 341).

The Ad-Dharm movement aimed at carving out a distinct identity for the untouchables, independent of the Hindus, Sikhs and Muslims.

The leadership of Ad-Dharm came from a small group of young SC members perhaps a dozen or so, who began meeting informally in Jalandhar city early in 1925. Among them, Swami Shudranand was from Jalandhar city, Vasant Rai from village Pandori Nijhran, district Jalandhar and Thakur Chand from village Kandola, near Nurmahal in Jalandhar district who later played a significant role in developing the Ad-Dharm organisation. These three and others, who were alleged to have been involved in that earliest group, had several characteristics in common, they came from the same geographical area; they were financially secure; educated and many had been associated with the Arya Samaj. Virtually, all the original activists came from the heart of the Doaba area including districts of Jalandhar, Hoshiarpur and the princely State of Kapurthala. This is an area characterised by fairly small landholdings, a large number of SCs.

The Ad-Dharm movement led local campaigns against discrimination agitated for Government reform, and registered themselves in the Census as a separate religious community. But perhaps the Ad-Dharm movement's greatest significance was in the fact that it existed as a movement for political identity and cultural pride. However, in 1929, the Ad-Dharm organisation split into two factions: the Ad-Dharm Mandal with its office in Jalandhar was headed by Mangoo Ram, and All Indian Ad-Dharm Mandal with its headquarter in Layalpur was headed by Vasant Rai. In fact, Vasant Rai group was lured back by the Arya Samaj in 1929, while Mangoo Ram group played an active part in the politics of Punjab between 1926 to 1952 (Chandra, 2004: 190). There were two epicentres of Ad-Dharm support: the Doaba area, including Jalandhar, Hoshiarpur, Kapurthala, and the area in western Punjab around Lyallpur, including districts Sheikharpura, Multan and Montgomery – many of these canal colonies to which lower caste people from the Doaba area had migrated.

As many as 14.9 per cent (5,32,129) of the 70,28,723 SCs of Punjab were listed as Ad-Dharmis in the 2001 Census, substantially more than those who registered themselves as belonging to the Ad-Dharmis *quam* in 1931. In religious terms, as many as 59.9 per cent of the Punjab SCs enumerated themselves as Sikhs and 39.6 per cent as Hindus. Only 0.5 per cent declared their religion as Buddhism

(Jodhka, 2009. *Op. cit*.: 82). The Ad-Dharmis of the Doaba region are mostly enumerated as Hindus, while in practice they worship the Sikh holy book, "Guru Granth Sahib" partly because it contains the writing of Guru Ravidass, who was a *Chamar* by birth. While the identity of Ad-Dharmis simply became a designation of a Hindu Caste group for official classification, the *Chamars* of Doaba did not go back to Hinduism. They began to develop their autonomous religious resources under the identity of Ravidassis. They have asserted through the Guru Ravidass deras which strengthened their identity. The most important of the Guru Ravidass deras in Punjab today is the *dera* located in the village Ballan, around 10 km. from the town of Jalandhar. It is locally known as Dera Sachkhand Ballan. In 1970, the Ad-Dharm movement was revived. On national issues Mangoo Ram was supportive of Ambedkar. In that sense the Ad-Dharm was the Punjab regional unit of a national network of support for Dr Ambedkar and his strategy for social reforms (Juergensmeyer, 1988. *Op. cit*.: 103).

Ad-Dharm was an anti-caste movement of the Chamar Dalits of the Doaba region launched during the 1920s and 1930s. The colonial rulers had conceded to their demand for being recognised as a separate religious community. However, after independence, they were included in the list of SCs and began to enumerate as such. Though most of them continue to enumerate themselves as Hindus, in practice, they, over the years, have moved closer to Sikhism. Apart from worshipping Guru Granth, the Sikh holy book, they have also begun to follow the Sikh rituals, such as getting married through an Anand Karaj. The primary reason for their attraction towards Sikhism is its explicit anti-caste message.

The *dera* was set up by Sant Pipal Das sometime during the early twentieth century.[1] Ravidassis have emerged as a strong and autonomous caste religious community, an outcome of vibrant Dalit identity movements in Punjab from the last eight decades. Over the years, Ravidassis have also evolved their own symbols and practices of worship, which distinguish them from Sikhs of Punjab. This provoked followers of this *dera,* who are Dalits and worship Bhagat Ravidass whose verses find a place of honour in Guru Granth Sahib.

Essentially, this is an assertion for equality by Dalits who despite Sikhism's egalitarian nature and its emphasis on a casteless society find the present state of affairs too stifling and unjust. Seen in this historical context, the street violence in Punjab following the Vienna attack on 24 May, 2009 leading to the death of a senior Ravidassi religious leader would appear more like a cause of assertion of the "*Ravidassis*" political strength and a statement of their united identity than a case of caste conflict.

A majority of Dalits in Punjab have neither converted to the mainstream religion nor have they assimilated the cultural ethos of the dominant castes. Ravidass deras and their unique way of social protest happened to be the main force behind Dalit upsurge. Dalits social protest is basically aimed at inventing Dalit cultural heritage (Ram, 2016: 32, 38). The figure of Ravidass, the fifteenth century poet-saint became the icon of Dalit assertion in Punjab who has provided a cultural space for Ad-Dharmis (Ram, 2004a: 167). The leading religiously-oriented activities of Sachkhand, Ballan seemed disinclined to approve of what the people of Doaba had allegedly learnt in foreign countries, and the arrogant and violent manner in which the new rich *Chamars* behaved, thereby disturbing the villages "peace and harmony" (Vairagi, 2003: 5). Dalit movement in Punjab was quite strong. Dalit leaders like Sant Brahma Das (Ludhiana), Sant Ram (Hoshiarpur), Swami Shudra Nand (Jalandhar), Prithvi Singh Azad (Ambala), Prabhati Ram (Amritsar), Kartar Chand Sulekh (Jalandhar), Mihan Singh (Patiala), Nanak Chand Rattu (Hoshiarpur) and many others endeavoured for the upliftment of their brethren.

Deras and Dalits: Is Dera Sacha Sauda a Dalit Citadel?

Political experts say that sect commands a strong presence among Dalits and economically backward sections of the society. Ashutosh Kumar (Rao, 2017: 11) stated that these sects offer dignity to their disciples by seeking to eradicate caste inequality. Acts like providing food, ration and money to the poor also help them win the allegiance of the disadvantaged. Rajiv Lochan (Rao, 2017. *Op. cit.*: 11) argues that joining *deras* fills them with a sense of optimism. They find a sense of belonging there or brotherhood helps one feel superior. Ronki Ram argues that the majority of the followers of Sacha Sauda-type deras come from the Dalit families (Ram, 2007: 4066). Ram (*Ibid.*: 11) said that the *dera* provides people with an alternative space for social, spiritual and cultural fulfillment. *Deras* can be understood as an alternative to mainstream religion, where faith creates social capital. Dera Ballan made concerted efforts for the construction of a separate identity, independent of both Sikhism and Hinduism. Dalit consciousness in Punjab emerged against the backdrop of the teaching of Guru Ravidass, who provided a middle path between assimilation and radical separatism (Ram, 2008: 1356, 1359). *Deras* are inclusive and have not only Sikh but Christian, Hindu and Muslim followers, many of them from Dalits and working class background. Jodhka (2017) in his interview on CNN-News18 said that these followers are from new rural middle class and low middle class. *Dera* had diverse audience. Empirically it is not true that these followers are only Dalits. They are OBCs, marginalised and SCs.

But the major question which strikes in minds, should we look at *deras* as open and casteless spaces where Dalits and the marginalised peasantry experience a sense of security and relief, away from the hostile realities of caste violence and agrarian crisis? There are wide talks of the anthropologists on this question. Some of them are blaming SGPC, which is not working meticulously to make an egalitarian society on the basis of Religious directions. Sikh religion is the religion of humanity. But when we see Sikh community, more or less, caste and caste discrimination both are still prevailed. Caste ridden Hinduism makes a distinction between pure and impure practices. Practices performed by certain castes are pure and members of other castes or women are excluded from them. For instance, women or Dalits may not be allowed entry into the inner sanctum of temples and in many cases even into the precincts of an upper-caste temple (Bhargava, 2017: 13). But such marginalised or dissenting sections of society do not cease thereby to have religious or spiritual lives. They invent gods, identify gurus, and develop forms of worship of them own.

Socio-Economic and Political Profile of Dalits in Punjab

As per Census, 2011, the State of Punjab, has the highest percentage of SC population amongst all the States of the country. The SC population in Punjab is 88.60 lakh which is 31.94 per cent of the total population (277.43 lakh) of the State. Punjab accounts

4.3 per cent SC population of India. The decennial growth rate of SC population in the State was 26.06 per cent as compared to 13.89 per cent for the State as a whole. However, a sizeable number of SC families still live below the poverty line. Over 60 per cent of households live below the poverty line, according to the Punjab Department of Welfare of SCs and BCs.

The SCs constitute 16.32 per cent of India's population; 36 per cent of them are workers, 48 per cent are agricultural labourers. Besides working as labourers or cultivators, many but not all are traditionally bound by certain caste occupations such as scavenging, which were in the past, a part of the *Jajmani* system. Out of the total SC population, SC labour force constitutes 35.88 per cent, out of which, 79.20 per cent and 20.80 per cent are main and marginal workers respectively. The majority of this segment of society is agricultural labourers or engaged in low wage and arduous occupations. The Punjab Government is committed to uplift this underprivileged section of the society by improving the socio-economic and educational development by providing them with technical skills for vocational jobs and link their present occupation/activity with the larger activity.

Major SC groups are Mazhabi, Chamar (including Ramdasias), Ad-Dharmis, Balmiki, Bazigar, Dumna (Mahasa), Megh, Sansi, Bauria, Kabirpanthi (Julaha) and Dhanak. These ten castes in order of composition make up 92 per cent of the SC population. Punjab had the highest percentage of SCs about 24.7 per cent in 1971; 26 per cent in 1981; 28.35 per cent in 1991; 28.85 per cent in 2001 and 31.9 per cent in 2011. Among SCs, the four largest Census categories are Mazhabis (31 per cent of the SCs population), Chamars including Ramdasia Sikhs (27 per cent), Ad-Dharmis (15 per cent), and Balmiki (12 per cent). The Census, for example, lists six caste names to be collectively coded as "Chamar" (Chamar, Jatia Chamar, Rehgar, Raigar, Ramdasi, and Ravidassi). These smaller categories, all differ from each other in social customs, religious practices, and traditional occupations.

According to the survey conducted by the Department of Rural Development and Panchayats for rural areas in the year 2002 and the State Urban Development Agency (SUDA) in urban areas in 2004, out of the total 5.23 lakh families living below the poverty line,

3.21 lakh families belong to the SCs which constitute 61.38 per cent of the total families below the poverty line in the State. As per Agricultural Census 2010-11, the number of operational holdings with SCs are 63,480 spreading over an area of 1,26,966 hectares comprising 6.02 per cent and 3.20 per cent of the total landholdings and area of the State respectively. Major bulks (85.54 per cent) of these holdings are unviable being less than the size of 5 hectares.

The SC population is predominantly rural by residence. As per Census 2011, 73.33 per cent of the SC population lives in the rural areas, whereas, the remaining 26.67 per cent resides in the urban areas of the State. The distribution of SC population among the districts of the State indicates that percentage of SC persons is higher in the districts of Shaheed Bhagat Singh Nagar (42.51 per cent), Sri Muktsar Sahib (42.31 per cent), Ferozepur (42.17 per cent), Jalandhar (38.95 per cent), Faridkot (38.92 per cent), Moga (36.50 per cent), Hoshiarpur (35.14 per cent), Kapurthala (33.94 per cent), Tarn Taran (33.71 per cent), Mansa (33.63 per cent), Bathinda (32.44 per cent), Barnala (32.24 per cent) and Fatehgarh Sahib (32.07 per cent). Out of the total 12,168 inhabited villages in the State, 57 villages have 100 per cent SC population; and 4,799 villages (39.44 per cent) have 40 per cent or more SC population. The village/tehsil/ district-wise detail of villages having 40 per cent or more SC population is given in Part-IV (II) of the document. Among 217 towns, 175 towns have 20 per cent or more SC population, and majority of them are either small towns or Census towns. As per Census 2011, the literacy rate among SCs is 64.81 per cent as compared to total literacy rate of 75.84 per cent of the State and 73.00 per cent of the country as a whole. The female literacy rate of SCs at 58.39 per cent in the State also lags behind that of total 70.73 per cent of the State. However, it is better than the SC female literacy rate at 56.46 per cent of the country. The SC male literacy rate at 70.66 per cent of the State is also lower than the total male literacy rate of 80.44 per cent in the State.

Although the Land Alienation Act of 1900 was aimed at preventing the transfer of land from the hands of agriculturist castes into the non-agricultural money-lending castes, it also debarred many castes from owning land. Untouchables who were already deprived of land according to the Hindu *Varna-Vyavastha* system were now legally debarred from land ownership. But the adoption of the Green Revolution technology during the 1960s and 1970s set the pace of economic change that led to a complete transformation of the agrarian social structure and village life. Dalit communities of rural Punjab used the new space opened up by the process of economic development to re-negotiate their relations with the locally dominant castes and rural social structure, eventually leading to a near complete breakdown of the *Jajmani* relations. These changes could perhaps be conceptualised through the categories of dissociation, distancing and autonomy (Jodhka, 2002: 1812-1813).

The onset of the Green Revolution has led to the increase of capitalism in agriculture giving rise to a small class of rich peasants co-existing with a majority of small and poor peasant households depending on subsistence farming. These changes have not only affected agrarian relations, but also have led to an overall shift in the occupational structure (Dhami, 1988. *Op. cit.*: 382). The Green Revolution added to economic and political clout of the land owning class in general, while further widening social inequality, the Jat control of the leadership of the SAD since 1962 has added to apprehensions in the lower caste Sikhs. Whereas much change under the impact of Dalit political assertion, social welfare measures and spread of education is visible, it has also led to tensions and conflicts.

The term "Dalit" in Ambedkarian framework includes SCs primarily–but a broader concept of it includes economically, socially and politically underprivileged section. On the contrary, caste continues to be important marker of social, economic and political life in contemporary Doaba region. Caste-based segregation is easily evident in the social life of rural Doaba region. Caste boundaries are maintained and reproduced with much keenness even within Dalit castes. Practice of untouchability has perhaps been most pronounced in the religious sphere. Brahminical Hinduism imposed restrictions on Dalits' participation in religious life. They were denied access to the classical religious traditions and scriptures. They could not even learn, read and write. Similarly, they were prohibited from entering the Hindu temples. Followers of Sikhism constitute nearly 80 to 90 per cent of the rural population of Punjab. Even among those who are registered as Hindus in the Census enumeration, many practice Sikh rituals and visit Sikh gurudwaras. Ibbeston discovered that the roots of Brahminical influence in Punjab were weak and that by religion "the then Punjab was more *"Mohammedan"* than Hindu and that instead of the rigorous ritual purity norms of the caste-hierarchy, the people are bound by the social and the tribal customs far more than by any rules of the religion" (Ibbeston, 1916: 14-15).

The social structure of Punjab presented complexities in the form of segmental division, namely, the existence of numerous castes and sub-castes within Hinduism as well as other religions. There were a large number of outcastes or untouchables. Among these were Chamars, Mochis, Dumnas and Chuhras, described as leather workers, menials and scavengers respectively placed in a socially, economically and politically disadvantageous position in relation to the high castes. The untouchables were either engaged in agricultural production as agricultural labourers or as carrying out certain unclean occupation such as scavenging. The Mazhabi Sikhs provide the bulk of the agriculture labour in Punjab. They are looked down by the Jat land-owners.

As per the 1991 Census, among the SCs, there were less than five per cent cultivators, but 60 per cent agricultural labourers. SCs shared 4.82 per cent of the number of operational holdings and 2.34 per cent of the total area under cultivation (Jodhka, 2006: 12). Emigration of Dalits from the Doaba belt of Punjab to the Gulf countries has set a mode for their brethren left behind within the folds of traditional structure of villages' society. Caste conflict has manifested itself in the distinction between the agricultural and non-agricultural castes on the one hand, and between the higher castes and the SCs on the other (Brar, 1989: 112). The percentage of Dalits owning land is quite low, that is 4.3 per cent and according to the Punjab Human Development Report (2004), more than half of them were agriculture labourers in 1991 (Judge and Bal, 2009: 5).

Squalor and hunger may not mark the faces of Dalits in Punjab, but this has not changed some key facts. While the percentage of literates in the State is higher than the national average, Punjab's Dalits are less likely to be educated than their counterparts nationwide. The future looks dismal with number of Dalits living below the poverty line having increased in the past decade (Kaur, 2004: 3, 4). Both in

Jalandhar and Hoshiarpur districts (in rural as well as in urban areas), Ad-Dharmis are far outnumber than other castes. The Balmikis and Chamars are distant second and third-ranking castes. New opportunities opened up by the growing demand of leather goods such as boots and shoes for the British army had brought relative prosperity to some of the enterprising members of the Chamar caste. This mobility was particularly evident in the Doaba sub-region of Punjab from where some of the Chamars had even gone to the United States of America and had been part of the left wing organisation there. The Chamars (including Ad-Dharmis and Ramdasis) have almost completely moved away from their traditional occupation of dealing with dead cattle. Among Balmikis and Mazhabis (earlier known as Chuhras), only a few families from these castes actually work as scavengers.

Looking into the impact by economic prosperity in the Doaba region through remittances from Dalit migrant workers in foreign land, Judge (1997: 57-62) points out to a prominent tendency in that section to flaunt their wealth so as to underline their high social status. The Ad-Dharmis of Boota Mandi in Jalandhar, who control the leather industry, are the richest among the SCs of Punjab. Similarly, some sections of the SCs, particularly the Chamar, and Ad-Dharmis, have acquired administrative positions in the State administration. Perhaps the single most visible feature and a proof of caste in rural Punjab is the distribution of agricultural land, the most important productive asset in any agrarian economy. Due to the various historical reasons, despite their numerical preponderance very few among Dalits own or cultivate land, less than 5 per cent of all Dalits in Punjab are cultivators. However, proportionally, Dalits of Punjab are less urbanised than the State average of urban population, large majority of them are part of the rural economy as dependent groups, working on land as labourers or doing menial jobs.

Commercialisation and mechanisation of agriculture, on the one hand, and the introduction of democratic political process on the other, have together transformed caste relations in rural Punjab fundamentally. Over the last twenty years or so, large proportions of Dalits in Punjab have consciously traditionally dissociated themselves from their occupations and have also been trying to distance themselves from everyday engagement with the agrarian economy (Jodhka, 2006: 11-12). The Chamars, and Ad-Dharmis of Boota Mandi have effectively used their resources and organisation to capture not only power at the local level but they are also striving towards the pan-Indian Dalit unity. Ad-Dharmis and Chamars are on the top of virtually every parameter like education, urbanisations, jobs, occupational change, cultural advancement, political mobilisation (Puri, 2004: 4). In the Doaba region, where Dalit mobility has been more pronounced than elsewhere in the State, very few of them worked as attached labourers. However, Malwa still had many who were working as attached labourers.

Business, however, was a different matter, especially those business ventures related to leather. Swami Shudranand's father came from Phagwara to set up a large boot-making operation in Jalandhar, where the British army cantonment had created a great market for boots and army shoes. The leather trade attracted the families of Vasant Rai, Thakur Chand, and many other early Ad-Dharmi leaders. Picking up of dead cattle has become a completely commercialised enterprise. There has been some degree of commercialisation of other Dalit or *"Jajmani"* occupations. Barbers, carpenters, blacksmiths–all have shops. Along with commercialisation, a process of 'dissociation of caste and occupation' is also underway. The percentage of agricultural labourers out of the total workers declined from 23.8 per cent in 1991 to 16.4 per cent in 2001 (Judge and Bal, 2005: 108). A large percentage of SC communities from Doaba, particularly Hoshiarpur, Jalandhar and Nawan Shahr have migrated to foreign countries.

It is not uncommon to come across people of the lower castes living in well-furnished houses or holding Government jobs in the Doaba region of Punjab. Villages around cities such as Jalandhar and Hoshiarpur have Dalit families whose relative economic prosperity has come from small businesses or migration to Western countries. However, improvement in the financial condition has not translated into improved social status. Dalits in the Doaba region, like their less fortunate counterparts in South Punjab, still face social boycotts and segregation in daily life. The term *Chuhre-Chamar* (scavenger and tanner) is freely employed by landlords belonging to the upper castes to refer to Dalits. As common as the segregation of Dalit colonies are illiteracy, unemployment and landlessness. Economically, the SCs, both Sikhs and Hindus, stand in subordinate relationship with Jat Sikh peasantry, for whom they work as agricultural labourers. Economic conflicts over wages with the dominant peasantry, therefore, are further factors which have contributed to the weakness of the religious and cultural ties of the SCs.

Education empowers Dalits and helps them in moving away from traditional occupation to their professions. This shift is more pronounced in the Doaba region of Punjab. Particularly, Dalits of Jalandhar district are engaged in manufacturing and other services in a big way. Though, education along with the reservation has empowered Dalits in a comprehensive manner, but it has created a different section within Dalit community which is not identifying itself with the community for any more.

The political leadership and active involvement in political process seem to be controlled by economically stronger communities but Punjab Christians are socio-economically backward. Hence, it is difficult for Christian community to make progress in Punjab politics. They are considered as negligible vote bank by the political parties. Basically, community lacks social pull which is essential in the political field. Dalits are assertive and no longer accept the suzerainty of the dominant castes or classes. Electoral politics over the period has given impetus to caste divisions and assertions. In some pockets/districts of the State, Dalits constitute up to 40 per cent of the total population. Although they are divided among different sub-communities, but together, there would be many villages of Punjab where their number would be larger than the locally and regionally dominant caste of Jats. Despite many radical changes in the society and economy of rural Punjab, their position remains marginal in local politics.

Note

1 Mark Juergensmeyer in his work on Ad-Dharm movement metions that when he (Sant Hiran Das) established his *Ravi Das Sabha*, in 1907, in village Hakim......several other *deras* including that of Sant Pipal Das, were founded soon afterward (Juergensmeyer, 1988: 87).

References

- Ambedkar, B.R. 1989. 'Revolution and Counter Revolution.' in *Ancient India, Writing and Speeches*, Vol. 4, Bombay: Government of Maharashtra.
- Beteille, Andre. 2008. 'Caste and Political Group Formation in Tamilnadu.' In *Caste in Indian Politics,* edited by Rajni Kothari, 245-282. New Delhi: Orient BlackSwan.

- Bhargava, Rajeev. 2017. 'In Defiance of Organised Religion.' *The Hindu*: 3 September.
- Brar, J.S. 1989. *The Communist Party in Punjab*, New Delhi: National Book Organisation.
- Chandra, Kanchan. 2004. *Why Ethnic Parties Succeed: Patronage and Ethnic Head Counts in India.* Cambridge: Cambridge University Press.
- Dhami, M.S. 1988. 'Religio-Political Mobilisation and Shift in the Party Support Base in the 1985 Punjab Assembly Elections.' In *Political Dynamic and Crisis in Punjab*, edited by Paul Wallace and Surinder Chopra, 382-89. Amritsar: Guru Nanak Dev University.
- Gerald, Barrier N. 2000. 'The Singh Sabha Movement.' In *Social and Political Movements, Reading on Punjab*, edited by Harish K. Puri and Paramjit Singh Judge, 57-92. New Delhi: Rawat Publications.
- Ibbeston, Denzil. 1916 (1970 rept. 1983). *Punjab Castes* (being a reprint of the chapter on 'Races, Castes and Tribes of the People in the Census of 1881'). New Delhi: Cosmo Publications.
- Jodhka, Surinder S. 2002. 'Caste and Untouchables in Rural Punjab.' *Economic and Political Weekly* XXXVII (19): 1812-13.
- ———. 2006. 'Caste and Democracy: Assertion and Identity among Dalits of Rural Punjab.' *Sociological Bulletin* 55 (1): 11-12.
- ———. 2009. 'The Ravi Dasis of Punjab: Global Contours of Caste and Religious Strife.' *Economic and Political Weekly* XLIV (24): 79-81.
- ———. 2017. Interviewed by Anuradha Sen Gupta, *CNN-News18*: 2 September.
- Judge, Paramjit S. 1997. 'Emerging Trends in the Caste Structure of Punjab.' *The Administrator* XLII, January-March: 55-65.
- Judge, Paramjit S. and Gurpreet Bal. 2005. 'Dalits and Urban Social Space.' *Indian Social Science Review* 7 (2): 108.
- ———. 2009. *Mapping Dalits, Contemporary Reality and Future Prospects in Punjab.* New Delhi: Rawat Publications.
- Juergensmeyer, Mark. 1988. *Religious Rebels in the Punjab: The Social Vision of Untouchables*. Delhi: Ajanta Publications.
- Kaur, Naunidhi. 2004. 'Social Boycotts, Segregation.' *Frontline* 21 (10): 1-4.
- Nahar, Emanual. 2007. *Minority Politics in India.* Chandigarh: Arun Publishing House Pvt. Ltd.
- Puri, Harish K., ed. 2004. *Dalits in Regional Context.* New Delhi: Rawat Publications.
- Ram, Ronki. 2004a. 'Limits of Untouchability, Dalit Assertion and Caste Violence.' In *Dalits in Regional Context*, edited by Harish K. Puri, 132-189. New Delhi: Rawat Publications.

- ———. 2004b. 'Untouchability, Dalit Consciousness, and the Ad-Dharm Movement in Punjab.' *Contributions to Indian Sociology* 38 (3): 323-351.
- ———. 2008. 'Ravidass Deras and social Protest: Making Sense of Dalit Consciousness in Punjab.' *The Journal of Asian Studies* 67 (4): 1341-64.
- ———. 2016. 'Sacralising Dalit Peripheries, Ravidass Deras and Dalit Assertion in Punjab.' *Economic and Political Weekly* LI (1): 32-39.
- Rao, Hitender. 2017. 'Why Ram Rahim's Dera became a Dalit Citadel.' *Hindustan Times*: 1 September.
- Sharma, Satish K. 2000. 'Arya Samaj Movement in Punjab.' In *Social and Political Movements, Reading on Punjab*, edited by Harish K. Puri and Paramjit S. Judge, 93-110. New Delhi: Rawat Publications.
- Vairagi, Karnail. 2003. 'Talhan Kand Dharmo Samaj Layee ik Sharmnaak Ghatna.' *Begumpura Shahr* (*Punjabi Weekly*), 23 June: 5.
- Virdi, S.L. 2000. *Punjab Da Dalit Itihas.* Phagwara: Dalit Sahit Acadamy (Punjab).
- Webster, John C.B. 2000. 'The Christian Movement in Punjab.' in *Social and Political Movements, Reading on Punjab*, edited by Harish K. Puri and Paramjit S. Judge, 111-134. New Delhi: Rawat Publications.

Chapter - 5

Dalits and their Support Base: A Study of the Congress and the SAD in Punjab

An analysis of vote share data between the Lok Sabha polls 2009 and 2014 shows that the BJP's vote share at national level has gone up to 31 per cent from less than 19 per cent during last election. During the same period, the Congress' vote share has dipped to nearly 19 per cent from over 28 per cent. The BSP's nationwide vote share has declined from over 6 per cent to 4.1 per cent and still remains third largest party in terms of vote share after the BJP and the Congress. In UP, the BSP has got nearly 19.6 per cent votes–third largest party after the BJP (42.3 per cent) and the Samajwadi Party (22.2 per cent), although it has failed to win a single seat. The outcome of 16th Parliamentary elections has thrown up intractable surprise, if not enigma, defying understanding and interpretation. It has strangely wiped out from the Indian Parliament. Though, it has the record and experience of holding the reins of power. The BSP was relegated to the third position in UP with just 19 seats out of the total 403, the party's performance in Punjab was also nothing short of an embarrassment. Though, the BSP contested all 117 seats in Punjab. Avtar Singh Karimpuri was the only candidate not to have lost his security deposit. He finished at fourth place in Phillaur. While BSP was relegated to the third position in UP with just 19 seats.

The 2017 Assembly election in Punjab was unprecedented in many ways. For the first time, there was a third party in the fray, offering voters the possibility of a change in politics and Government that was dominated for decades by just two parties. Before this, Punjab voters alternated between the SAD and the Congress. The Congress party won 77 out of 117 seats, just one short of a two-third victory for any single party in Punjab since the SAD's victory with 75 seats in 1997. In that election BJP won 18 seats, while the Congress won just 14. Exactly two decades later, the SAD-BJP combination which ruled the State together over two terms beginning from 2007, won just 18 seats. The BJP itself was reduced to a mere 3 seats, down from its tally of 12 in 2012 while the SAD won 15, compared to its previous tally of 56. Doubtless, the Congress victory in Punjab rests on the fierce anti-SAD vote. But the decision of the voters to choose the Congress over the AAP cannot be explained simply as anti-incumbency. This vote could have just as well gone to the AAP. The voters decided that party, with a known, familiar chief ministerial Amarinder Singh was a bet than a party that went into the election with ambiguous signaling about who its Chief Minister would be.

The SCs in Punjab have never voted en bloc, and the BSP dwindled to a minuscule 1.5 per cent in 2017 from 4.29 per cent in 2012, 1.91 per cent in the 2014 Lok Sabha election. The BSP's failure over the years is attributed to the absence of the kind of social discrimination that Dalits experience elsewhere, the absence of a strong Brahmin community, and the division among the two main Dalit castes –Valmikis and the Ravidassias. The AAP had aimed to occupy the space vacated by the BSP. Among the separate Manifestos, the AAP brought out of different sections of voters such as farmers, youth and women, one was Dalit manifesto, which promised that there would be a Dalit deputy Chief Minister if it came to power. But the party did not invest much of its campaign energy outside Malwa, believing perhaps that a "wave" in its favour in that region would carry it through in the other two. In the event, while nine of its 20 members of Legislative Assembly are Dalits, only two are from Doaba. The Congress used to count Doaba as a stronghold, but in 2012 was defeated in all but 6 of the region's 23 seats, with the rest going to the SAD. This time the roles were reversed, with the SAD winning 6 seats.

Politics in Punjab continued to vacillate between the extremes of religio-caste identity to secular Punjabi identity as per the electoral and political needs. The religious reforms' movements among the Sikhs and Hindus (Singh Sabha and Arya Samaj, respectively) radically transformed the behavioural aspects of inter- and intra-caste practices which formed the third axis. This provided regional dimension to the caste dynamics in Punjab. The SCs acquired more social and political bargaining space. They found representation across political parties rather than merely in a caste-based political party such as the BSP. The long-term implications of SCs finding accommodation in the mainstream Punjab parties has been that the BSP's vote share has been continuously declining. It has come down from 7.98 per cent in 1997 to 4.29 per cent in 2012 Assembly election, and from 4.29 per cent to 1.5 per cent in 2017 Assembly election in Punjab.

It is relevant to point out that they got representation in all the political parties, including the Jat-dominated SAD. For instance, out of the total 11 Assembly elections of Punjab, in six, more SC legislators were elected on the Akali tickets than any other party. In 1969 (44 per cent), 1977 (48 per cent), 1985 (62 per cent), 1997 (77 per cent), 2007 (55 per cent), 2012 (62 per cent) were presented in the Akali Dal. In remaining five elections, the Congress gave higher representation to the SC legislators – in 1967 (52 per cent), in 1972 (61 per cent), in 1980 (45 per cent), in 1992 (63 per cent) and in 2002 (48 per cent) were presented in the Congress party. Of the 1248 legislators between 1967 and 2012, SCs constituted 25.16 per cent, OBCs 8.97 per cent, and Jat Sikhs 43 per cent (Kumar, 2017: 46).

The BSP lost a substantial portion of its Dalit vote base to the BJP in UP, Haryana, Delhi, Madhya Pradesh, and Maharashtra. The AAP became the principal beneficiary of the losses incurred by the Congress and the BSP among Dalit voters in Delhi and Punjab. It would not be an exaggeration to say that the BSP's vote base outside UP is largely made of Dalit electorates. The BSP failed to win a single seat in 2014 Parliamentary elections and 2017 Assembly election in Punjab. Though the party's decline in national vote share is largely due to the drubbing it received in UP, its poor performance outside the State added to the misery. By 2007, the BSP was totally fragmented in Punjab and it polled only 4.10 per cent votes. It could not improve its condition in 2012 Assembly elections. The SAD won 56 seats; the Congress had the largest share of 40.11 per cent votes. While Congress had focused on wooing the Dera Sacha Sauda, it failed to tackle Dera Ballan which is patronised by Ravidassia sect. The party leadership in the State informed that whenever the BSP remained strong in the State it had caused major dent to the Congress vote bank, but in 2014 Lok Sabha election in Punjab, its decreasing vote share could benefit only the AAP. The senior leaders of the party said that the policies of the BSP's State leadership led to its decreasing share and many good leaders have left the BSP and joined other parties. The AAP had joined the battle for the Assembly election riding on the back of its spectacular showing in 2014 Lok Sabha elections, where it won 4 seats and the third largest vote share (24.4 per cent) after the Congress (33.19 per cent) and the SAD (26.37 per cent). The BJP got 8.77 per cent, a slight increase over its 7.18 per cent showing in the 2012 Assembly elections. But the BSP plunged from 4.29 per cent in 2012 to 1.91 per cent in the Lok Sabha polls.

The story of Dalit vote in the 2014 election has two intertwined accounts. First, nationally, the BJP has managed to win more votes among Dalits than the Congress has. Second, the decline of the BSP (even among Dalit voters) suggests that the party's ambition of scaling up nationally is now a distant dream. The BJP has surpassed both the Congress and the BSP in attracting a larger share of Dalit vote. The BJP's Dalit vote base is largely the upwardly mobile sections (urban, educated, middle classes, with high media exposure). Much of the BJP's gain among Dalit voters came at the expense of the Congress and the BSP. UP remains a laboratory for the shifting of multi-caste alliances and political coalition governing Indian politics. The State's Dalit community ideologically remains committed to the BSP, while all other social groups in the BSP rainbow coalition remains wary and aloof from the BSP's overtly pro-Dalit agenda. In 2017 UP's Assemby election, the BSP has created a formidable combination of Dalits, Muslims and Brahmins. Dalits, who constitute about 21 per cent of the State's population, have been BSP's strongest support base. In 2014, BJP was able to masterfully craft an alliance of upper castes, forward castes and OBCs under a power Hindu nationalist, development-oriented umbrella.

The BSP in Punjab

The real presence of Dalits as a political force could only be felt after Kanshi Ram's BSP emerged on the political scene. The early cadre base of the BSP in Punjab as elsewhere in India came from

BAMCEF founded by Kanshi Ram to prepare the ground for a political party. This organisation offered Kanshi Ram, himself from among their ranks, a concentrated pool of resources with which to launch a political party. But unlike UP, the BSP failed to make a significant impact on the already existing political configuration in Punjab. Since independence and most especially since the creation of *Punjabi Suba*, a persistent dualism has characterised party politics and inter-party relationship in Punjab in which the Congress and the Akali Dal have been the principal contenders for power. The BSP aimed at creating a broad front of Dalits and becoming an important player in the politics of Punjab. Dalits visualised this party as their own which could lead them towards empowerment through the political goals.

In the context of Dalit politics, Punjab has the highest proportion of SCs in its total population. Low caste Sikhs among SCs are the only Dalits from a non-Hindu religious community listed among the SCs. Dalits in Punjab have experienced political power through the Congress and the SAD or through the BSP which has been claiming to be their true representative. In Punjab, the factors such as religion, caste, region, language and leadership combine differently in every election to produce contrasting electoral outcomes. Over the last three decades, a virtually bipolar system has come to stay in the State, where power has alternated between the Congress and the SAD. In 2014 Lok Sabha election the AAP won 4 seats out of 13 Parliamentary seats in Punjab. The attempts of the BSP to carve out an independent space in Punjab politics have not paid dividend so far.

In 1970, the Congress in Punjab sought to identify with and build a stronger base of support among non-Jat Sikhs from both the Scheduled and, "lower backward" castes and from the urban Sikh trading castes. The policy was largely successful. However, as everywhere in North India, the Congress lost support even among the Scheduled and BC Groups in the post-emergency 1977 election, and was defeated in the Punjab by a coalition of the Akali Dal and Janata Party (Brass, 1989: 5). During this coalition, the Congress sought to restore its base among non-SC Sikhs and also to divide the Akali Dal itself by supporting Bhindranwala and other militant groups. It succeeded for the most part in doing so and won support in 1980 especially from Hindus and Sikh SCs and even from "a small section" of the Sikh peasantry. The Congress was unable to maintain the broad based coalition of the 1970s. Nevertheless, even in the 1985 election, the Congress got 37.9 per cent of the votes, virtually the same vote share as the Akali Dal. The Congress retained its base among the Hindus and the SCs, including most Sikh SCs (Dhami, 1987: 27).

In 2004 Lok Sabha election, out of the 13 Lok Sabha seats in Punjab, the SAD-BJP combine won 11 Lok Sabha seats with the SAD winning 8 out of 10 seats it contested, with 34.3 per cent of vote share and the BJP winning all the 3 seats it contested, polling 10.5 per cent votes. Thus, the combined SAD-BJP vote share came to 44.8 per cent of the total votes. The Congress won 2 out of 9 seats and it polled 34.2 per cent of the total votes. Its allies the CPI and the CPM drew blank, contesting 1 seat each, with a share of 2.6 and 1.8 per cent of the votes respectively. It was obvious that notwithstanding the presence of smaller political parties as well as the independents, the contest mainly remained between the traditional rivals the Congress and the SAD. Compared to the 1999 Lok Sabha elections and the 2007 Assembly elections, the electoral outcome is a complete reversal of the electoral fortunes of the two major parties. In the 1999 Lok Sabha elections, a resurgent Congress won 8 seats polling 38.4 per cent votes as against the SAD winning 2 and the BJP winning 1 seat (the alliance won 28.6 and 9.2 per cent of the total votes polled respectively). The SAD (Mann) won the remaining 1 seat polling 3.8 per cent votes. In the 2002 Assembly elections, the Congress, the SAD and the BJP had polled 35.8, 31.1 and 5.7 per cent of the votes respectively giving the Congress-CPI alliance 64 assembly seats compared to 44 seats won by the SAD-BJP combine (Kumar, 2004: 5441).

The BSP put up a creditable performance in this election to the discomfort of the Congress. There was a clear-cut three-way split of votes with the BSP emerging as a distant third alternative. Like Akalis, the BSP also fared poorly in 1999 as the party at the time was divided into three "*bahujan*" parties, namely, the BSP, the BSP (Ambedkar) and the Democratic Bahujan Samaj Morcha (DBSM). In 1999, the BSP had contested the three constituencies and polled 3.8 per cent votes. In 2004, it contested all the 13 seats and polled 7.7 per cent votes. The final tally of votes reveals that a tie up with the BSP would have paid rich dividends to the Congress, which had made an attempt to have pre-poll alliance that did not materialise in the absence of any national alliance between the two parties. As the results show, the BSP continues to have a strong base among Dalits, especially in the Doaba region, besides certain parts of Malwa such as Ferozepur. If the BSP can get rid of factionalism, it is capable of repeating its performance in 1998 elections when the party had emerged as a strong third force (Kumar, 2005. *Op.cit.*: 5443).

Deras, Dalits and Party Politics: Views on Dera Sacha Sauda

The rise of the *deras* and their ability to attract marginalised sections of the society–mostly the landless, the Dalits and the underprivileged in Punjab (especially Malwa)–resulted in political forces such as the BSP and the Left steadily losing out on potential voters. CPI suffered losses ever since the *deras* became a refuge for the landless and Dalits. Poverty was the main reason why Dalits move towards the sects. While religion wouldn't provide them with equal rights, political parties never looked at them as anything beyond vote banks. Head of the *dera* chief Gurmeet Ram Rahim Singh's conviction on 25th August, 2017 in rape case has become a matter of immense political interest across the country. Because, if his *dera* was to lose out on its followers as a consequence, there are many who would like to swoop in and claim them as their own. *Dera* Sacha Sauda was the only among the various *dera*s, which openly asked its supporters to vote for particular political parties. The *dera* Sacha Sauda took the plunge into electoral politics by supporting the Congress in the 2007 Punjab Assembly elections. Neither Panthic groups nor the Akalis were pleased with the fact that a large number of Dalit Sikhs were being weaned away by the sect. The group later floated a political affairs wing, which made a dent in the traditional Akali vote in Punjab's Malwa region. The *dera* endorsed the Congress in the 2009 Haryana Assembly elections, but later switched sides to support the BJP in its 2014 edition. All the major parties in Punjab have been in bed with the *dera* at one point or the other in recent history.

Dalits and the Congress Party in Punjab

The Congress, established in 1885, continues to occupy a place in the national political arena. The Congress party is as fractured as the social cleavage theory of party system would predict from the heterogeneity of Indian society. The Congress is a coalition of State and local parties which differ substantially among themselves in the groups and interests they represent. In terms of its supporters, the Congress is several parties, with a social base in some parts of the country that is at odds with its social foundation in other regions. Looking from the national level, the Congress supporters represent a variety of social classes, occupational groups, religions, and languages. The electoral support base of the Congress is quite homogeneous. Clearly, no caste group alone formed the social foundation on which the Congress based its massive electoral majority. (Chhibber and Petrocik, 2002: 60-61).

Existing as a coalition of interests' support for the Congress cuts across major ethnic, regional, and class barriers, not because it was designed as a heterogeneous catch-all party, but because its role in the independence movement allowed it to sweep up and retain voters and group who were first mobilised into mass politics during the independence movement. The task of building the Congress coalition was eased by traditional values and roles of conciliation that the Congress men astutely took up and the Rudolph's contention is traditional element of the caste system assisted the development of modern representative politics in India (Rudolph and Rudolph, 1967:1).

The Congress enjoyed a distinct advantage over sectional and regional parties. It is still the party that manages to garner the largest amount of support from the underprivileged (Yadav, Kumar and Heath, 1999: 40). This support, however, comes to the Congress by default and is not the outcome of a systematic effort to create a counter-bloc of the underprivileged, or to build a social coalition based on social democratic politics (Kothari, 2002: 48). Similarly, the broadening of the social and ideological base of the Indian polity depended upon the broadening of opportunities within the Congress as it would be suicidal for new sections and interests to join in opposition party and invite the hostility of the ruling party.

At the all-India level, the Congress provided the institutional basis and leadership for aggregating and directing this diverse collection of sub-groups in a massive onslaught against colonial rule, successful mobilisation and accommodation of these groups into the Congress party not only resulted in an independent India, but in a pluralist political system (Wallace, 1981: 7). The Congress was a broad-based coalition, consisting of former *Zamindars*, the locally dominant proprietary castes of Brahmins, Rajputs and Bhumihars' sections of the middle status cultivating castes with self-sufficient holding, the bulk of the lower backward Dalit and the Muslim minority vote (Brass, 1985: 15). The local upper caste leaders, who headed these coalitions, were used to mobilise the lower castes on the basis of patron-client relationship and thereby build vote bank or caste coalitions.

Off and on since independence, political parties with various names have sought to represent specifically and exclusively the SCs. These parties have included the SCF, which contested the 1952 and 1957 elections, the RPI which replaced between 1962 to 1972 and the DS-4 contested 1985 State Legislative Assembly elections since the formation of the *Punjabi Suba*, however, no such party has been able to win above two per cent of the popular vote. There is no question that the main political parties in the Punjab, especially the Congress and the Akali Dal, the two leading contenders for power, draw differential support from the two religious communities and from their internal segments. Since the creation of the *"Punjabi Suba"* in 1966, the Congress has been the more broadly-based of the two main parties. Its strongest support has tended to come from Hindu and SC population, but there have been elections in which it has won considerable support from rural non-SC Sikhs as well.

Organisation of the Congress Party in Punjab

Unlike the Akali Dal, the Congress party in Punjab first shot into prominence with the Jallianwala Bagh tragedy on 13 April, 1919. At that time it could not become a mass party owing to a variety of reasons. The organisation continued to be dominated by the upper and upper middle class people belonging mainly to the upper castes. This party has monopolised the support of the majority of the rural population, cutting across the religious ties. This was possible as it claimed to protect the interests of the small as well as large landowners against the urban commercial and money lending groups. It was able to win over a substantial section of the peasantry, including Muslims, Hindus and Sikhs.

Being a national party, the Congress has set up a uniform pattern of party organisation in all the States of the Indian Union. The Punjab Pradesh Congress Committee (PPCC henceforth) is the highest organ of the party in the State. The members of the PPCC elect from among themselves a president, a vice-president and a treasurer. They also elect a twenty-one members' Executive Committee to look after the day-to-day party affairs. The PPCC president is also the Chief of the Executive Committee. The president is vested with the power to appoint two General Secretaries to look after the party affairs in the State. It has many frontal organisations in the State, Congress Seva Dal, Indian Youth Congress, All India Mahila Congress, Indian National Trade Union Congress (INTUC) and National Students Union of India (NSUI).

Support Base of the Congress Party in Punjab

The process of politicisation of castes acquired a great deal of sophistication in the politics of the Congress party, which scrupulously avoided taking any theoretical-ideological position, on the issue of caste versus class. As against the Akalis, who mainly follow the strategy of winning the Sikh support, the Congress follows the strategy of the aggregative party in its organisation structure and maintains an inter-communal character in both the electoral and legislative arenas (Brass, 1975: 12). In other words, the Congress seeks to give representation to both the Sikhs and Hindus in accordance with their strength in Punjab. In Punjab, the Congress has always been for all practical purposes, the only major secular party of the non-communist left. It is, in fact, the Congress Party which is both multi-communal in theory and practice, and moderate socialist in ideology. The Congress alone occupied the central position in the party system in both communal and ideological respects. The party was politically aware of the change in the agrarian context. Thus, by relying on the caste calculus for its electoral politics and at the same time, articulating political issues in terms of national economic development and integration, the Congress was able to evolve durable electoral bases across castes (Sheth, 2002: 116).

During 1985 Assembly elections, the Akali Dal scored a spectacular tally of 73 seats in the 117 member State Assembly. The Congress trailed far behind with 32 seats. This dent was made into the Congress vote by DS-4 etc. The situation changed only marginally after the rise of the BSP. The Akali-Dal led Government in Punjab between 1985 and 1987 allotted one important portfolio to a SC minister. However, the Congress Government, which took power in 1992, did not allot any important portfolio of SC ministers. In both the Akali Dal and the Congress Government, the ratio of SC representation in the Council of Ministers to percentage of SC in the population rose only slightly from 4 to 6. The Congress classical formula prepared over the distinctive identities of castes and communities. It was sustained by the distribution of patronage and co-option of leaders. It was only after independence that the Congress was able to aggregate rural interests in order to primarily to win elections. But in spite of its broad based complexion after independence, it was unable to direct its disparate elections toward the path of a secular ideology (Dhami, 1975: 46). By contrast, the BSP's coalition is based on an explicit recognition of group identities but under the overarching presence of Dalits (Bidwai, 2007: 98). The party must do so wisely and with inclusive and universalist perspective that was central to Ambedkar's vision. That would be the best way of carrying forward his legacy and addressing India's many unfinished social agendas.

Dalits and the SAD

The SAD founded on December 1, 1920, is the main contender for political power in the State of Punjab. Due to its faith in the inseparability of religion and politics, the party stands committed in furthering the interests of the Sikhs, the Panth and in promoting the interests of all "Sarbat da Bhala". The party is committed to "creating such an environment wherein the manifestation of national aspirations and nationality of the Sikh Panth may find complete realisation." The SAD is the political mouthpiece of the Sikhs. It has been vociferously emphasising the need to maintain the distinct socio-cultural identity of the Sikhs and to protect their interests. The word *"Akali"* has been derived from *"Akal"*, which has its origin in the Sanskrit word "*Kal*" (Time). Thus, *"Akal"* literally means one who 'does not die' and belongs to Akal the immortal or God. The Akali Dal, thus, means 'the party of immortals'. The Akali concept of the inseparability of religion and politics has its origin in the days of the Sixth Guru, Hargobind

Rai, who used the two words of *'Miri'* and *'Piri'*.[1] The relationship between religion and politics is also evidenced by the symbolic relationship of the SGPC and the Akali Dal. Thus, the Akali Dal openly stands for the inextricable mixture of religion and politics, in repudiation of the ideal of secular State (Nayer, 1968: 448). In fact, this frank confession of the inseparability of religion and politics by the Akali Dal is its major feature that distinguishes it from other parties.

The origin of the Akali Dal lies in the awakening among Sikh community to protect their distinct identity. This process was initiated in the last quarter of the nineteenth century when the challenge from renascent Hinduism, mainly represented by the Arya Samaj, further accentuated the Sikh elites' apprehension of the community being absorbed into the Hindu fold. This created an urge among the Sikh elites to preserve and promote their distinct identity and to make the boundary definition with the Hindu less ambiguous. This objective was taken up by the Sikh socio-religious movement, particularly the 'Singh Sabha Movement' of 1873. The Chief Khalsa Diwan, an offspring of the Singh Sabha Movement, was established in 1902 with the aim of safeguarding Sikh rights vis-à-vis the other communities to fight for adequate representation of Sikhs in various services, particularly in the army (Singh, 1974: 145).

The Akali Dal since its very inception is a religio-political force interested in self-salvation, making claims disproportionate to its size and importance, and obtaining results more than its due. The Sikhs were only 13 per cent of the population of Punjab in 1919; Chelmsford Reforms secured 18.5 per cent and in 1932 under the Communal Award, 19 per cent of the total legislative representation. The Akali Dal, for the first time in 1942, was split into two groups; the one under Udham Singh Nagoke joined the national movement, while the other led by Giani Kartar Singh cooperated with the British Government and trenchantly criticised Gandhi and the Congress. The Akali Dal is a party which has benefited immensely by the agitational strategy. Its retreat or advance is determined by the quantum of gains it can secure in a political situation. Its multiplication has not materially affected its capacity to make effective demands in national politics on behalf of its community.

Before independence, the Akali Dal was proved to factional fight among the party leaders due to their vested interests. After independence a new trend emerged in the politics of the Akali Dal that it became caste-oriented. Jat Sikh peasantry became politicised after having suffered the pain of partition. During the Akali Dal agitation for *Punjabi Suba*, the leadership of the Akali Dal stepped from the hands of traditional non-Jat urban Sikhs into the hands of newly emerging rural Jat Sikh leaders.

Singh Sabha Movement was one of the 'classic' expositions was made by Bhai Kahn Singh in his book '*Hum Hindu Nahin*' (We are not Hindus). One of the major arguments, as referred to above, was the total rejection of caste in Sikh religion. In 1953, after the demand for *Punjabi Suba* had been raised, Master Tara Singh and the SAD asked for inclusion of all the 'untouchable castes' converted to Sikhism in the list of SCs. Only four major castes (covering 85 per cent of all Sikh untouchable/Backward Classes) were included in the list, was condemned as highly discriminatory "a conspiracy to crush the religion. Master Tara Singh threatened to go on a fast unto death if all the *Achhuts* who had become Sikhs were not given the same rights as were given to Hindu Achhuts" (Puri, 2004: 213).

All major ideological doctrines of the Akali Dal originate from the basic postulate of the inseparability of religion and politics. One among them is the Akali doctrine that the Sikhs should act as a separate political entity. The main justification given by the Akali Dal leaders in favour of this doctrine is that being a minority, they should act as a separate entity; otherwise, their cultural identity would be endangered (Dhami, 1975. *Op. cit.*: 19). From this doctrine stems the Akali demand for autonomy to the States in India, which, in the words of SGPC President, G.S. Tohra, is essential and necessary for preserving the being and identity of the nations, nationalities and minorities that constitute the fabric of multi-national Indian society (Tohra, 1981: 6). The 'practical' consideration for reservation for the Sikh SCs was not confined to the secular domain. By an amendment made in 1953 to the (Punjab) Sikh Gurudwara Act, 1925, a provision was made for reservation of 20 seats for the SC Sikhs, out of total of 140 elected seats in the SGPC. The Jat control of leadership in the SAD since 1962 added to the fear and apprehension in the lower caste Sikhs (Puri, 2004. *Op. cit.*: 215).

The caste distinctions play an important role in the politics of the State. The Jat Sikhs, being the dominant caste in Punjab, find greater representation in the power structure of the State. Jat Sikhs predominate in the Congress party, whereas the BJP (the former Jan Sangh) finds its main support base in the urban Hindu castes. The SCs, constituting highest percentage of the total population, maintain the political balance in the State on account of their numerical strength, divided in Hindus and Sikhs. This fact compels every political party to woo the SCs in order to ensure their electoral support.

An analysis of election results since the reorganisation reveals that majority of the rural constituencies of the reorganised Punjab have always been returning the Sikh legislators, irrespective of their political affiliations, while the Hindu candidates have been winning from the urban constituencies. There are, however, a few mixed constituencies that have sometimes been returning a Hindu and sometimes a Sikh candidate to the Assembly. This shows that almost every political party in Punjab keeps in mind the strength of various religious communities while distributing the party ticket to the candidates for the Assembly elections. Generally, a Sikh candidate is selected in a Sikh majority constituency. Even in the selection of the Chief Minister, in the reorganised Punjab, the Congress too has always opted for a Sikh Chief Minister. Some amount of polarisation is witnessed amongst various Sikh caste groups. The persistent as well as significant pattern is that the non-Jat caste groups—the Mazhabis, Ad-Dharmis, 'Bhappas' (Sikh Khatris) and artisan castes–join hands against the dominance of the Jat Sikhs. This is also true in regard to their role in the major two political parties of the State–the Akali Dal and the Congress (Sharma, 1986: 18-19).

Organisation and Ideology of the SAD

The organisational structure of the SAD, like other parties is hierarchical. At the root of the hierarchy are the villages, Kasba (towns), cities, Akali Jatha, known as the Sathanak (local) Akali Jathas, with a minimum strength of the members. These local organs of the Akali Dal play an important part in organising the party and carrying its message to the masses at large. Each Jatha has its own Jathedars (Senior and Junior), two General Secretaries, a secretary and a treasurer elected by its members among themselves. Whatever ideological principles the Akali Dal professes, are reflected mainly in the policy pronouncement of its leaders and its elections manifestos. There are many frontal organisation of the SAD, Students Organisation of India, Youth Akali Dal etc. Since the Akali Dal is a politico-religious organisation of the Sikhs, its ideology is a theo-political ideology. It controls Sikh religious bodies, the SGPC, Delhi Sikh Management Committee. The basic philosophy of the SAD is Sikhism, Punjabiyat and Punjabi nationalism. By the word, theo-political is meant the inseparability of religion and politics. The Akali leadership is of the firm view that politics cannot be run properly without the sanction of the religious authority of the Sikh religion which cannot be safeguarded without holding political power. Both go hand in hand. From this angle, acquisition of political power is not an end in itself, at least in theory, for the Akali Dal.

Support Base of the SAD

The Congress support for Sikh militants caused great strains both between the latter and moderate Akali Dal politicians as well as within the ranks of the Akali Dal itself. The division increasingly took the form of a competition concerning which party, faction or leader was most militant and determined to protect and promote the interests of Sikh Panth (community) (Brass, 1989. *Op. cit.*: 1). There has been a decline in inter-elite cooperation and communication across the Hindu and Sikh boundaries, but there are good ground to doubt and permanence of that change in the situation. The SAD has always maintained that religion cannot be separated from politics. Essentially, a party representing the Sikhs, the Akali Dal invariably raised issues that concerned the Sikhs' religious interest in normal times. The Akali Dal also controls the SGPC and plays the role of regulating affairs of the community. The Singh Sabha Movement and later on, the movement of the Akalis for the control over the Sikh shrines tended to define, regulate and control the Sikh religious tradition. As a result of the formation of the SGPC, it became possible to ensure that the tradition is observed (Judge, 2005: 28). The SGPC relied on the SAD which was formed less than one month after the founding of the SGPC in December 1920 (Wallace, 1981. *Op. cit.*: 13). The SAD took essentially exclusive and extremist position before the 1971 Parliamentary and the 1972 Assembly elections.

The popularity of the *deras*, however, is directly linked to the perception among the BCs in Punjab and Haryana that the SGPC is dominated by the upper castes. The SGPC is close to the Shiromani Akali Dal (Badal) in Punjab is also a source of discomfiture for these sections. Many within the Sikh community feel that only a genuine effort on the part of Sikh institutions to involve the lower and BCs will help, stem the increasing sense of alienation that these sections feel and the periodic violent outbursts, which are the symptoms of this alienation.

All the Sikh organisations like Sikh *deras*, the SGPC, and the SAD are under the control of the Jat Sikhs. It is found that 80 per cent of its administrative posts are under the control of Jat Sikhs, 15 per cent under other castes and only 5 per cent are with Dalit Sikhs (Mazhabis and Ramdasias). By this caste-wise discrimination, and social exclusion, Dalits have been veering away from the mainstream of Sikh religion and enrolling themselves into various forms of non-Sikh *deras* in Punjab (Ram, 2007: 4066-67). The mass support base of the Akali Dal upto 1960 was almost evenly upon the Sikh rural peasantry as well as urban Sikh traditional classes, with the Jat peasantry forming its backbone. With the 1962 split in the Akali Dal, the Sant Akali Dal became predominantly, a Jat Akali Dal whereas the master Akali Dal's support base shrank to certain sections of urban Sikhs. There is no doubt that the Sant Akali Dal was also supported by some liberal sections of the Hindu community of various political shades. But still, the Akali Dal has faced split in the years 1962, 1980, 1986, 1989 and 1991. It has many factions like Akali Dal (Badal), the Akali Dal (Mann), the Akali Dal (Manjit), the Akali Dal (Longowal), the Akali Dal (Talwandi), the Akali Dal (Babbar) and the Panthic Akali Dal.

Akalis claim to represent all Sikhs; there have always been sharp political difference within the Sikh community. Caste has remained an important factor that shapes the internal power structure of the Sikh community. The support base of the Akali Dal witnessed an improvement with the reorganisation of the State in 1966. This is evidenced by the 1967 Assembly elections' result; mainly three factors contributed in this regard, namely, (a) the State's changed demographic profile in 1960, (b) success of the Green Revolution and its impact on the socio-economic and political status of the peasantry who, by and large, rallied behind the Akali Dal and (c) the general decline in the image of the Congress party from the early sixty onward (Verma, 1987: 273).

One of the important features of the Akali Dal's support base is that its electoral performance has always been better in the Malwa region as compared to the Majha and Doaba regions of Punjab. It is due to various factors; one is that the Malwa region has more proportion of the Sikh population as against the Majha and Doaba regions which have large proportion of Hindu population. Secondly, the later regions have more proportion of the SCs than the former. Since both the Hindus and the SCs, Sikhs as well as Hindus, have traditionally been supporters of the non-Akali parties in Punjab, therefore, the Akalis' performance has been relatively poor in these regions. Moreover, the bulk of the Akali Dal top leadership has generally been coming from the Malwa region. On the whole, the rural Jat Sikhs peasantry contributes the main support base of the Akali Dal. There is a definite pattern in the party preference of SCs who have gradually shifted from the Congress and opted for alternatives wherever they could find them. This change in allegiance is more guided by the secular concern to assert in the power structure in order to gain benefits that may accrue from it, than by mere parochial interests. This has led them to search for alternatives as they are no longer prepared to accept the role of a passive voter-supporter in the overall environment subjugation and subordination (Pushpendra, 2001: 338).

The phenomenon of the BSP has resulted in the decline of the Congress support base among the SCs and OBCs in Punjab. For instance, in 1985 Assembly elections the impact of the BSP then working in the name of DS-4 was felt in the Doaba region. No doubt, its candidates did not win any seat yet they polled more than one lakh votes in the Doaba region which were otherwise supposed to go to the Congress candidates. The drift of the SC voters from the Congress (I) in 1985 elections gave maximum benefit to the Akalis in the rural constituencies. Out of the total 12 seats in the Jalandhar district, the Akali Dal captured 6 seats, while the Congress could get only 4 seats as against 8 in the 1980 elections. This decline in the Congress's electoral performance was attributed to the phenomenon of DS-4. M.S. Dhami has observed regarding 1985 elections that the major factor which accounts for the Congress (I) vote is the sizeable shift in the support base of the Congress-I vote in 1985, partly a continuation of a trend noticed earlier in 1977 and 1980 Assembly elections and partly the result of religio-political mobilisation. The shift from the Congress to the Akali Dal has taken place mainly in the case of SC voters, may be around 10 to 15 per cent have voted for the Akali Dal, whereas earlier rarely two to five per cent voted for it.

In the Doaba region, many castes among Dalit category prefer the BSP than other political parties. The BSP's base in Punjab, which also happens to be the home turf of the BSP founder Kanshi Ram, has gradually shrunk since 1992, reducing it to a fringe player in the State politics. The BSP, however, has seen better times. The party's best electoral performance was in the 1992 Assembly elections in which it won 9 seats–though it was largely due to the Akali boycott of the polls. It did well in the 1996 Parliamentary polls too, when it forged an alliance with the SAD to win 3 seats then–the BSP supremo Kanshi Ram from Hoshiarpur, Harbhajan Singh Lakha from Phillaur, and Mohan Singh Phalianwala from Ferozepur. The BSP downfall began in the 1998 Lok Sabha polls and failed to retain any of its 3 seats. The decline in Punjab compared to the success in UP underlined the importance of a charismatic leader like Mayawati; it also means that the BSP's growth in the country's largest State was not being applied anywhere else.

Since positions of power in Punjab Congress Organisation and Governments were monopolised by upper and intermediate castes, emerging SC elites saw little chance of obtaining office themselves by joining the Congress party. The Akali Dal, the principal opposition party in Punjab did not offer better prospects. Since SC elites had little hope of rising up the ladder in the Congress or any other party in Punjab they turned instead to the BSP. In its first election in Punjab, the BSP found a critical mass of joiners comparable to that of UP.

Prior to the emergence of the BSP in 1984, there was no electoral incentive for the Congress to incorporate SCs and BCs in Punjab. There has never been a BCs' party in Punjab and the SC parties (SCF and RPI) that preceded the BSP obtained only marginal support.[2]

Caste has for long been viewed as the defining reality of the Indian social structure. Almost everyone saw caste as the primary institution around which the social life in India was organised. Not only in India but it was present all over the sub-continent, as its structure and ideology was neither more nor less the same everywhere. The contemporary Dalit politics in Punjab seems to be reformed by a similar kind of understanding of caste. In the Doaba region, majority of the population follows the tenets of Sikhism, which ideologically and theologically decries the caste system. Punjab has been a relatively prosperous region of India. However, in recent times the Doaba region witnessed growing instances of caste related conflicts. The available literature also tends to point towards a process of mobility among Dalits and other categories of population of Punjab.

Dalit politics in the State is increasingly influenced by this ground reality. However, the political parties in the State are ready to take the political mileage and electoral gains. For instance, the political parties tried to exploit the Talhan issue for electoral gains. It is reported that the BSP has been trying to continue the simmering to make the best out of the situation. The BJP attempted to communalise the issue between Sikhs and Hindus. The Congress party did not try to examine the issue in its totality and the Government did not direct the administration to ease the tension and work out an amicable solution with the consent of all groups, especially from the perspective of the victims, Dalits. It is significant that despite their efforts, political parties could not politicise the issue of Dalit assertion at Talhan.

The ideological and social make up of the Congress has made it less welcoming to highly assertive advocates of the untouchable cause. It would be pertinent to note here that while the untouchables were a crucial Congress vote bank in India as a whole and in a majority of individual States, even before the recent flux they did not cling to the Congress in regions where another party or movement rose to dominance.[3] Basically, in Punjab both the Congress and the SAD vie for power. These parties attract the votes of Dalits. The BSP is basically a Dalit party, but even after that it could not come into power. In 2012, the BSP–said to have been in an undeclared alliance with the SAD–contested all 113 seats and became a crucial agent in the defeat of the Congress, even though it did not win a single seat itself. There were Dalits within parties across the whole political spectrum. Dalits are the key element in the constituency of the BSP, and also active in numerous other parties. Together, it makes up Dalit movement in its widest sense.

Dalits' Demography in Punjab

SCs' population in India comprises 16.6 per cent of total population. The distinguishing feature of Dalits in Punjab is that Dalits constitute the numerical strength of the SC population, i.e., 31.9 per cent (2011 Census). In terms of population share, Punjab accounts for 4.4 per cent of the total SCs population in India. During this decade, two more castes, namely, Mochi and Mahatam/Rai Sikh castes have been notified as SCs in Punjab. Today, it is estimated that the proportion of Dalits may have risen above 32 per cent in the State of Punjab.

Dalits are sharply divided into various sub-castes, scattered in different religions (Hinduism, Sikhism, Christianity and Buddhism), mostly landless, economically marginalised, socially oppressed and politically neglected. Among these Chamars, Ad-Dharmis and Balmiki are the most numerous castes (Judge, 2004: 187). The major groups of SCs are Mazhabi, Ad-Dharmis, Ramdasia, Balmiki, Bazigar, Mahasha, Megh, Sansi, Bauria, etc. Most of the castes are either engaged in agricultural production as agricultural labourers. Landlessness is primary cause for weak Dalit voice in Punjab. Dalit share under cultivation is only 2.3 per cent. As per the SCs and STs Amendment Act, dated 18th September 1976, a total of 38 Castes were identified for inclusion in the Scheduled list by the Ministry of Home Affairs, New Delhi. According to the official list, Punjab has 39 castes of Dalits including Mahatam/Rai Sikhs. No community in the State was listed as a ST.

Table 5.1: Scheduled Castes in Punjab

Scheduled Castes, 2011		
1. Ad-Dharmi	14. Darain	29. Parna
2. Barar, Burar, Berar	15. Deha, Dhaya, Dhea	30. pherera
3. Banagali	16. Dhogri, Dhangri, Siggi	31. Sanhai
4. Batwal	17. Gagra	32. Sanhal
5. Bauria, Bewaria	18. Ganadhila, Gadeil	33. Sansoi
6. Bazigar	19. Kabirpanthi or Julaha	34. Sansi, Bhedkut, Manesh
7. Balmiki, Chura, Bhangi	20. Khatik	35. Sapala
8. Bhanjara	21. Marija, Marecha	36. Sarera
9. Chamar, Jatia Chamar, Rehgar, Raigar, Ramdasia, Ravidassia	22. Kori-koli 23. Mazhabi 24. Megh	37. Sikligar 38. Sirkiband
10. Chanal	25. Mochi	39. Rai Sikh/Mahatam
11. Dagi	26. Nat	
12. Dhanak	27. Od	
13. Dumna, Mahasha, Doom	28. Pasi	

Source: Census of India, 2011. Chandigarh.

Table 5.2: Scheduled Castes' Population and Decadal Change by Residence in the Doaba Region: 2001-2011

State/District	*SC Population, 2011*			*Decadal Change 2001-2011*			*Percentage of SC Population*		
	Total	*Rural*	*Urban*	*Total*	*Rural*	*Urban*	*Total*	*Rural*	*Urban*
1	**2**	**3**	**4**	**5**	**6**	**7**	**8**	**9**	**10**
Punjab	88,60,179	64,96,986	23,63,193	26.1	22.2	38.2	31.9	37.5	22.7
Kapurthala	2,76,707	2,12,013	64,694	22.6	22.3	23.3	33.9	39.8	22.9
Jalandhar	8,54,444	5,15,342	3,39,102	15.5	9.2	26.6	39.0	49.9	29.2
Hoshiarpur	5,57,504	4,65,037	92, 467	9.8	7.4	23.5	35.1	37.2	27.6
Nawan Shahr	2,60,284	2,12, 889	47,395	9.5	1.0	75.9	42.5	43.7	37.8

Source: Census of India, 2011. Chandigarh.

The SC population is growing at a rate higher than the rest. Being relatively less urbanised than the other caste groups, their proportions are obviously higher in the rural areas of the State. In the State of Punjab, Dalits comprise up to 42 per cent of the Doaba region, which consists the districts of Nawan Shahr, Kapurthala, Jalandhar and Hoshiarpur. The highest numerical strength of SC population is found in Nawan Shahr which is 42.5 per cent. In Kapurthala, Jalandhar and Hoshiarpur, the corresponding proportion of SC population ranges 33.9, 39.0 and 35.1 per cent.

Table 5.3: Percentage of Major Scheduled Castes in Punjab, Census, 2011

Sl. No.	*Caste*	*1991*	*2001*	*2011*
1.	Ad-Dharmis	15.9%	14.9%	11.48%
2.	Chamar/Ravidassia/Ramdasia/Raigar	25.8%	26.2%	23.45%
3.	Balmikis	11.1%	11.2%	9.78%
4.	Mazhabis	30.7%	31.6%	29.73%
5.	Remaining Castes	16.5%	16.1%	25.56%
	Total	**100**	**100**	**100**

Source: Census of India, 2011. Chandigarh.

Table implies that there are two groups which comprise up to 74.44 per cent of the total SC population. One group consists of Balmikis and Mazhabis and the other group consists of Ad-Dharmi, Chamar, Raigar, Ramdasia, Ramdasia Sikh, Ravidassia, and Ramdasia Sikh. The population of first group as per the Census of 2011 is 39.51 of SC population and the second group's population is 34.93 per cent.

Studies on Dalits in Punjab

There are some studies which focus on Dalits, their socio-economic and political conditions in Punjab. They include among others, D.C. Ahir, Kanchan Chandra, M.S. Dhami, Surinder S. Jodhka, Mark Juergensmeyer, Ronki Ram, Harish K. Puri, Paramjit S. Judge, Gurpreet Bal and Ashutosh Kumar. Ahir (1992) has focused on the contribution made by B.R. Ambedkar regarding the assertion of Dalits in Punjab. Chandra's (2000) article is an analysis of the success of the BSP in 1992 Assembly elections in Hoshiarpur district of Punjab. This study compares the relative performance of the Congress and the BSP and analyses the comparative ability of the BSP to provide political representation as a key explanation for its success. He expressed that the rise of the BSP in Punjab was due to the previous attempts of mobilisation of SCs, such as Ad-Dharm movements which had already prepared the ground of Scheduled Castes Federation (SCF) and Republican Party of India (RPI). Chandra (2004) in his another study uses the term 'SC' as the BSP's target ethnic category; and defines the success of ethnic category, if it captures the votes of at least a majority of the members of its target ethnic category. Dhami (1981) in his study finds that the caste structure in Punjab lacks the hierarchical quality common in some other parts of the country.

It does not conform to the *Varna* model with Brahmins at the apex followed by twice-born castes, and with Shudras at the bottom.

Jodhka's (2004) article looks at caste in relation to Sikhism in the regional context of contemporary Punjab. He concludes that while caste is nearly dead in contemporary Punjab, as an ideology, it survives and thrives as a source of identity. Taking a cue of the case of conflict in Talhan of the Doaba region of Punjab, he analyses that it was an experience of Dalit assertion. It was a case of demanding equal rights and share in the resources, material as well as symbolic. He also discussed that classical Brahminical notion of hierarchy did not work in Punjab; Sikhism has a parallel structure of hierarchy. Jodhka (2005) in his another study, analyses the changing caste relation and the rise of Dalit identity in contemporary Punjab. Keeping in mind the existing diversity and sub-variations, a total of six villages and four towns were identified for the primary survey. He finds that the Doaba region has been a region of vibrant Dalit social and political movements, economically, also Dalits of the Doaba region are better off than their counterparts elsewhere. The study is significant to understand the socio-economic aspects of Dalits.

Juergensmeyer (1988) in his work, studies a particular segment of Punjabi society the so-called "untouchables". He has tried to understand the career of Ad-Dharm movement in political and cultural terms. He has raised some basic questions about the role of religion in social change. Ram (2004a) in his work, has studied the phenomenon of untouchability and caste violence in Punjab. He analysed that many castes among Dalits have converted to Sikhism, but they have not been considered equal by the upper Sikh castes, which refuse to associate with them even at the time of religious ceremonies. Even in Sikhism, the spectre of untouchability kept haunting them. He also analyses that in Punjab, the discourse of the Brahminical principal of purity pollution has never been strong as in other parts of India, the main reason behind the caste conflicts was not the factor of communalism, rather it was a sense of assertion for their rights. Untouchability in Punjab was more associated with asymmetrical structure of the agrarian rural economy. Ram (2004b) in his another work, analyses that the Ad-Dharm movement in Punjab aimed at securing a separate and respectable space for the SCs to seek social recognition through cultural transformation and spiritual regeneration. He argues that Ad-Dharm had become an identity for political power, their real objective was to create an egalitarian social structure and the BSP has the same objective. By the ideology and objectives of Ad-Dharm, the BSP has now become the torch bearer. Puri (2004) in his study, points out that the upper castes of Punjab have relatively more liberal attitude towards Dalits in terms of purity and pollution than other States.

Judge (2004) examines and analyses the changing status of Dalits of Punjab. He analyses that the caste system among the Sikhs is largely based on power and privilege paradigm, whereas the Hindu caste system has strong ideological basis. He finds three major changes among Dalits of Punjab, particularly the Doaba region, viz. education, emigration and empowerment in the political process. Judge and Bal (2009) in their study, examine and interrogate the changing status of Dalits in Punjab by taking into consideration four variables, namely, education and accusation, empowerment, entrepreneurship and emigration. The study shows that castes that have suffered all kinds of discrimination for centuries are demanding equal share in all aspects of collective life of the society. Kumar (2004) in his study, argues that if the BSP can get rid of factionalism, it is capable of repeating its performance of 1998 elections, when the BSP emerged as a third strong political party. In 1998 elections, the BSP secured more than 40 per cent votes in the districts of Hoshiarpur, Ferozepur and Phillaur.

There is lack of investigation in the existing literature to provide an answer to the question as to why the BSP has not been able to mark among Dalits in Punjab? It is in this context that the survey conducted on Dalits in the Doaba region of Punjab assumes greater significance.

Selection of Villages

Keeping in view the broad objectives of the study, twenty villages having a relatively high Dalit population were identified. The selection of these villages was made on the basis of available official data. Interviews were conducted on the basis of the voter lists of 2012, which were collected from village to village. The population for interviews was divided into rural and urban. Table 5.4 provides a list of the selected villages falling in the four blocks of the Doaba region under study. The data pertaining to the population of the SCs in these villages is also presented.

Table 5.4: Selected Blocks and Villages with Total Population of the Scheduled Castes

Sl. No.	*Block*	*Total number of Villages*	*Selected Villages for the Study*	*Total Population*	*Total Population of SCs*	*Total Percentage of SCs*
1.	**Hoshiarpur II**	124	Phuglana	3314	2049	61.83
			Ahrana	2105	1625	77.20
			Bohan	2798	1093	39.06
			Sahari	3038	1716	56.48
			Shergarh	2456	1395	56.80
2.	**Jalandhar I**	100	Khambra	4035	3146	77.97
			Partapur	2434	1836	75.43
			Jamsher	8426	3577	42.45
			Sofipind	5549	2872	51.76
			Dhin	4641	2775	59.79
3.	**Phagwara**	102	Chak Prema	621	185	29.79
			Mann	867	800	92.27
			Rawal Pindi	1087	701	64.49
			Jamalpur	1877	1572	83.75
			Khalwara	2544	1825	71.74
4.	**Banga**	92	Behram	3511(SC+BC)	3398	96.78
			Khothran	4430(SC+BC)	4338	97.92
			Mahal Gehla	3684(SC+BC)	3380	91.75
			Mehli	3431(SC+BC)	3227	94.05
			pharala	3750(SC+BC)	3496	93.23

Source: Data collected during the field study from the Block Committees of the Doaba region, 2014.

A Framework of the Study

The field study in this chapter is concerned with the support base of Dalits among three political parties of the State of Punjab, the Congress, the SAD and the BSP. As explained earlier, Doaba region has the highest proportion of SCs in the country. The study covers the entire Doaba region. Keeping in mind the existing diversities and regional variations, in all four blocks and twenty villages were identified for the primary survey. Blocks and villages were selected on the basis of the numerical strength of Dalit population in Doaba

Table 5.5: Respondents' Opinion regarding Political Parties' Representation to Dalits

Sl. No.	*Block (City) N=120*	*Political Parties*			*Total*	*Block (Village)* N=180*	*Political Parties*			*Total*
		Congress I	*SAD*	*BSP*			*Congress I*	*SAD*	*BSP*	
1.	Hoshiarpur	10 (33.33)	3 (10.00)	17 (56.67)	30 (100.00)	Hoshiarpur	18 (40.00)	4 (8.89)	23 (51.11)	45 (100.00)
2.	Jalandhar	9 (30.00)	3 (10.00)	18 (60.00)	30 (100.00)	Jalandhar	15 (33.33)	4 (8.89)	26 (57.78)	45 (100.00)
3.	Phagwara	8 (26.67)	3 (10.00)	19 (63.33)	30 (100.00)	Phagwara	14 (31.11)	4 (8.89)	27 (60.00)	45 (100.00)
4.	Banga	8 (26.67)	4 (13.33)	18 (60.00)	30 (100.00)	Banga	12 (26.67)	5 (11.11)	28 (62.22)	45 (100.00)

Note: The asterisk mark* shows the selection of 5 villages from each block. The figures given in the parentheses denote the percentage share.

region. The study was qualitative in nature and tactfully conducted. It is an analysis of the interactions with 300 members of the targeted SC population.

In the political dynamics of Punjab, there are two major players and contenders of power, namely, the Congress and the Akali Dal. The BSP forays in the region have so far had little success. In the absence of caste as a defining parameter Dalit find presentation in all political parties. The respondents' opinion with regard to the representation given to Dalits in the organisational structure of the different political parties in Punjab is reflected in the Table 5.5.

Table 5.5 clearly shows which party gives more representation to Dalits in its organisational structure. It can be seen that as far as the Block (City) in all the four blocks is concerned, it is the BSP which gives more representation to Dalits in its organisational structure. The percentage is high in all the four blocks. The percentage in the Block (City) is 56.67 per cent in Hoshiarpur, 60.00 in Jalandhar, 63.33 per cent in Phagwara and 60.00 per cent in Banga. The Congress-I appears next with the percentage of 33.33 in Hoshiarpur, 30.00 per cent in Jalandhar, 26.67 each in Phagwara and Banga respectively. The SAD is the party which has given least representation to Dalits in its organisational structure. This representation is 10.00 per cent in Hoshiarpur, Jalandhar and Phagwara respectively, and 13.33 per cent in Banga.

Similarly at the Block (Village) level, the BSP leads all the political parties in giving high representation to Dalits in its organisational structure. In its case, this representation is 51.11 per cent in Hoshiarpur, 57.78 per cent in Jalandhar, 60.00 per cent in Phagwara and 62.22 per cent in Banga. The Congress-I appears next in this regard with Dalits representation of 40.00 per cent in Hoshiarpur, 33.33 per cent in Jalandhar, 31.11 per cent in Phagwara, and 26.67 per cent in Banga. As far as the SAD is concerned, it has given least representation to Dalits in its organisational structure. This presentation at the Block (village) level is 8.89 per cent in Hoshiarpur, Jalandhar and Phagwara respectively and 11.11 per cent in Banga. The BSP, basically, concentrates on capturing the votes of Dalit category. In this sense, it does not appear a secular party, while the Congress tries to represent Dalits on the secular basis and considers the ability of a member in its

Table 5.6: Dalit Respondents' Party Preferences.

Sl. No.	*Block (City) N=120*	*Political Parties*				*Total*	*Block (Village)* N=180*	*Political Parties*				*Total*
		Congress I	*SAD*	*BSP*	*None of these*			*Congress I*	*SAD*	*BSP*	*None of these*	
1.	Hoshiarpur	5 (16.67)	3 (10.00)	7 (23.33)	15 (50.00)	30 (100.00)	Hoshiarpur	10 (22.22)	6 (13.33)	12 (26.67)	17 (37.78))	45 (100.00)
2.	Jalandhar	5 (16.67)	4 (13.33)	7 (23.33)	14 (46.67)	30 (100.00)	Jalandhar	12 (26.67)	4 (8.89)	11 (24.44)	18 (40.00)	45 (100.00)
3.	Phagwara	7 (23.33)	4 (13.33)	11 (36.67)	8 (26.67)	30 (100.00)	Phagwara	8 (17.78)	6 (13.33)	15 (33.33)	16 (35.56)	45 (100.00)
4.	Banga	8 (26.67)	4 (13.33)	10 (33.33)	8 (26.67)	30 (100.00)	Banga	9 (20.00)	6 (13.33)	16 (35.56)	14 (31.11)	45 (100.00)

Note: The asterisk mark* shows the selection of 5 villages from each block. The figures given in the parentheses denote the percentage share.

organisational structure. However, educational qualification of a member gets least consideration in the organisational structure of the BSP. It adversely affects the organisational structure of the party and its strategies. The SAD can also not be called a secular party, and it mainly represents the peasantry class. The BSP has always failed to garner full support of Dalits as other political parties such as the Congress and the Akali Dal also give them due representation in their organisational structure, and Dalits due to their division of votes fail to protect their interests fully. The data pertaining to the respondents' preference for different political parties is provided in Table 5.6.

It can be observed from the table that percentage is quite high in all the four Blocks (City) with the BSP leading the front. Hoshiarpur and Jalandhar exhibit the same percentages i.e., 23.33 per cent while Phagwara and Banga represent the percentages of 36.67 per cent and 33.33 per cent respectively. For the Congress I, it is 16.67 per cent in Hoshiarpur and Jalandhar respectively, 23.33 per cent in Phagwara and 26.67 per cent in Banga. As for the SAD, it is 10.00 per cent in Hoshiarpur, 13.33 per cent each in Jalandhar, Phagwara and Banga respectively. It is seen that respondents' percentage in Block (city) is quite high for 'None of these'. It is 50 per cent in Hoshiarpur, 46.67 per cent in Jalandhar and 26.67 per cent in Phagwara and Banga respectively.

Again, in Block (Village), the most preferred political party is the BSP. In Hoshiarpur, it is 26.67 per cent, 24.44 per cent in Jalandhar, 33.33 per cent in Phagwara and 35.56 per cent in Banga. Preference-wise, the Congress I appears after the BSP. It is 22.22 per cent in Hoshiarpur, 26.67 per cent in Jalandhar, 17.78 per cent in Phagwara and 20.00 per cent in Banga. Only 13.33 per cent in Hoshiarpur, 8.89 per cent in Jalandhar, 13.33 per cent in Phagwara and Banga respectively prefer the SAD party. It is seen that respondents' percentage in Block (Village) is also quite high for 'None of these'. In Hoshiarpur, it is 37.78 per cent, 40.00 per cent in Jalandhar, 35.56 per cent in Phagwara and 31.11 per cent in Banga. It implies that Dalit category is not fully satisfied with any political party. Voters are likely to prefer the parties that have chance to come to power. The SC is the core ethnic category of the BSP but in the Doaba region the SCs votes are also leading to the Congress and the SAD at large numbers. TINA (there is no alternative) factor always works in this region. If Dalit votes for the BSP, it might have been a TINA factor. Voters likely to prefer that party which will give them access to the benefits.

Table 5.7: Overall Percentage of Dalits' Vote Preferences

Sl. No.	*Vote Preference*	*Overall preferences*	
		Urban (N=120)	*Rural (N=180)*
1.	Congress I	32 (26.67)	60 (33.33)
2.	SAD	21 (17.50)	30 (16.67)
3.	BSP	55 (45.83)	75 (41.67)
4.	None of these	12 (10.00)	15 (8.33)

Source: The figures given in the parentheses denote the percentage share.

Table 5.7 indicates quite high Dalits' vote preference for the BSP. It is 45.83 per cent and 41.67 per cent in urban and rural areas respectively. The Congress I is the second vote preference of Dalits in the region. It is 26.67 per cent and 33.33 per cent respectively. For the SAD, it is 17.50 per cent and 16.67 per cent respectively. The percentage is quite high for 'None of these.' It is 10.00 per cent and 8.33 per cent respectively. To conclude and looking at the objective of the chapter to examine the support base of Dalits among other political parties like the Congress and the SAD, the study explores that religious allegiances and the political parties such as the Congress and the SAD which have a sizeable support base among Dalits, weaken the support base of the BSP. By these factors, the BSP finds difficult to mobilise Dalit voters. It is interesting to note that even the SAD which is dominated by the Jats, leads Dalits' representation. The Akali Dal has produced many Dalit leaders like Dhanna Singh Gulshan, Gursev Singh Badal, Charanjit Singh Attwal, Satwant Kaur Sandhu, Basant Singh, Gulsan Singh Ramke, Mahinder Kaur Josh, Desh Raj Dhugga, Sarwan Singh Philour, have remained the State ministers in the Centre Government.

Similarly, the Congress party has given eminent place to Dalit leaders from whom the central ministers Buta Singh, Master Gurbante Singh, Joginder Singh Mann, Darshan Singh, Chaudhury Jagjit Singh, Mahinder Singh, Shamsher Singh Doolan, Chaudhury Santokh Singh, Chaudhury Ram Lubhaya and Santosh Chaudhury. Moreover, out of these Dalit leaders the Congress party gave party chief place to

Shamsher Singh Doolon and Mahinder Singh at State level. It is precisely because of the intra-Dalit cleavages that Dalits could not emerge as a cohesive force to reckon within the politics of Punjab. In the absence of a common platform some of Dalits and their local elites seek their salvation through different political outfits including the Congress and the Akali Dal. In the age of Neo-liberalism, democracy is reduced to management, especially of votes – that enables a political party to form a Government. The political establishment seeks glory in managing a crisis rather than resolving it. The success of a politician is measured in the micro-management of elections. The main opposition party, the Congress is riven with factionalism. The crisis within the AAP has dampened its political fortunes and has damaged the prospects of an alternative political space in Punjab. So, both the parties are virtually inconsequential in the current political crisis. There is mistrust and anger against these political parties. A handful of the ministers among all the political parties in Punjab want to gain political mileage in the name of religion and caste.

In spite of high percentage of Dalit population, the BSP has better prospects of becoming an important player than parties other than the Congress and the Akali Dal. The representational blockage of Dalits in the Congress, the SAD and in the entire party system in Punjab presents the BSP with an opportunity that it could attract Dalit support base in the State of Punjab. The major shift from grassroots level movement to the formal political participation in elections as a means to empowerment is quite visible among Dalits. Dalit Sikh did not get equal treatment in the Gurudwaras of the upper caste Sikhs. Mazhabis were forbidden to enter the Golden Temple for worship, their offering of Karah Prasad was not accepted and Sikhs denied them access to public well and other utilities. SCs, which were the most under-represented, were obviously the most susceptible to the BSP's appeal. With the lessening of Hindu-Sikh tension in Punjab, and the presence of the BSP, religion is now being replaced by caste as the dominant political cleavage in Punjab.

Notes

1. According to Sikh tradition, the word 'miri' stands for worldly power and the word 'piri' stands for religious authority.

2. The highest percentage of votes obtained by the SCF/RPI in Parliamentary elections was 6.2 per cent in 1957 (Brass, 1975: 22).
3. The major examples of long term non-Congress dominance are West Bengal and Tamil Nadu.

References

- Ahir, D.C. 1992. *Selected Speeches of Ambedkar.* New Delhi: Blue Moon Publications.
- Bidwai, Praful. 2007. 'Creating History.' *Frontline* 24 (10): 98-99.
- Brass, Paul R. 1975. 'Ethnic Cleavages in the Punjab Party System (1952-1975).' In *Studies in Electoral Politics in the Indian States,* edited by Myron Weiner and John Osgood Field, 12-16. Delhi: Manohar Book Service.
- ———. 1985. *'Caste, Faction and Party in Indian Politics, Election Studies.'* Vol. 2, New Delhi: Chanakya Publications.
- ———. 1989. 'Socio-economic Aspects of the Punjab Crisis.' *Punjab Journal of Politics* XIII (1-2): 5-14.
- Chandra, Kanchan. 2000. 'The Transformation of Ethnic Politics in India: The Decline of Congress and the Rise of the Bahujan Samaj Party in Hoshiarpur.' *The Journal of Asian Studies* 59(1):26-61.
- ———. 2004. *Why Ethnic Parties Succeed: Patronage and Ethnic Head Counts in India.* Cambridge: University of Cambridge.
- Chhibber, Pradeep K. and John R. Petrocik. 2002. 'Social Cleavages, Elections and the Indian Party System.' In *Party and Party Politics,* edited by Zoya Hasan, 60-61. New Delhi: Oxford University Press.
- Dhami, M.S. 1975. *Minority Leader's Image of the Indian Political System: An Exploratory Study of the Akali Leaders.* Jalandhar: Sterling Prakashan.
- ———. 1981. 'Caste, Class and Politics in the Rural Punjab: A Study of two Villages in Sangrur District.' In *Political Dynamics of Punjab,* edited by Paul Wallace and Surendra Chopra, 292-317. Amritsar: Guru Nanak Dev University.
- ———. 1987. 'Religio-Political Mobilisation and Shift in the Party Support Base in 1985 Punjab Assembly Elections.' *Punjab Journal of Politics* 11 (1-2): 21-42.
- Jodhka, Surinder S. 2004. 'Sikhism and the Caste Question: Dalits and their Politics in Contemporary Punjab.' *Contributions to Indian Sociology* XXXVIII (1&2): 165-93.
- ———. 2005. *A Research Report 'Social Mobility and Changing Identity.'* New Delhi: Indian Social Institute.
- Judge, Paramjit S. 2004. 'Interrogating Changing Status of Dalits of Punjab.' In *Dalits in Regional Context*, edited by Harish K. Puri, 100-131. New Delhi: Rawat Publications.

- ———. 2005. 'Emerging Trends in Social Conflicts in Punjab.' *Journal of Sociology* 26 (1): 28-32.
- Judge, Paramjit S. and Gurpreet Bal. 2009. *Mapping Dalits, Contemporary Reality and Future Prospects in Punjab.* New Delhi: Rawat Publications.
- Juergensmeyer, Mark. 1988. *Religious Rebels in the Punjab. The Social Vision of Untouchables*. Delhi: Ajanta Publications.
- Kaur, Kuldeep. 1989. *Akali Dal in Punjab Politics: Splits and Mergers.* New Delhi: Deep & Deep Publications Pvt. Ltd.
- Kothari, Rajni. 2002. 'The Congress System in India.' In *Parties and Party Politics,* edited by Zoya Hasan, 48. New Delhi: Oxford University Press.
- Kumar, Ashutosh. 2004. 'Punjab in Search of New Leadership.' *Economic and Political Weekly* XXXIX (51): 5441-44.
- Kumar, Pramod. 2017. 'Punjab Politics, Contesting Identities and Forging Coalition.' *Economic and Political Weekly* LII (3): 44-49.
- Nayer, Baldev R. 1968. 'Punjab.' In *State Politics in India*, edited by Myron Weiner, 448-452. Princeton: Princeton University Press.
- Puri. Harish K., ed. 2004. *Dalits in Regional Context.* New Delhi: Rawat Publications.
- Pushpendra. 2001. 'Dalit Assertion through Electoral Politics.' In *Dalit Identity and Politics*, edited by Ghanshyam Shah, 311-339. New Delhi: Sage Publications.
- Ram, Ronki. 2004a. 'Untouchability in India with a Difference: Ad-Dharm, Dalit Assertion and Caste Conflict in Punjab.' *Asian Survey* XLIX (6): 895-912.
- ———. 2004b. 'Untouchability, Dalit Consciousness, and the Ad Dharm Movement in Punjab.' *Contributions to Indian Sociology* 38 (3): 323-51.
- ———. 2007. 'Social Exclusion, Resistance and Deras: Exploring the Myth of Casteless Sikh Society in Punjab.' *Economic and Political Weekly* XLII (40): 4066-4074.
- Rudolph, l. Lloyd and Susanne Hoeber Rudolph. 1967. The *Modernity of Tradition: Political Development in India.* Chicago: University of Chicago Press.
- Sharma, T.R. 1986. *New Challenges of Politics in Indian States*. New Delhi: Uppal Publishing House.
- Sheth, D.L. 2002. 'Caste and Class: Social Reality and Political Representations.' In *Caste and Democratic Politics in India*, edited by Ghanshyam Shah, 108-133. New Delhi: Permanent Black.
- Singh, Khuswant. 1974. *A History of the Sikhs*. Princeton: Princeton University Press.
- Tohra, G.S. 1981. *Five Points' Porgamme of SGPC*, Amritsar: Shiromani Gurdwara Prabandhak Committee.

- Verma, P.S. 1987. 'The Akali Dal History, Electoral Performance and leadership profile.' In *Punjab Today*, edited by Gopal Singh, 273-275. New Delhi: Intellectual Publishing House.
- Wallace, Paul. 1981. 'Religious and Secular Politics in Punjab: The Sikh Dilemma in competing Political System.' In *Political Dynamics of Punjab,* edited by Paul Wallace and Surendra Chopra, 156-176. Amritsar: Guru Nanak Dev University.
- Yadav, Yogendra, Sanjay Kumar and Oliver Heath. 1999. 'The BJP's New Social Bloc.' *Frontline:* 19 November.

Chapter - 6

The BSP and Dalits: An Analysis of the State of Punjab

In 2014 Lok Sabha, only three of the 85 Dalit MPs belong to a Dalit-led party–the Lok Janshakti Party, led by Ram Vilas Paswan. The BSP won no seats in the 2014 Parliamentary election. The overwhelming majority of Dalit MPs belong to parties with a leadership that is either forward caste or, less often, from the BCs: 40 Dalit MPs belong to the BJP, another 7 Dalit MPs belong to the Congress, one Dalit MP belongs to the CPI(M), and the remaining 34 to regional parties. In the State Assemblies, taken together, there are currently 612 Dalit MLAs. Only three per cent belong to a Dalit led party, and most of these MLAs belong to the BSP. The largest single group of Dalit MLAs also belongs to the BJP (25 per cent), with another 14 per cent belonging to the Congress, and 4 per cent to the two communist parties. The remainders belong to regional parties with non-Dalit leaders (Chandra, 2016: 11).

The BSP has contributed substantially to the social deepening of Indian democracy. It is the only Dalit party that has achieved considerable electoral success and handled State power in UP. The BSP has brought upon the issues of social emancipation and political rights to centre-stage. Within a short period of time the BSP has emerged as a strong party within the emerging multi-party system. The major development in 1980s that culminated into the full-fledged Dalit assertion in 1990s was the formation of the BSP under Kanshi Ram regarded as the only successful player in the history of Dalit politics. The BSP has historically drawn a loyal base of voters from

India's lowest caste (Dalit). It has attempted to grow nationally as well, but has met limited success so far. The party emerged from the activities under taken by Kanshi Ram to protect the interests of SC Government employees. Kanshi Ram was able to promote the organisation in the States of Punjab, UP, Haryana and Madhya Pradesh. Although the BSP was recognised by the Election Commission as a national party, it effectively functioned in certain North Indian States only. Its ideology is based on the argument that the majority are oppressed by the selected upper class. It aims to change this by using the Government power.

An Analysis of the BSP in Punjab

I

This Chapter explores as to why the high concentration of Dalit population in Punjab, has not translated into success for the BSP? For answering this question, the study examines two aspects, one, the nature of the party organisation and two, political strategy of the BSP. The study was qualitative and tactfully conducted with the same methodology and the framework mentioned in chapter V. It is an analysis of the interactions with 300 respondents of the targeted SC population and 20 leaders of the BSP and its factional political parties.

The BSP began a system of alliances that proved to be of minor political gains, because the BSP faced split and many parties emerged that dissipated all its advantages. In the case of Punjab, the BSP entered the Assembly polls in 1985, in almost all the Assembly constituencies in the Doaba region and failed to win any seat, it was polled a significant proportion of the total votes which ended the support base of the Congress, helped the Akalis to win especially in rural areas. The BSP contested 51 Assembly seats all over the State in 1985. In this election, the BSP candidates polled 18 per cent of the total votes in Jalandhar North constituency where SCs, largely Chamars constitute 24 per cent of the voting population (Juergensmeyer, 1988: 12). In 1989 Lok Sabha elections, it won Phillaur reserved seat. In 1992 Assembly elections, it won 6 seats from the Doaba region. It won 2 seats from Sangrur and 1 from Ferozepur districts. The Ferozepur parliamentary seat also went in its favour. The BSP became main opposition political party in Assembly in Punjab by winning 9 seats.

In 1996 Parliamentary election, it could win 3 Parliamentary seats of Phillaur, Hoshiarpur and Ferozepur to the Lok Sabha and gave a lead in as many as 17 Assembly segments; however, it failed to continue its alliance with the Akali Dal Badal. It disassociated itself from main Akali Dal and could not form alliance with the Congress party in 1997 Assembly elections. In result, it could get only 1 seat in the elections. In 1998 Parliamentary elections, it fought elections in alliance with the Indian National Congress (INC) but it could not open its account in Lok Sabha. In September 1999 parliamentary polls, the BSP joined the United Front but could not get any seat (Verma, 1999: 17-18). The BSP has reduced its vote share from 16.32 per cent in 1992 to 1.9 per cent in 2014 General election. The BSP failed to inspire voters. The BSP's shocking result in 2014 Punjab General election put Mayawati and the party in an existential crisis. In 2017 Punjab Assembly election, the BSP's vote share has been decreased to 1.5 per cent in Kanshi Ram's home State. It proves that the people are no longer interested in just caste or religion based politics. The prospect of real development is more important and attractive than dry words like 'Ethnic Identity' and 'assertion of caste identity or Dalit identity'.

Despite the strong proportion of SCs in the Punjab population and the fact that they are the best off across India, Dalits of Punjab have still been unable to assert themselves on the political scene. The mobilisation of Dalits began on the question of distinct religious identity. Interestingly, Ambedkar's rejection of Hinduism when he led his followers to conversion to Buddhism; the struggle of Dalits began and ended on the issue of religious identity. Dalits in Punjab fought for a distinct religious identity; they were able to achieve their goal and were recorded as Ad-Dharmis in 1931 Census. Dismal performance could be the division of SCs into numerous castes scattered across varied religions, *deras* and sects. Among Dalits Ramdasias, Mazhabis, Rai Sikhs, and Sansis follow the Sikh religion. Balmikis are primarily Hindus. Ravidassias and Ad-Dharmis have recently founded a separate Dalit religion–Ravidassia Dharm. In terms of political affiliation, the SCs in Punjab are also highly heterogeneous. Chamars and Balmikis are generally considered to be closer to the Congress party whereas the Mazhabis, Ramdasias, Rai Sikhs and

Sansis support the Akali Dal. However, political affiliations remain mercurial (Ram, 2017: 54).

Politics in Punjab operates within the given social boundaries. The composite religio-cultural tradition lends a distinct flavour of the otherwise divisive politics. Caste hierarchy is pervasive in society, but in electoral politics, it could not emerge as an exclusive factor for vote catching machine, even the lower rung in caste hierarchy, Dalits do not constitute a captive vote bank. A typical example is most of the writings on caste in Punjab. These start with the argument that caste has been weak in Punjab (Jodhka, 2004: 165-167) because Punjab has liberal religious practices. Both Sikhism and the Arya Samaj have liberated Dalits from the stringent purity pollution based behavioural patterns. Further, the political orientation of the BSP has been unable to capture the regional, cultural and economic specificity of Punjab. The purity pollution and Manuwad that are the BSP's main ideology do not find expression in this region in view of the role of the Arya Samaj and the Sikhism. In Punjab, there has always been a parallel spiritual syncretic tradition, epitomised by the teachings of Sufis, *Faqirs* and *Pirs* that could be invoked for egalitarian politics, a pre-condition for a sound democracy.

Sikhism is a religion without caste. Not only the Sikh Gurus were beyond all doubt vigorous and practical denouncers of caste, but Sikh reformers in the late nineteenth century also used its anti-caste message to establish Sikhism's distinctiveness from Hinduism. Contemporary Sikh scholars also underline this point very sharply. With regard to caste discrimination, the idea of caste has become weaker than what it used to be in the past. Sikhism is supposed to have been one of the liberalised aspects in the lives of Dalits of Punjab which has also provided enormous scope for Dalit identity formation and assertion. The Sikh Gurus' opposition to Brahminical orthodoxy and caste reduced the oppressive nature of casteism in Punjab.

The practice of untouchability at religious places among the Sikhs is almost absent in the Doaba region. There is widely held belief that there is caste hierarchy among the Sikhs, though caste system lacks rigidity that is prevalent in other parts of the country. There is a general impression that there is a caste basis of the Gurudwaras. Each caste tends to have its own Gurudwara. Such an observation is partially true. For Dalits, the caste system is oppressive due to discrimination and exclusion. But at the same time it situates them in the system as a collective identity. The decline of untouchability however, does not imply that caste has disappeared. When compared with other sections of the population, Dalits of Punjab continue to be a deprived community. Their relative deprivation is clearly reflected when we compare their economic standing and the quality of life with the non-Dalits in the villages. In the emerging scenario, Dalits have begun to assert for equal rights. Dalit assertions are actively resisted by the erstwhile dominant castes. The obvious result of this is an increase in the incidents of caste-based conflicts. One section of elite among Dalit has preferred to be Sanskritised rather than remaining with Dalit masses and giving them appropriate directions.

Ramdasias and Ad-Dharmis originated from Chamars and Mazhabis from Balmikis. But Ramdasias, Ad-Dharmis and Mazhabis consider themselves superior to their erstwhile castes. On the other hand, the distinctive pattern of caste hierarchy in Sikhism which points to a new pattern of competing hierarchies, parallel to that of the Hindus, calls deeper insight into the dynamics of political power and economic relation both at local and regional level. Sikhism doctrinally does not support the practice of caste; it may be interesting to see that Dalits of Punjab have made use of this available 'cultural resources' while trying to negotiate their identities with the dominant communities in their immediate social context. Such an understanding may help us to unravel the nature of Dalits politics in Punjab today. The Talhan episode has revealed two contradictory trends. Firstly, the political assertion of Dalits took place in a region which has always remained more vibrant and socially and economically well informed region of Punjab, as far as the position of Dalits is concerned. Secondly, despite the social mobility in the Doaba region particularly among Dalits, the inter-caste power equation has yet not changed, though the inter-caste relations are cordial but the inter-caste equation is highly imbalanced in the disadvantage of Dalits. The inequalities are inherited and institutionalised in the social structure of Punjab. Ambedkar seriously contemplated conversion to Sikhism much before he decided in favour of Buddhism. It is not certain why he changed his decision, but one of the conjectures is that the (upper caste) Sikh theologians were appalled at the thought of millions of converted Dalit Sikh taking over their religious institutions.

The larger discourse of Dalit politics that calls upon the different caste groups to come together under a common political banner has also played some role in the process of identity formation. With growing self-consciousness, individual caste groups, such as Balmikis or Ad-Dharmis also invest in consolidating their own community identity. It hardly helps that the BSP in Punjab has mostly been a divided house. The ties between Government employees and the BSP ruptured in 1985, when internal dissension led to a nationwide split between BAMCEF and the BSP. The split was particularly debilitating for the BSP in Punjab, where BAMCEF workers left the party almost en masse. Today there is no united BSP in Punjab. Rather, it is divided into the BSP (Ambedkarite), the BSP (Democratic), the Bahujan Samaj Morcha, the BSP (Nahar), the Bahujan Kranti Dal, the BSP (Kainth), the Bahujan Samaj Vikash Party and the Bahujan Shakti Party which are leading to the division of Dalit votes. These various factions have rendered the BSP ineffective in Punjab.

Dalit question has recently come into limelight in context of the controversy around the burgeoning *deras* and *baba* cults in the State. Though these *deras* are certainly manifestation of a pluralistic culture in the State and attract many Dalits, it is too optimistic for them as places of Dalit assertion. Although Dalits visit *deras* frequently, there are at least 60 sects boasting of large followers. More than half of these are located in the four districts of Doaba region, considered to be the heartland of Ad-Dharmis–those Sikhs who joined Ravidassias. At least 40 per cent of Doaba's population comprises Ad-Dharmis. S. R. Heer, the general secretary of Sant Sarwan Dass Charitable Trust run by the Ballan-based sect said that there are over 60 *deras* in Punjab that have exclusively Ravidassias' identity. Dalit activist and the BSP leader Ramesh Kaul said, if the small *deras* are included, the numbers could well touch 100. These sects preach the words and philosophy of Guru Ravidass, a prominent figure in the Bhakti movement that flourished in the fourteenth and fifteenth centuries. In Punjab, Dalit politics has shifted to the *deras* and saints who have established themselves as the sole and soul spokesman of Dalits particularly the Ad-Dharmis and Chamars. A result of this participation of the man of God in public, social and political affairs of Dalits is the newly emerged context of Dalit assertion. According to the Dalits informants there are 176 *deras* of Ad-Dharmis Saints that follow Guru Ravidass as their deity.

There has always been a sharp political difference within the Sikh community. Caste has remained an important factor that shapes the internal power structure of the Sikh community. The Akali Dal has been dominated by the Sikh upper caste, the Khatris and the Jats. On the other hand Dalits among them, who constitute between 25 per cent and 30 per cent of the total Sikh population, have remained on the margin of community affairs. Besides the complicated and contested listings of communities, the Indian political system over the past seven decades produced a three-fold framework of hierarchy: the generals, the backwards and the Dalits, some States further dividing the 'backwards' and 'Dalits' into sub-categories on the basis of degrees of backwardness. The internal classification of the SCs in Punjab is certainly much more than instances of competitive vote bank politics (Jodhka and Kumar, 2007: 20-23).

Dalits especially in the Doaba region have moved up economically over the past few decades, but have no improvement in their social position. In other places, the emphasis by the *deras* on social service and campaign against alcohol and narcotic abuse has helped in garnering more numbers of devotees. The Ad-Dharmis in Doaba region have more NRIs among SCs today. The SC people live in a separate neighbourhood; their place of worship is separate. However, their visibility in the State politics has so far been rather poor. Even at the local level, they have not been able to acquire power. Despite many radical changes in the society and economy of villages, their position remains marginal in local politics. Hierarchical differentiation among Dalits has played an important role in preventing them from becoming a major political force in Punjab. What have prevented Dalits in Punjab from emerging as a political alternative despite high concentration of their population is that they have not been able to consolidate themselves as a homogenous group. Dalit consciousness, instead of transcending caste and caste-based hierarchies, strengthened caste identities. In Doaba region where youngsters proudly uttered "*put Jattan de* (sons of Jats)" today it is "*put Chamaran de* (sons of Chamars)." The sustainability of Dalit assertion has become a possibility largely due to the emergence of sizeable middle class among

Dalits, which find it difficult to be assimilated in the caste society as equals. Caste distinction is relatively stronger in rural Punjab. With the economic rise of some sections of Dalits, there has been a spate of separate Dalit gurudwaras in the State. In urban areas probably the distinction is less antagonistic, though not absent. In some places like Jalandhar, for example, the leather trade and production of leather related sports goods for a long time ensured that it was possible for at least to some sections.

II

In Punjab, however, the split left no such leadership vacuum, and the SC elites are not strong enough to displace dominant elites from within, remain in subordinate position. The phenomenal rise of the BSP under the leadership of Mayawati has baffled political pundits. Conventional wisdom suggests that a party rocked by so many defections should be struggling to find its feet. Mayawati hounded out virtually every party veteran who helped to build the BSP from its infancy, and this should-again, according to conventional wisdom – led to her own political demise. The absence of senior and middle level leaders in Punjab should have stunted the growth of the BSP. Leaders and activists are normally reluctant to remain in political parties where most of the tickets to State Assembly and Parliamentary elections are bartered to the ignorant persons. The BSP's first step in politics was the establishment of an "independent Dalit political leadership" instead of a "dependent Dalit political leadership." Kanshi Ram produced an independent Dalit political leadership in a party that was led and dominated by Dalits with an independent agenda.

Dalits of Punjab constitute a motley group of castes, economic stratas and religious identities, besides there is no able BSP leader in Punjab to mobilise them across religious and regional dividends. All political parties namely the BSP, the BJP, the CPI and the AAP are minor players and become effective only if they fight elections by forging an alliance with any of these parties. This time, Dalits of the Doaba region are leaderless, have no party to turn to for help. Dalits across the Doaba region disenchanted with the three major parties– the Congress, the Akali Dal and the BSP. Basically it happens that when a Dalit votes for the BSP, it is because of the TINA (there is no alternative).

After 1997, the BSP suffered decline in its political fortune with local leadership having no autonomy in decision-making process and all power lying with BSP supremo Mayawati. Further, the BSP suffered from lack of intra-party democracy. In 2002, the BSP suffered a major jolt when senior leaders quitting the party in protest against the "dictatorial attitude" of the BSP High Command. Accusing the BSP of "exploiting Dalit sentiments for selfish motives," 17 senior BSP leaders, including some former district presidents, resigned from the party and joined the Bahujan Samaj Morcha, headed by Satnam Singh Kainth. The BSP leadership in Punjab could not evolve an integrated ideology that could unite the different Dalit castes in the State under one umbrella. Mr. Satnam Singh Kainth claimed that his party the BSM is a true representative of Dalits and the downtrodden in the country. He alleged that the BSP had practiced opportunistic politics and totally ignored the real issues and problems faced by Dalits. But the voters had realised the designs of the BSP and rejected the Congress-BSP alliance (Interview with the BSP leaders, December, 2016).

Bahujan base on caste identity may seem to work–as in the case of the BSP–in strategising electoral wins. But it cannot effect the slightest change for the better in the social contradictions of castes on the ground. In Punjab, many strong leaders have left the party due to the monopoly of High Command. Most of the leaders are of the opinion that the party's problem is to replicate the alchemy, it has been able to work in UP. The BSP's record in Punjab despite its high proportion of Dalit voters, has been dismal and after Kanshi Ram's death, it has been dominated by a few leaders of the party with little prospect of other.

Traditionally, Dalit voted for the Congress till the BSP started the direct Dalit politics which led to social and political awakening in them. But after the party's founder Kanshi Ram death, Dalit leadership in the BSP splintered and many of his foot soldiers in Punjab parted away. Most of the key Akalis are Jat Sikhs. Relatively the Congress party has offered slightly more space to BCs and Dalit Sikhs like Giani Zail Singh (a tarkhan, a relatively BC) and Buta Singh, a Dalit Sikh. A majority of the SGPC members are Jats. The BSP's approach is fundamentally different from other parties. For it, political society is constituted by groups, and not individuals. It treats group identity as defining one and does not consider class, gender, or occupation as relevant. Hence, its political strategy hinges on activating this identity. In accordance with this strategy, the BSP advocates a one point programme: proportional representation for all groups in Government, bureaucracy, and educational institutions (Galanter, 1989: 133).

III

Organisation studies are badly needed because the BSP's organisation has received remarkably little attention in recent years. Analysts have concentrated on its discourse and its social base share of votes in various elections instead of the party strategies. The breaking of party organisation that is the process by which a party's members are induced to defect to other parties – has been a significant theme in recent years in several States. Lack of organisation is meant purely lack of reliable instrument for reaching more votes. Organisationally, the BSP has divided the State of Punjab into district zones, sectors and booths level.

(a) The State is divided into five zones: Jalandhar, Patiala, Amritsar, Bathinda, Ferozepur. Coordinator, president, general secretary and cashier are appointed in each of the zones.

(b) State president and coordinator organise cadre camp in every Constituent Assembly.

(c) There are 160 Booths in the State of Punjab; each booth constitutes its own booth committee, which comprises of one president, six organiser secretaries, and one member of BAMCEF. The fee of membership is deposited to the High Command (UP Govt.).

(d) Ten Booths comprise one sector, the region is divided into 16 sectors, and each sector is comprised with its own in-charge, president and general secretary.

(e) For 2017 Punjab Assembly election, the BSP organised four-members' panel for each constituency. The BSP was also planned a social media campaign to shed its pro-Dalit tag.

A Sector Level Committees

1. Polling Booth Committee is the most unified organisation. It is the strength of the Booth Committee.

2. The in-charge of Lok Sabha constituency organises Cadre camp at every 10 polling booths; in which 30 workers participate from each booth. The total strength of this cadre camp is 300 (Interview with the BSP leaders, May 2015).

Table 6.1: Zonal Co-ordinators of the BSP in Punjab.

Sl. No.	*Zone*	*Designation*	*Caste*
1.	Jalandhar	Coordinator	Ad-Dharmi
2.	Jalandhar	Coordinator	Ad-Dharmi
3.	Patiala	Coordinator	Ravidassia
4.	Patiala	Coordinator	Chamar
5.	Amritsar	Coordinator	Ad-Dharmi
6.	Amritsar	Coordinator	Ravidassia
7.	Bathinda	Coordinator	Ravidassia
8.	Ferozepur	Coordinator	Rai Sikh
9.	Ferozepur	Coordinator	Ravidassia

Source: Interviews with the BSP officials in Jalandhar, 2014.

Table 6.2: Caste-wise Lok Sabha Constituencies' Presidents of the BSP in Punjab.

Sl. No.	*Constituency*	*Designation*	*Caste*
1.	Jalandhar	President	Ad-Dharmi
2.	Hoshiarpur	President	Ad-Dharmi
3.	Gurdaspur	President	Prajapati
4.	Khadur Sahib	President	Mazhabi Sikh
5.	Patiala	President	Ravidassia
6.	Ferozepur	President	Dhanak
7.	Anandpur Sahib	President	Ad-Dharmi
8.	Faridkot	President	Mazhabi Sikh
9.	Sangrur	President	Ramdasia Sikh
10.	Ludhiana	President	Ramdasia
11.	Bathinda	President	Ramdasia
12.	Fatehgarh Sahib	President	Ravidassia
13.	Amritsar	President	Mazahabi Sikh

Source: Interviews with the BSP officials in Jalandhar, 2014.

The BSP has good organisational stracture. But in practical sense, it has not been able to attract Dalit community. The BSP faces a strategic predicament. Its autonomous politics has raised the political profile of Dalits at the local level, which requires the Government to support local resistance. But tackling local problems entails a class approach to pressurise the Government for implementation of economic redistribution, which a caste based following cannot achieve and which the party wants to avoid.

A major dimension of Dalit politics is that of the politics of identity i.e. the distinct identity of the exploited and the broken people who tended to define themselves as Dalits. The political articulation of the organisation of Dalits, whether belonging to the BSP, the BSP Ambedkar, the BSP Kanshi Ram, the BSP Democratic, the Bahujan Samaj Morcha or any other faction of the BSP, has been focused primarily on the share in the political power, reservation and check on atrocities on Dalits, whereas the society has underlined the political weightage of this segment of the society. It is important to notice that Dalits' organisations have failed to emphasise and ensure the effective implementation of Government schemes.

In Punjab, the uniqueness of Kanshi Ram's political lineage, as compared to the leaders of other parties, also explains why they rejected a functional multi-tiered hierarchical party organisation. As outsider that carried no political baggage from other parties, Kanshi Ram and Mayawati could afford to knock off several rungs in the BSP's internal organisational ladder. In the early days, while building the BSP organisation brick by brick, Kanshi Ram was not completely averse to delegating authority to subordinates, but this changed as the party took off. Most of the leaders are compelled by their organisational structure to search for candidates primarily from within the party, even though parties like the Congress have increasingly introduced a quota of outsider candidates, most notably film stars. In the case of the BSP, there is no such organisational imperative for Mayawati since nobody in the party is encouraged to even think that they will move upwards in the hierarchy. After all, if there is no ladder worth the name, it is impossible to climb. Former activists of the BAMCEF, DS-4 and even Dalit Panthers and Naxalite groups are the ones who fought the daily battles of oppressed group in the State against the upper caste establishment.

Among SCs, Ad-Dharmis are the best represented and have typically been given about half of the seats in Assembly elections over the 1985-2012 periods, while BCs have not been given adequate representation in the BSP organisational structure. The early BSP organisation in Punjab was dominated by the Chamars and Ad-Dharmis. The two State level organisers of BAMCEF and then DS-4 were both Ad-Dharmis (Chandra, 2004: 192). In such a situation the Mazhabis and Balmikis felt threatened by increasing influence of the Ad-Dharmis. The Success of the BSP in 1992-1997 Legislative Assembly elections in Hoshiarpur is the historical role played in this district by the Ad-Dharm movement, and preexisting political parties, including the SCF and RPI (Chandra, 2000: 51).

Since the BSP organisation lacked the multi-tiered hierarchy of other political party that led the senior and middle-level leaders leaving the party. This is quite unique since even in parties that have strong leaders who take most of the decisions, there are still rungs in the organisational ladder down which power percolates. Mayawati, on the other hand, has completely dispensed with this hierarchical structure. Internal organisational elections do take place in the BSP regularly in accordance with Election Commission regulations, but these are even more of a farce than those carried out by dynastic parties like the Congress. The BSP's core Dalit voters have been shifting to the Punjab Congress in sizeable numbers, as they happen to be the main beneficiaries of the NREGA and mid-day meal scheme that has given them some security in a relatively bleak scenario.

IV

The BSP's predecessor, DS-4, had aptly described what *Bahujan Samaj* stood for through its evocative slogan. It establishes that caste based political mobilisation will help in transferring power from leaders who belonged to the historically most powerful castes to those who belong to the most oppressed and suppressed. Ambedkar's vision that caste, apart from being socio-spiritual institution, is also a political and ideological institution, and that it needs to be attacked through political means. The signature slogan raised in the mid-80s described the party's attitude towards the non-*Bahujan Samaj*:

(1) 85 par 15 ka raj nahin chalega, nahin chalega (85 per cent living under the rule of 15 per cent, this will not last, this will not last)

(2) Vot hamara, raj tumhara, nahin chalega, nahin chalega (We have the votes, you have the power, this will not last, this will not last)

(3) Tilak, taraju aur talvar Isko maro joote char. (The tilak [emblem of the sectarian affiliation of the Hindus which is on the forehead and symbolises the Brahmin], the balance [symbol of the merchant castes] and the sword [symbol of the warrior castes], hit them with their shoes [symbol of the work of the Chamars, the principal untouchable caste of North India, who work with leather).

The BSP dramatically altered its traditional and trenchant anti-Brahmin, anti-upper caste political position. Mayawati told that the BSP is now a party of all castes, all religions, announced *"Haathi nahi Ganesh hai, Brahma, Vishnu, Mahesh hai."* The party also coined the slogans *"Jiski jitni sankhya bhaari, uski utni bhagidari"*, *"Jiski jitni hai taiyari, uski utni hissedari"* and *"Brahmin shankh Bajayega, hathi badhta jayega"* which meant that representation in ticket distribution will be as per the participation by various castes in party's growth. The politics of the BSP does not ask for the revision of the category of Dalit, but goes for sudden rejection. Similarly it does not go for the modification of the category of the Bahujan instead it seeks to ensure the latter into *Sarvajan* without any consideration for the historical role that this category has played in consolidating Dalit Bahujan solidarity (Guru, 2005: 26). The BSP have rebuilt the Congress-style rainbow coalition and has succeeded in garnering the support of non-Dalit voters at a level. Mayawati has affected a paradigm shift in Indian politics. The BSP for the first time in 2007 in UP Assembly elections, succeeded in building a social coalition that inverts the pyramid of caste/class hierarchy by building a rainbow alliance of social groups, now dominated by that greatest under class of all Dalits. The strategy of the BSP has mostly been to prefer the political empowerment of Dalits in Punjab. The process of social engineering strategy proves counter-productive because in Punjab, the process of Dalit consciousness slows down. Whether to keep its

Dalit identity intact or to open its door for twice-born castes is still a paradox for the BSP. It has not come out of this paradox clearly. However, now the party officially stands for 'Sarvjan hitay, sarvjan sukhay'. By 2006-2007, keeping the exigencies of parliamentary politics in mind, the party firmly led by Chief Minister started experimenting with a new social engineering formula of wooing the same upper castes against which the BSP social movement had been mobilised.

"Dalit-Brahmin-Muslim" combination had gone to be the axis of the BSP's 2017 Assembly election gambit. Higher share of Brahmin and Muslim candidates eating into the share of OBCs was learnt to be the major bone of political contention for the BSP's gambit in 2017 Assembly election. The BSP was appeared to slot more than half the candidates from among Brahmins and Muslims. The BSP believes that *"Dalit-Brahmin-Muslim bhaichara"* experiment can be replicated at least in Madhya Pradesh, Rajasthan and Punjab with minor variations; the aim is to advance the central idea of *"Dalit-Brahmins-Muslim"* combinations. The reformulation of *Manuwad* automatically creates background condition for the BSP to transmute the vague *Bahujan Samaj* into *Sarvajan.* At least *Bahujan* promises broad polarisation between the three and half per cent and rest of them who are numerically majority. The Bahujan category can be defined in terms of the formal power framework, while the former could be defined in terms of the socio-cultural framework. *Sarvajan* obliterates all the contradictions in its vagueness. It does not have contours as if the social reality itself is without polarity and sharpness. In 2009, out of 80 BSP candidates, only 18 per cent were Dalits. Dalits voted for the party both because its leader was a Dalit, and because its programme was 'pro-Dalit.' In fact, most of the 'caste parties' are placed in this category because of the caste of their leader, as is evident from the 'Yadav parties.' But the BSP played an additional caste card in 2009 by nominating a record number of Brahmin candidates (20 per cent) in order to send a signal to this caste group which had joined hands with Dalits against the Yadav-Rajput alliance in 2007. Tables 6.3, 6.4 and 6.5 show the BSP's caste-wise candidates' representation in 2012 and 2017 Assembly elections and 2009 and 2014 Lok Sabha elections in Punjab.

Table 6.3: Caste-wise Presentation by the BSP in 2012 Punjab Assembly Election

Sl. No.	*Castes*	*Caste-wise Presentation*
1.	Chamar/Ad-Dharmi/Ramdassia	47.00
2.	Mazhabi Sikh/Balmikis	22.22
3.	Bajigar/Rai Sikh	2.56
4.	BCs	10.25
5.	Upper Castes	14.52
6.	Muslims	1.70
7.	Charistians	1.70

Source: Interviews with key functionaries of the BSP in Punjab, 2013. Jalandhar.

Table implies that in 2012 Assembly elections, seats were also distributed to upper caste candidates, in total 117 Assembly seats, tickets were distributed to Chamarss, Ad-Dharmis, Chuhras, Jats, Muslims, Christians, and OBCs. As far as caste-wise representation is concerned, the BSP fielded nearly half of the seats to the Chamars/ Ad-Dharmis/Ramdassia, which is 47.00 per cent, Mazhabi Sikhs/ Balmikis 22.22 per cent, Bajigar/Rai Sikh 2.56 per cent, BCs 10.25 per cent, upper castes 14.52 per cent and the representation of religious minority groups was not impressive, proportion was 1.70 per cent each to Muslims and Christians. Data shows that Chamar/Ad-Dharmis are dominating the representation over the rest. Yet the realisation on the part of the BSP as a party, its base was largely limited to the SCs and that too mainly the Chamars and Ad-Dharmis among them.

Table 6.4 implies that as far as caste is concerned, five SC candidates were fielded in the Punjab Lok Sabha elections 2009. Rai Sikh caste was not a scheduled caste till 2009. Three candidates were from Chamars/ Ramdasias caste among the five SCs candidates. While four seats were distributed to the upper castes and three seats were to the BCs. The Representation of religious minorities groups was not impressive. In 2014 Lok Sabha election, five seats were distributed to the Chamar/Ravidassia and Ad-Dharmi caste, two seats were fielded of the Mazahabi caste and other seats were distributed to the upper and BCs. One can infer that Chamar caste among the SCs is dominating the representation. In a bid to gain ground in Punjab after suffering a humiliating defeat in the 2014 Lok Sabha polls, the BSP was decided to shed its image as a pro-Dalit party in the 2017 Assembly election. Taking a major step towards it, the party chalked out a plan, which aimed to reach around 55 lakh families in the State. To make this plan a reality, the party launched a 'Ghar Ghar Chalo' campaign. In 2017 Assembly election in Punjab, the BSP promised 10 per cent quota for 'poor upper castes'.

Table 6.4: Caste-wise BSP Candidates' list of Lok Sabha Elections in Punjab, 2009 and 2014

Sl. No.	*Constituency*	*Caste of the Candidate, 2009*	*Caste of the Candidate, 2014*
1.	Gurdaspur	Muslman	Ravidassia
2.	Amritsar	Brahmin	Khatri
3.	Khadoor Sahib	Sunhar	Mazhabi Sikh
4.	Jalandhar	Chamar	Ad-Dharmi
5.	Hoshiarpur	Chamar	Chamar
6.	Anandpur Sahib	Gujjar	Jat
7.	Ludhiana	Tarkhan	Jat
8.	Fatehgarh Sahib	Chamar	Prajapat
9.	Faridkot	Mazhabi Sikh	Mazhabi Sikh
10.	Ferozepur	Rai Sikh	Prajapat
11.	Bathinda	Bania	Chamar
12.	Sangrur	Rajput	Chamar
13.	Patiala	Brahmin	Ramgaria

Source: Interviews with the leaders of the BSP, 2014. Hoshiarpur.

Table 6.5: Caste-wise Distribution of the Seats by the BSP in 2017 Punjab Assembly Election

Sl. No.	*Category*	*Seats*
1.	General	10
2.	BCs	08
3.	SCs	93

Source: Interview with president and zonal president of the BSP, 2017. Chandigarh.

Table denotes that the BSP contested at 111 constituencies in 2017 Punjab Assembly election, where it had distributed 93 seats to the SCs, 10 to General category and 8 to BCs. Among 93 SC seats, about 65 per cent seats were given to the Chamars/Ad Dharmis/Ramdasias.

Rest of the seats were alloted to other SCs like Mazhabis/Balmikis, Rai Sikhs, Bazigar etc. In Punjab, Kanshi Ram's "Bahujan" Strategy as a key for political power seems totally failure. Kanshi Ram's "Bahujan" assimilated all castes and communities, except for the upper castes, glossing over their different histories, cultures and more importantly, their material contradictions. They were supposed to snatch political power from the 15 per cent strong upper castes. But in Punjab, as a matter of fact, Kanshi Ram's Bahujan could not transcend this caste confine. The BSP has persistently been ignoring its own promises to the Bahujan. It refused to learn from the systematic erosion of its mass base in the State.

Anyone with leadership ambitions in the BSP runs smack into the obvious lack of opportunity to represent the party in either the State Assembly or Parliament. The overwhelming majority of the election tickets in State and national polls are distributed on a piecemeal basis to candidates depending on their caste, community and the financial resources at their command. They do not even have to be the BSP members, let alone leaders or key functionaries who have worked for the party for a long time. It means that those who belong to the party organisation have little chance to further a career in the party. This is again quite different from other parties where even though top leaders distribute election tickets to favourites, most candidates are found from within the party and affiliated organisation.

The BSP is the only party which has no social and political programme in Punjab. It never issued any manifesto. Dr Ambedkar, on whose name is trying to cash in, had pleaded for land reforms in order to give land to the landless, the bulk of who belong to Depressed Classes. The BSP's strategy is to dazzle by demonstrating her glamorous personality. Mayawati thinks differently: in her opinion this class comes en bloc to her because of the hardship and sacrifices they endure, there will be no reason to support her once their oppressive misery is no more. The shift in the party's ideology from *"Bahujan Samaj*" (majoritarianism) to *"Sarvajan Samaj*" (whole society) would mean an ideological turnaround as the political raison detre of the BSP has been to take up the exclusive cause of Dalits. The social engineering formula to some extent worked in UP because Dalits already consolidated as a political force and hence best placed to cash in on anti-incumbent sentiments. In 2017 Assembly election in UP, Mayawati had entered into new experiment of Muslims-Dalit combine. It gave 99 tickets to Muslims more than their population and 87 tickets to Dalits. Besides taking Brahmins to its fold by allowing them to contest on 66 Assembly seats as they account for 12-13 per cent population share, BSP trusted non-Yadav OBCs and gave 106 tickets to them. She fielded 45 other than Brahmin upper caste candidates justifying its balanced approach for all the communities. The same conditions do not exist in Punjab. The most distinctive trait is that in Punjab, the BSP and its leaders have displayed their reluctance to be involved in mass agitation. Strangely, despite the BSP's aggressive agenda representing the cause of deprived and oppressed Dalits, lower castes and minorities against the upper-caste establishment, party leaders and activists have stayed away from protests and demonstrations. They have, instead, devoted all their organisational energies towards promotional activities projecting the party and its leaders mostly in preparation for the next elections. During election campaigns these publicity exercises turned into poll campaigns conducted with elaborate strategy and meticulous planning.

V

The uncertain religious allegiances of Dalits and in the absence of caste as defining parameter for social position, Dalits find the representation in the Congress and the SAD organisational structure in the Punjab. It might explain the allegiance of Dalits to both the SAD and the Congress. Dalits in the Doaba region have experienced political power through two main political parties, the Congress and the SAD. Voters are likely to cast their votes to that party which has a chance to come to power. But Dalits resent both the SAD and the Congress for taking them as vote bank only. For the BSP to act as an alternative to both the parties, it must involve itself with Dalits at ground level in their day-to-day problems. In the absence of such involvement with their day-to-day problems, many Dalits fail to see them as a promising alternative to the Congress and the Akali Dal.

In 1992 Assembly elections, the inter-caste alliance among the SCs, Rai Sikh, Kamboj, Ramgarhia, Jat Sikhs, Gujjars, Sainis, Kumhars (Potters) has worked well in parts of the State of Punjab to the benefits of the BSP. The BSP along with the Panthic allies faced a humiliating defeat at the hands of the Akali-BJP combine during the February 1997 Assembly polls in the State. This belied all hopes of Kanshi Ram to form a Government in Punjab. It was only on August 28, 1994 that Kanshi Ram announced at a mammoth gathering at Dareshi Ground (Ludhiana) that this party would come into power in Punjab in the next Vidhan Sabha elections. What a fall that his party was reduced to only 1 seat in 1997 from 9 in the previous Assembly polls, held in 1992. He blamed the party MLAs and the State unit for this debacle and also said that the lack of poll alliance with the Congress party in Punjab was another reason for its defeat. Interestingly enough, during the February 1998 Parliamentary polls, the BSP entered the fray as an ally of the Congress party. However, both failed to open their account in the new Parliament. In 1997 elections, the BSP succeeded in weaning away Dalit votes at the cost of the Congress. The success of the SAD in six constituencies was an attempt to draft support among Dalit Sikhs by giving them representation in the reconstituted political affair committee and distributing the tickets them in large numbers (Kumar, 2007: 2043-48).

The alliance can take advantage of the winner to magnify the support bases of each of two parties, catapulting them into control of the Government. Once in control of Government, the party can expand pool of offices to distribute and can attract new elites (Interview, 2016: 28 August). It is to ensure success of the social alliance which would emerge as the most viable alternative to the traditional bi-polar contest between the Akali-BJP combine and the Congress. In the process they also created their own base among Dalit activities. Hence, opportunistic alliances have usually proved costly to the BSP, even reducing its mobilising potential of its own vote bank. In fact the support bases of the BSP and its regional ally, in most cases, have been interest wise poles apart.

The BSP was created as a champion of the *Bahujan Samaj*, which it defined as the majority constituted by a coalition of downtrodden minorities: Dalits, Adivasis, Backwards and Religious Minorities or, in its own words, everyone but the Hindu upper caste. Under Kanshi Ram's leadership, the BSP held regular cadre camps, study sessions and political rallies in which it propagated a vision of the

Bahujan Samaj as a rainbow coalition of subaltern groups. The BSP's cultural pantheon has from its inception included important figures from across these groups in addition to Ambedkar, it includes Jyotirao Phule, Narayana Guru, Chhatrapati Sahuji Maharaj, and Periyar. It also built a second- and third-line leadership from among BCs and other Bahujan categories through the allocation of posts in the party organisation. After Kanshi Ram, the BSP neither has an organised political cadre in the Doaba region nor a solid social base. The BSP has neither an organisational network nor a sufficiently large mass base. National president has little to boast about her party's stakes in Punjab, the State with highest percentage of Dalit voters. The BSP founder had single mindedly focused on the pursuit of Ambedkar's master key of political power which he felt was essential to have before he could change society. The BSP leadership has over the years scrupulously eschewed any kind of mass actions that would pit the party cadre against the State, instead of emphasising the priority of political power over social reforms. Significantly, the BSP has viewed agitation methods that are normally used by most parties to accelerate their political interests, as damaging to the purpose of capturing power through elections. Of all differences between the BSP and other parties and movements, this distinctive attitude to mass agitation is the most fascinating. If the BSP is not to become just another blip in the political landscape, it will have to return to the early investment in constructing a Bahujan ideology and organisation that it lost along the way.

The BSP has radically altered the nature of collective self-assertion of Dalits. The BSP in Punjab could not muster Dalit votes on the issues of caste discrimination, untouchability and Brahminical ideology. In addition, the BSP failed to capture the regional, cultural and economic specificities of Punjab. First, the dismal performance of the BSP can be attributed to the internal divide within Dalit community along the lines of religion and caste. The socio-economic condition of Dalits in Doaba region has far better than the rest of India. Religiously, Sikhism, Christianity and Arya Samaj forbid subjecting Dalits to caste based harassment. But religious identity of Dalits in Doaba region makes it difficult to treat Dalits as a homogeneous category in terms of their electoral choices. It is apparent that in the absence of a clear support for the BSP by Dalit communities, the main stream political parties in Punjab are on a spree to woo Dalit vote bank. Clearly the BSP is out of sync with the political, cultural and economic realities of Punjab.

Second, the purity-pollution issue and *Manuvad* that are the BSP's main ideological planks do not find expression in the socio-cultural domain of Punjab in its fundamental form, as say, it exists in Uttar Pradesh. Sikhism doctrinally does not support the practice of caste. Third, there is less possibility of untouchability on the basis of caste in the form of purity and impurity to catch Dalit voters. Fourth, the weak leadership of the BSP and the dictatorship nature of High Command could not develop any strong organisational structure in the State of Punjab. Fifth, the BSP strategy of social engineering and *Sarvajan* politics could not be successful in the State of Punjab in comparison to UP. Sixth, the voting pattern of SCs has become very complex due to the shifting votes of Dalits, their party preference during the election time. Some of Dalits and their local elites seek their salvation through different political outfits including the Congress and the Akali Dal. Seventh, the BSP in Punjab has failed to mobilise Dalits in Punjab despite entering into all types of alignment and electoral adjustment. In fact, the BSP has entered into electoral alliance with almost all political parties or groups in the State from one election to another, but it has neither chosen any perspective or path of fighting for justice for Dalits nor given any weightage to the consideration of ideology or like mindedness before aligning with various political parties. The BSP has failed to evolve a comprehensive ideological basis and consistent line of action in Punjab politics. Eighth, some castes within the SCs have progressed more than others. They try to distance themselves from the less fortunate castes. Division within Dalits along caste lines have meant that community votes are dispersed. This fact of disunity among different castes has been exploited by other main political parties of the Doaba region in their favour to the BSP's disadvantage. In fact they form a conglomerate of thirty nine Dalit castes with different sub-identities and diverse religious affiliations. The rules of grammar of caste hierarchy are also followed by SCs in the region.

Should the BSP concentrate only in UP or should the party also focus on other States? The dilemma is due to the fact that Mayawati is, perhaps, the only vote getter for the party. If she decides to take a national trajectory and move beyond UP campaigning for party, she may garner a few more votes for her party but it is difficult to say whether she would be able to convert them into seats. The BSP is still a one person centric party and terribly short of star campaigners. The BSP leaders may not motivate voters in other States. If she is engaged elsewhere, she may not be available for campaigning in UP which might adversely impact the party in its home turf. That will obviously hamper the vote capturing ambitions of the BSP at national level. During the election time, some of the opportunist leaders of the BSP have self-interest and try to compromise with other political parties. These leaders keep silent so that vote bank of other parties could remain secure in Punjab. Many BSP leaders of Punjab have been very critical of their political ideology.

BSP has also failed to construct and communicate a narrative of growth and development. Demagoguery around selective reading and interpretation of *Manusmriti* will not have traction among the generation. To paraphrase Henry Ford, the only history Dalit youth is interested in, is the history they are making today. More or less, despite the high concentration of Dalit population, inability of the BSP to gain electorally/politically can be attributed to the failure of the party in terms of its organisation and strategy. It has no grass root level organisational structure and has no planning to collects the votes of SCs. The BSP is the only party that has no social and political programme in Punjab. It is worthwhile to examine how the BSP fought an election yesterday under different agenda could bury their differences to produce a floor majority. The danger would always be hanging overhead of one of the partners withdrawing its support. It has no planning of coalition with other political parties due to the domination of High Command.

The absence of co-ordination among the various organisations of the party, the failure of the party leadership to focus on regional and specific socio-cultural issues, wide spread factionalism and the absence of dedicated party workers who could genuinely identify with the poor sections of the society, the BSP's refusals of ideology, refusal of alliances, refusal to place itself in the political spectrum, its assessment of all parties by the single criterion of their orientation to break the caste system prove it to be an anti-party entity. In 2017 Assemblies' elections, the BSP's loss is an indication of the declining identity-based politics. If Mayawati and her leaders do not re-think their strategy, they are looking at a complete wipeout, that left the BSP with its limited appeal and caste calculations wanting. The BSP's defeat is its failure to unite the socially-ostracised with the upper castes. The disenchantment was growing and the BSP looks failure to read the undercurrent. The BSP has emerged as a new political entity, the most worrisome issues of social and economic discrimination in egalitarianism continued to haunt Dalits. It might be a hollow victory of the BSP if these problems which form the backbone of the BSP's ideology, remain unsolved.

References

- Chandra, Kanchan. 2000. 'The Transformation of Ethnic Politics in India: The Decline of Congress and the Rise of the Bahujan Samaj Party in Hoshiarpur.' *The Journal of Asian Study* 59 (1): 26-61.
- ———. 2004. *Why Ethnic Parties Succeed: Patronage and Ethnic Head Counts in India.* Cambridge: University of Cambridge.
- ———. 2016. 'Back to the BSP's Roots.' *The Hindu*: 18 October.
- Galanter, Marc, ed. 1989. *Group Membership and Group Preferences in India.* New Delhi: Oxford University Press.
- Guru, Gopal, ed. 2005. *Atrophy in Dalit Politics*. Mumbai: Vikas Adhyayan Kendra.
- Jodhka, Surinder S. 2004. 'Sikhism and the Caste Question: Dalits and their Politics in Contemporary Punjab.' *Contributions to Indian Sociology* XXXVIII (1 and 2): 165-93.
- Jodhka, Surinder S. and Avinash Kumar. 2007. 'Internal Classification of Scheduled Castes: The Punjab Story.' *Economic and Political Weekly* XLII (43): 20-23.
- Juergensmeyer, Mark. 1988. *Religious Rebels in the Punjab: The Social Vision of Untouchables*. Delhi: Ajanta Publications.
- Kumar, Ashutosh. 2007. 'Punjab Elections: Exploring the Verdict.' *Economic and Political Weekly* XLII (22): 2043-2048.
- Ram, Ronki. 2017. 'Internal Caste Cleavages among Dalits in Punjab.' *Economic and Political Weekly* LII (3): 54- 57.
- Verma, P.S. 1999. *'Dalit Consciousness and the BSP in Punjab.'* A paper presented at the seminar on 'Dr B.R. Ambedkar and Social Transformation: Democracy, Diversity and Resistance' held on 17-18 December at ICSSR Complex, Punjab University Chandigarh.

APPENDIX - I

Study of Dalit Masses in the Doaba Region

Table I: Which Political Party gives more Representation to Dalits in its Organisation?

Sl. No.	*Block (City) N=120*	*Political Parties*			*Total*	*Block (Village)* N=180*	*Political Parties*			*Total*
		Congress I	*SAD*	*BSP*			*Congress I*	*SAD*	*BSP*	
1.	Hoshiarpur	09 (30.00)	3 (10.00)	18 (60.00)	30 (100.00)	Hoshiarpur	18 (40.00)	4 (8.89)	23 (51.11)	45 (100.00)
2.	Jalandhar	9 (30.00)	3 (10.00)	18 (60.00)	30 (100.00)	Jalandhar	15 (33.33)	4 (8.89)	26 (57.78)	45 (100.00)
3.	Phagwara	8 (26.67)	3 (10.00)	19 (63.33)	30 (100.00)	Phagwara	14 (31.11)	4 (8.89)	27 (60.00)	45 (100.00)
4.	Banga	8 (26.67)	4 (13.33)	18 (60.00)	30 (100.00)	Banga	12 (26.67)	5 (11.11)	28 (62.22)	45 (100.00)

Note: The asterisk mark* shows the selection of 5 villages from each block. The figures in the parentheses denote the percentage share.

Table II: Respondents' Vote Preference for the Major Political Parties

Sl. No.	*Overall Preference*	*Political Parties*				*Total*
		Congress I	*SAD*	*BSP*	*Any other*	
1.	**Urban (N=120)**	32 (26.67)	21 (17.50)	55 (45.83)	12 (10.00)	120 (100.00)
2.	**Rural (N=180)**	60 (33.33)	30 (16.67)	75 (41.67)	15 (8.33)	180 (100.00)

Note: The figures in the parentheses denote the percentage share.

Table III: Dalits' Vote Preferences

Sl. No.	Block (City) N=120	Political Parties				Total	Block (Village)* N=180	Political Parties				Total
		Congress I	SAD	BSP	Rest of the Respondents			Congress I	SAD	BSP	Rest of the Respondents	
1.	Hoshiarpur	9 (30.00)	5 (16.67)	13 (43.33)	3 (10.00)	30 (100.00)	Hoshiarpur	16 (35.56)	7 (15.56)	18 (40.00)	4 (8.88)	45 (100.00)
2.	Jalandhar	8 (26.67)	6 (20.00)	12 (40.00)	4 (13.33)	30 (100.00)	Jalandhar	15 (33.33)	7 (15.56)	18 (40.00)	5 (11.11)	45 (100.00)
3.	Phagwara	8 (26.67)	5 (16.67)	15 (50.00)	2 (6.66)	30 (100.00)	Phagwara	14 (31.11)	8 (17.78)	20 (44.44)	3 (6.67)	45 (100.00)
4.	Banga	7 (23.33)	5 (16.67)	15 (50.00)	3 (10.00)	30 (100.00)	Banga	15 (33.33)	8 (17.78)	19 (42.22)	3 (6.67)	45 (100.00)

Note: The asterisk mark* shows the selection of 5 villages from each block. The figures given in the parentheses denote the percentage share.

APPENDIX - II

Table I: Respondents' Opinion regarding the Immediate Socio-Economic Problems of Dalits in their Town/Village

Sl. No.	Block (City) N=120	Lack of Unity among Dalits	Internal Discrimination	Lack of Political Awareness	Any other	Total
1.	Hoshiarpur	14 (46.67)	9 (30.00)	6 (20.00)	1 (3.33)	30 (100.00)
2.	Jalandhar	12 (40.00)	7 (23.33)	8 (26.67)	3 (10.00)	30 (100.00)
3.	Phagwada	16 (53.33)	9 (30.00)	5 (16.67)	-	30 (100.00)
4.	Banga	15 (50.00)	6 (20.00)	5 (16.67)	4 (13.33)	30 (100.00)
Sl. No.	***Block (Village)* N=180***	***Lack of Unity Among Dalits***	***Internal Discrimination Awareness***	***Lack of Political***	***Any other***	***Total***
1.	Hoshiarpur	20 (44.44)	10 (22.22)	8 (17.78)	7 (15.56)	45 (100.00)
2.	Jalandhar	18 (40.00)	12 (26.67)	9 (20.00)	6 (13.33)	45 (100.00)
3.	Phagwada	23 (51.11)	13 (28.89)	7 (15.56)	2 (4.44)	45 (100.00)
4.	Banga	22 (48.89)	11 (24.44)	8 (17.78)	4 (8.89)	45 (100.00)

Note: The asterisk mark* shows the selection of 5 villages from each Block. The figures in the parentheses denote the percentage share.

Table II: Respondents' Opinion regarding the Domination of Major Castes/Caste Groups in the Organisation of the BSP

Sl. No.	Overall Percentage	Name of the Caste/Castes: Ad-Dharmis/ Chamars	Each Socio-political Active Caste has Domination	Any other	Total
1.	**Urban (N=120)**	77 (64.17)	18 (15.00)	25 (20.83)	120 (100.00)
2.	**Rural (N=180)**	117 (65.00)	35 (19.44)	28 (15.56)	180 (100.00)

Note: The figures in the parentheses denote the percentage share.

Table III: Respondents' Opinion regarding the Various Causes behind the Factions of the BSP

Sl. No.	Block (City) N=120	*Causes behind the Various Factions of the BSP*				Total
		Leaders have Different Ideology	*Leaders are against the Sarvajan Politics*	*Internal Controversies*	*Any other*	
1.	Hoshiarpur	6 (20.00)	4 (13.33)	18 (60.00)	2 (6.67)	30 (100.00)
2.	Jalandhar	5 (16.67)	3 (10.00)	21 (70.00)	1 (3.33)	30 (100.00)
3.	Phagwada	4 (13.33)	2 (6.67)	22 (73.33)	2 (6.67)	30 (100.00)
4.	Banga	3 (10.00)	4 (13.33)	21 (70.00)	2 (6.67)	30 (100.00)
Sl. No.	*Block (Village)* N=180*	*Leaders have Different Ideology*	*Leaders are against the Sarvajan Politics*	*Internal Controversies*	*Any other*	*Total*
1.	Hoshiarpur	8 (17.78)	6 (13.33)	25 (55.56)	6 (13.33)	45 (100.00)
2.	Jalandhar	9 (20.00)	7 (15.56)	24 (53.33)	5 (11.11)	45 (100.00)
3.	Phagwada	8 (17.78)	7 (15.56)	26 (57.78)	4 (8.88)	45 (100.00)
4.	Banga	9 (20.00)	8 (17.78)	26 (57.78)	2 (4.44)	45 (100.00)

Note: The asterisk mark* shows the selection of 5 villages from each block. The figures in the parentheses denote the percentage share.

Table IV: What are the Causes behind the Weak Support Base of the BSP?

Sl. No.	*Block (City) N=120*	*Weak Leadership*	*Various Factions of the BSP*	*Weak Organisation*	*Changing Ideology and Strategy*	*Total*
1.	Hoshiarpur	21 (70.00)	2 (6.67)	6 (20.00)	1 (3.33)	30 (100.00)
2.	Jalandhar	22 (73.33)	2 (6.67)	4 (13.33)	2 (6.67)	30 (100.00)
3.	Phagwada	20 (66.67)	4 (13.33)	5 (16.67)	1 (3.33)	30 (100.00)
4.	Banga	23 (76.67)	1 (3.33)	3 (10.00)	3 (10.00)	30 (100.00)
Sl. No.	*Block (Village)* N=180*	*Weak Leadership*	*Various Factions of the BSP*	*Weak Organisation*	*Changing Ideology and Strategy*	*Total*
1.	Hoshiarpur	26 (57.78)	3 (6.67)	9 (20.00)	7 (15.55)	45 (100.00)
2.	Jalandhar	27 (60.00)	4 (8.89)	9 (20.00)	5 (11.11)	45 (100.00)
3.	Phagwada	31 (68.89)	4 (8.89)	8 (17.78)	2 (4.44)	45 (100.00)
4.	Banga	32 (71.11)	3 (6.67)	5 (11.11)	5 (11.11)	45 (100.00)

Note: The asterisk mark* shows the selection of 5 villages from each block. The figures in the parentheses denote the percentage share.

Table V: Queries/Questions on the Political Strategy of the BSP in Punjab

Sl. No.	*Block (City) N=120*	*Do you rely upon the ideology of the BSP?*				*Should the BSP ally with other political parties?*				*Do you agree with the Sarvajan Politics of the BSP in Punjab?*			
		Yes	*No*	*Others*	*Total*	*Yes*	*No*	*Others*	*Total*	*Yes*	*No*	*Others*	*Total*
1.	Hoshiarpur	20 (66.67)	7 (23.33)	3 (10.00)	30 (100.00)	14 (46.67	13 (43.33)	3 (10.00)	30 (100.00)	15 (50.00)	9 (30.00)	6 (20.00)	30 (100.00)
2.	Jalandhar	21 (70.00)	6 (20.00)	3 (10.00)	30 (100.00)	18 (60.00)	10 (33.33)	2 (6.67)	30 (100.00)	19 (63.33)	8 (26.67)	3 (10.00)	30 (100.00)
3.	Phagwada	17 (63.33)	6 (20.00)	7 (16.67)	30 (100.00)	19 (63.33)	8 (26.67)	3 (10.00)	30 (100.00)	17 (56.67)	9 (30.00)	4 (13.33)	30 (100.00)
4.	Banga	18 (60.00)	6 (20.00)	6 (20.00)	30 (100.00)	20 (66.67)	9 (30.00)	1 (3.33)	30 (100.00)	16 (53.33)	5 (16.67)	9 (30.00)	30 (100.00)
Sl. No.	*Block (Village)* N=180*	*Do you rely upon the ideology of the BSP?*				*Should the BSP ally with other political parties?*				*Do you agree with the Sarvajan Politics of the BSP in Punjab?*			
		Yes	*No*	*Others*	*Total*	*Yes*	*No*	*Others*	*Total*	*Yes*	*No*	*Others*	*Total*
1.	Hoshiarpur	32 (71.11)	8 (17.78)	5 (11.11)	45 (100.00)	27 (60.00)	15 (33.33)	3 (6.67)	45 (100.00)	22 (48.89)	9 (20.00)	14 (31.11)	45 (100.00)
2.	Jalandhar	30 (66.67)	9 (20.00)	6 (13.33)	45 (100.00)	29 (64.44)	13 (28.89)	3 (6.67)	45 (100.00)	21 (46.67)	14 (31.11)	10 (22.22)	45 (100.00)
3.	Phagwada	28 (62.22)	9 (20.00)	8 (17.78)	45 (100.00)	26 (57.78)	14 (31.11)	5 (11.11)	45 (100.00)	23 (51.11)	12 (26.67)	10 (22.22)	45 (100.00)
4.	Banga	26 (57.78)	9 (20.00)	10 (22.22)	45 (100.00)	27 (60.00)	15 (33.33)	3 (6.67)	45 (100.00)	21 (46.67)	13 (28.89)	11 (24.44)	45 (100.00)

Note: The asterisk mark* shows the selection of 5 villages from each block. The figures in the parentheses denote the percentage share.

Study of the Leaders of the BSP and its Factional Political Parties

Table VI: Leaders' Response regarding the Various Factions of the BSP

Sl. No.	*Reasons behind the Varioius Factions*	*Numbers of Respondents (N=20)*
1.	Lack of trust	3 (15.00)
2.	Domination of High Command	7 (35.00)
3.	Internal controversies	10 (50.00)

Note: The figures in the parentheses denote the percentage share.

Table VII: Leaders' Opinion regarding the Domination of Major Castes/ Classes/High Command in the Organisational Hierarchy of the BSP

Sl. No.	*Leaders' Response*	*Numbers of Respondents (N=20)*
1.	Domination of Ad-Dharmis/Chamars	8 (40.00)
2.	Domination of High Command	4 (20.00)
3.	Each caste which is socially and politically active, has sway	7 (35.00)
4.	Any other	1 (5.00)

Note: The figures in the parentheses denote the percentage share.

Table VIII: Has the BSP adequate Dalits' Representation in Party Organisation?

Sl. No.	*Leaders' Response*	*Numbers of Respondents (N=20)*
1.	Yes	12 (60.00)
2.	No	7 (35.00)
3.	Others	1 (5.00)

Note: The figures in the parenthesis denote the percentage share.

Table IX: Is the BSP Organisational Structure plagued by Autocratic Tendencies or governed by Democratic Principles?

Sl. No.	*Leaders' Response*	*Numbers of Respondents (N=20)*
1.	Plagued by autocratic tendencies	12 (60.00)
2.	Governed by democratic principles	8 (40.00)

Note: The figures in the parentheses denote the percentage share.

Table X: Do you support the Social Engineering Formula of the BSP in Punjab?

Sl. No.	*Leaders' Response*	*Numbers of Respondents (N=20)*
1.	Yes	15 (75.00)
2.	No	4 (20.00)
3.	Others	1 (5.00)

Note: The figures in the parentheses denote the percentage share.

Table XI: Leaders' Opinion regarding the Various Reasons behind the Weak Support Base of the BSP in Punjab

Sl. No.	*Leaders' Response*	*Numbers of Respondents (N=20)*
1.	Weak leadership	10 (50.00)
2.	Lack of strong organisational	6 (30.00)
3.	Changing ideology/strategy	4 (20.00)

Note: The figures in the parentheses denote the percentage share.

APPENDIX - III

Table I: Scheduled Castes' Population and Decadal Change by Residence: 2001-2011

State/ District	*SC Population, 2011*			*Decadal Change 2001-2011*			*Percentage of SCs' Population to total Population 2011*		
	Total	*Rural*	*Urban*	*Total*	*Rural*	*Urban*	*Total*	*Rural*	*Urban*
1	*2*	*3*	*4*	*5*	*6*	*7*	*8*	*9*	*10*
Punjab	88,60,179	64,96,986	23,63,193	26.1	22.2	38.2	31.9	37.5	22.7
Gurdaspur	5,80,576	4,35,930	1,44,646	11.5	6.3	30.9	25.3	26.6	21.9
Kapurthala	2,76,707	2,12,013	64,694	22.6	22.3	23.3	33.9	39.8	22.9
Jalandhar	8,54,444	5,15,342	3,39,102	15.5	9.2	26.6	39.0	49.9	29.2
Hoshiarpur	5,57,504	4,65,037	92,467	9.8	7.4	23.5	35.1	37.2	27.6
SBS Nagar	2,60,284	2,12,889	47,395	9.5	1.0	75.9	42.5	43.7	37.8
F G Sahib	1,92,493	1.54,570	37,923	16.5	14.0	28.1	32.1	37.3	20.4
Ludhiana	9,23,358	5,59,471	3,63,887	21.8	14.1	36.1	26.4	39.2	17.1
Moga	3,63,417	3,07,098	56,319	27.5	24.4	47.6	36.5	40.0	24.8
Ferozepur	8,55,726	7,09,922	1,45,804	114.8	130.0	62.5	42.2	48.1	26.4
Muktsar	3,81,554	2,95,179	86,375	30.0	24.1	54.9	42.3	45.4	34.2
Faridkot	2,40,328	1,71,199	69,129	20.6	20.1	21.9	38.9	42.8	31.8
Bathinda	4,50,473	3,21,533	1,28,940	27.0	18.3	55.8	32.4	36.2	25.8
Mansa	2,58,878	2,17,553	41,325	23.9	24.4	21.3	33.6	35.9	25.3
Patiala	4,65,359	3,48,587	1,16,772	28.5	20.3	60.9	24.5	30.8	15.3
Amritsar	7,70,864	4,64,984	3,05,880	30.7	30.2	31,5	31.0	40.2	22.9
Tarn Taran	3,77,468	3,39,558	37,910	25.3	23.0	49.6	33.7	34.7	26.7
Rupnagar	1,80,905	1,38,597	42,308	13.5	7.2	40.1	26.4	27.3	23.8
SAS Nagar	2,16,231	1,32,713	83,513	27.1	5.4	88.9	21.7	29.5	15.3
Sangrur	4,61,609	3,61,376	1,00,233	17.5	13.1	36.5	27.9	31.7	19.4
Barnala	1,92,001	1,33,435	58,566	21.1	17.7	29.8	32.2	33.0	30.7

Source: Census Commission of India, 2011. Chandigarh.

Table II: Percentage of Male/Female Scheduled Castes' Population in Punjab, 2011

Sl. No.	*Total*	*Rural*	*Urban*	*Total*	*Rural*	*Urban*
Males	46,39,875	33,96,329	12,43,546	31.7	37.3	22.4
Females	42.20,304	31,00,657	11,19,647	32.2	37.6	23.1
Total	**88,60,179**	**64,96,986**	**23,63,193**	**31.9**	**37.5**	**22.7**

Source: Election Commission of India, 2011. Chandigarh.

Table III: Vote Percentages of the BSP in Punjab Assembly Elections, 1992-2017

Vidhan Sabha Term	*Punjab Assembly Election*	*Seats Contested*	*Seats Won*	*Vote Percentage*
10th Vidhan Sabha	1992	105	9	16.32
11th Vidhan Sabha	1997	67	1	7.48
12th Vidhan Sabha	2002	100	0	5.69
13th Vidhan Sabha	2007	115	0	4.13
14th Vidhan Sabha	2012	117	0	4.30
15th Vidhan Sabha	2017	110	0	1.50

Source: *Punjab Election Commission, 2017. Chandigarh.*

Table IV: Result of 2017 Punjab Assembly Election

Political Party	*Seats Contested*	*Seats Won*	*Popular Vote*	*Vote Share %*
Indian National Congress	117	77	5,945,899	38.5
Aam Aadmi Party	112	20	3,662,665	23.7
Shiromani Akali Dal	94	15	3,898,161	25.2
Bharatiya Janata Party	23	3	833,092	5.4
Lok Insaaf Party	5	2	189,228	1.2
Bahujan Samaj Party	111	0	234,400	1.5
Aapna Punjab Party		0	37,476	0.2
RMPOI		0	37,243	0.2
SAD(M)		0	49,260	0.3
Communist Party of India		0	34,074	0.2
Independents		0	323,243	2.1
None of the above			108,471	0.7
Total		**117**	-	
Turnout:78.6%				

Source: Punjab Election Commission, 2017. Chandigarh.

Table V: Punjab Scheduled Castes' Seats in Lok Sabha, 1967-2014

Lok Sabha	*Period*		*Total Seats*	*Reserved Seats*	*Balmikis/ Mazhabis*	*Chamars*
	From	*To*				
4th	16.03.1967	27.12.1970	13	3	2	1
5th	19.03.1971	18.01.1977	13	3	2	1
6th	25.03.1977	22.08.1979	13	3	1	2
7th	21.01.1980	31.12.1984	13	3	2	1
8th	15.01.1985	27.11.1989	13	3	2	1
9th	18.12.1989	13.03.1991	13	3	0	3
10th	09.07.1991	10.05.1996	13	3	1	2
11th	22.05.1996	04.12.1997	13	3	0	3
12th	23.03.1998	26.04.1999	13	3	0	3
13th	20.10.1999	06.02.2004	13	3	1	2
14th	02.06.2004	18.05.2009	13	3	2	1
15th	01.06.2009	18.05.2014	13	4	1	3
16th	04.06.2014	Till today	13	4	0	4

Source: A Report of Election Commission of India, 2014. Chandigarh.

Table VI: Scheduled Castes' Representation in Punjab Assembly, 1967-2012

Year	Total	Reserved	Indian National Congress			SAD			BJP/Bhartiya Jansangh			BSP			Others Parties (CPI/CPM, Indepenents and RPI)		
			Balmikis, Mazhabis	Chamars	Others	Balmikis, Mazhabis	Chamars	Others	Balmikis, Mazhabis	Chamars	Others	Balmikis, Mazhabis	Chamars	Others	Balmikis, Mazhabs	Chamars	Others
1967	117	23	3	9	-	4	2	-	-	-	-	-	-	-	2	3	-
1969	117	23	4	5	-	4	7	-	-	1	-	-	-	-	1	1	-
1972	117	23	6	7	-	4	3	-	-	-	-	-	-	-	1	2	-
1977	117	29	1	2	-	8	7	-	1	2	-	-	-	-	2	6	-
1980	117	29	5	8	-	2	7	-	-	-	-	-	-	-	4	3	-
1985	117	29	4	6	-	8	10	-	-	1	-	-	-	-	-	-	-
1992	117	29	7	12	-	1	-	-	-	-	-	1	6	-	2	-	-
1997	117	29	-	1	-	12	11	-	-	2	-	-	-	-	1	-	-
2002	117	29	5	8	1	7	5	-	-	-	-	-	-	-	2	1	-
2007	117	29	3	5	1	8	7	-	-	3	1	-	-	-	1	-	-
2012	117	34	3	5	2	11	10	-	-	2	1	-	-	-	-	-	-

Source: Election Commission of India, 2012. New Delhi.

Table VII: Category-wise Analysis, Punjab Assembly Elections 2012

Category	*Total Seats*	*Turnout (Per cent)*	*Congress*		*SAD/BJP*		*BSP*	
			Won	*Vote (Per cent)*	*Won*	*Vote (Per cent)*	*Won*	*Vote (Per cent)*
Reserved	34	78.0	10	40.1	24	42.3	0	6.1
General	83	78.8	36	40.1	44	41.8	0	3.5
Total	**117**	**78.6**	**46**	**40.1**	**68**	**41.9**	**0**	**4.3**

Source: Data aggregated and recomputed by CSDS data unit, 2012. New Delhi.

Table VIII: Assembly Results in Uttar Pradesh, 2012, 2017

Political Party	*Seats Won in 2012*	*Seats Won in 2017*	*Vote Per cent, 2017*
Bhartiya Janata Party	312	47	39.75
Samajwadi Party	47	224	21.8
Bahujan Samaj Party	19	80	22.2
Apna Dal (Soneylal)	09	01	1
Indian National Congress	07	28	6.2
Suheldev Bhartiya Samaj Party	04	-	0.7
Rashtriya Lok Dal	01	09	1.8
Nirbal Indian Shoshit Hamara Aam Dal	1	-	0.65
Independents	03	06	2.6

Source: Election Commission of India, 2012-2017. New Delhi.

Table IX: Caste-wise Vote Percentage in Uttar Pradesh Assembly Election, 2017

Class	*BJP*	*SP+Congress*	*BSP*
Dalits	41%	26%	25%
OBCs	42%	28%	23%
General	44%	24%	21%
Jaat	45%	22%	21%
Yadav	38%	32%	22%

Source: Election Commission of India, 2017. New Delhi.

Table X: Caste Profile of the BSP in Uttar Pradesh, 1993-2012

Caste Group	*1993*	*1996*	*2002*	*2007*	*2012*
UC	2 (2.9)	9 (13.4)	21 (21.9)	60 (29.1)	17 (21.3)
OBC	30 (42.9)	28 (41.8)	36 (37.5)	53 (25.7)	28 (35.0)
SC	26 (37.1)	19 (28.4)	26 (27.1)	62 (30.1)	16 (20.0)

(contd...)

Muslims	12 (17.1)	11 (16.4)	13 (13.5)	30 (14.6)	15 (18.8)
Unidentified	0	0	0	01	04(5.0)
Total	**70 (100)**	**67 (100)**	**96 (100)**	**206 (100)**	**80 (100)**

Source: UP State Assembly Legislature, data set. 2012. New Delhi.

Table XI: Region-wise and District-wise Analysis: Turnout and Performance of Major Alliances and Parties in the Assembly Elections in Punjab, 2012

Region/ District	*Total seats*	*Turnout (Per cent)*	*Congress*		*SAD-BJP*		*BSP*	
			Won	*Vote (Per cent)*	*Won*	*Vote (Per cent)*	*Won*	*Vote (Per cent)*
Majha	25	75.0	9	41.2	16	47.2	0	1.1
Gurdaspur	10	76.3	5	42.7	5	45.8	0	1.4
Amritsar	11	71.8	3	38.5	8	48.9	0	1.0
Tarn Taran	4	79.6	1	43.9	3	46.6	0	0.9
Doaba	23	76.4	6	37.1	16	41.3	0	12.1
Kapurthala	4	79.0	2	43.4	2	44.1	0	7.4
Jalandhar	9	75.6	0	37.9	9	43.2	0	12.7
Hoshiarpur	7	75.2	2	35.9	4	40.9	0	9.5
Nawan Shahr	3	79.3	2	29.6	1	32.9	0	21.9
Malwa	69	80.6	31	40.6	36	40.3	0	3.0
Rupnagar	3	77.5	1	37.9	2	41.4	0	5.0
SAS Nagar	3	75.8	2	30.7	1	38.3	0	7.7
Fatehgarh Sahib	3	81.9	2	33.7	1	35.5	0	4.1
Ludhiana	14	76.0	6	40.7	6	39.9	0	3.3
Moga	4	80.5	1	43.2	3	45.2	0	1.5
Ferozepur	8	83.4	3	37.4	5	39.5	0	1.9
Muktsar	4	85.2	2	40.2	2	41.0	0	2.6
Faridkot	3	84.1	1	38.8	2	43.2	0	2.3
Bathinda	6	82.6	2	40.9	4	42.0	0	1.6
Mansa	3	84.4	1	38.4	2	39.6	0	2.6
Sangrur	7	84.5	2	40.0	5	41.5	0	2.9
Barnala	3	81.8	3	45.9	0	40.1	0	4.0
Patiala	8	78.5	5	49.9	3	37.6	0	2.8
Total	**117**	**78.6**	**46**	**40.1**	**68**	**41.9**	**0**	**4.3**

Source: Data aggregated and recomputed by CSDS data unit, 2012. Chandigarh.

Table XII: Dalit Leaders in Various Political Parties, 1967-2002

Year	*Congress*		*Akali Dal*		*CPI*		*CPM*		*BJP*		*BSP*		*Others**		*Grand Total*	
Total	*Dalit*	*Total*	*Dalit*	*Total*	*Dalit*	*Total*	*Dalit*	*Total*	*Dalit*	*Total*	*Dalit*	*Total*	*Dalit*	*Total*	*Dalit*	
1967	48	12	26	5	5	2	3	1	9	-	-	-	13	1	104	21
1969	38	9	43	11	4	1	2	1	8	1	-	-	9	-	104	23
1972	66	13	24	7	10	2	1	1	-	-	-	-	3	-	104	23
1977	17	3	58	15	7	3	8	5	25	3	-	-	2	-	117	29
1980	64	14	37	9	9	3	5	3	1	-	-	-	1	-	117	29
1985	32	10	73	18	1	-	-	-	6	1	-	-	5	-	117	29
1992	87	20	3	1	4	-	1	-	6	-	9	7	7	-	117	29
1997	14	1	75	23	2	1	1	-	18	4	-	-	6	-	117	29
2002	62	14	41	12	2	2	-	-	3	-	-	-	9	1	117	29
Total	**428**	**96**	**380**	**101**	**44**	**14**	**21**	**11**	**76**	**9**	**10**	**7**	**55**	**5**	**1014**	**243**

Source: Punjab Vidhan Sabha Compendium Who's Who, 1960-2002.

* Including smaller parties like RPI, PSP, SSP, Swatantra and Independent.

Table XIII: Caste Profile of Parties' Organisations, the Congress and the SAD in 1997

Castes	*Congress*	*Akali Dal*
Upper Caste	9	5
Intermediate Caste (Jat)	8	-
BC	1	-
SC	1	-
Unknown	1	-
Total	**20**	**21**

Source: Chandra, Kanchan. 2000. 'The Transformation of Ethnic Politics in India: The Decline of Congress and the Rise of the Bahujan Samaj Party in Hoshiarpur.' The Journal of Asian Studies 59(1):26-61.

Table XIV: Caste Profile of the BSP Candidates in Hoshiarpur, 1985-1997

Category	*1985*	*1992*	*1997*
Upper Castes	-	-	-
Intermediate Caste (Jat)	-	-	-
BCs	0%	20% (2)	10% (1)
SCs	100 (9)	70% (7)	90% (2)
Ad-Dharmi	33 (3)	40% (4)	50% (5)
Ramdasias	11 (1)	10%(1)	30% (3)
Balmikis	22 (2)	0%	10% (1)
Other SCs	11 (1)	0%	10% (1)
Unknown SCs	22 (2)	-	-
Unknown	-	10%	-
Total	**99 (9)**	-	**100% (10)**

Source: Chandra, Kanchan. 2000. 'The Transformation of Ethnic Politics in India: The Decline of Congress and the Rise of the Bahujan Samaj Party in Hoshiarpur.' The Journal of Asian Studies 59(1):26-61.

Table XV: Party-wise Numbers of Seats Won and Percentage of Votes polled in Punjab Assembly Elections 1967-1977

Sl. No.	*Party*	*1967*		*1969*		*1972*		*1977*	
		Seats	*Per cent*	*Seats*	*Per cent*	*Seats*	*Per cent*	*Seats*	*Per cent*
1.	The Congress	48	37.5	38	39.18	66	42.84	17	33.48
2.	Jan Sangh/Janata	9	9.8	8	9.01	-	4.97	25	14.96
3.	The PSP/SSP	1	1.2	3	1.33	-	0.97	New constituents of the Janata Party	

(contd...)

4.	The Swatantra/BLD	-	-	1	0.98	-	0.01		
5.	The Congress (O)	-	-	-	-	-	-		
6.	The Akali Dal/its factions	26	24.7	43	30.23	24	27.64	58	31.50
7.	The CPI	5	5.2	4	4.84	10	6.51	7	6.71
8.	The CPI (M)	3	3.3	2	3.07	1	3.25	8	3.59
9.	The RPI	3	1.8	-	-	-	0.28	-	-
10.	Independent	9	16.0	5	12.30	3	12.43	2	9.78
	Total	**104**	**100**	**104**	**100**	**104**	**100**	**117**	**100**

Source: 1967 Assembly election figures are based on Paul Brass, 'Ethnic Cleavages in the Punjab Party system.' 1972 election figures are taken from the report of the General elections to the Punjab Vidhan Sabha. Dhamis, M.S. 1978. 'The Punjab Assembly elections–June 1977.' Punjab Journal of Politics: II (1).

Table XVI: Electoral Performance of the BSP in Punjab Vidhan Sabha Election, 1985

Sl. No.	*Name of the Constituency*	*Total No. of Valid Votes polled*	*Votes polled by the BSP Candidates*	*Vote Percentage*
1.	Nawan Shahr	80148	17038	21.26
2.	Banga (SC)	59503	11006	48.50
3.	Balachaur	60250	11028	18.30
4.	Jalandhar North	50348	7420	14.74
5.	Sham Chaurasi	58467	7845	13.41
6.	Kapurthala	49894	6385	12.80
7.	Garshankar	52692	6360	12.07
8.	Mahilpur (SC)	49661	5693	11.46
9.	Nakodar	64770	6190	9.55
10.	Phillour (SC)	62629	5738	9.16
11.	Nurmahal	66541	5902	8.87
12.	Adampur	59221	4785	8.08
13.	Kot Kapura	64491	3651	5.66
14.	Gamdiwala	54316	3077	5.66
15.	Phagwara (SC)	67286	3388	5.03
16.	Dasuya	51483	2224	4.32
17.	Banur	64292	2331	3.63
18.	Hoshiarpur	57858	1824	3.15
19.	Ferozepur Cantt	57792	1788	3.09
20.	Tunda	59139	1802	3.05
21.	Ludhiana North	59625	1813	3.04

(contd...)

22.	Valtoha	51327	1562	3.04
23.	Guru Harsahai	65966	1984	3.01
24.	Dhuri	70265	2101	2.99
25.	Ludhiana Rural	78711	2347	2.98
26.	Anandpur Sahib	56035	1627	2.90
27.	Majitha	51705	1477	2.86
28.	Sangrur	64960	1832	2.82
29.	Rampura Phool	58278	1591	2.73
30.	Sherpur (SC)	60779	1469	2.42
31.	Mukatsar	63946	1544	2.41
32.	Barnala	57232	1344	2.35
33.	Morinda	69357	1594	2.30
34.	Patiala	49641	1099	2.21
35.	Attari (SC)	40991	849	2.07
36.	Sirhind	76190	1497	1.96
37.	Malout (SC)	56198	1068	1.90
38.	Pathankot	53913	853	1.58
39.	Kartarpur (SC)	57634	667	1.55
40.	Malerkotla	76310	1154	1.51
41.	Narot Mehra (SC)	49799	696	1.40
42.	Ghanaur	59200	730	1.23
43.	Rajpura	63364	683	1.08
44.	Sujanpur	48111	520	1.08
45.	Giddarbaha	66772	698	1.05
46.	Samana	67907	700	1.03
47.	Amloh (SC)	69776	711	1.02
48.	Ferozepur	59462	469	0.79
49.	Dakala (SC)	73873	579	0.78
50.	Jandiala (SC)	51403	362	0.70
51.	Jalandhar Central	47026	409	0.69
52.	Dina Nagar (SC)	56116	302	0.54
53.	Nabha	81838	401	0.49
54.	Jalalabad	64722	313	0.48
55.	Shutrana (SC)	60200	241	0.44

Source: The Oppressed Indian, January 1986, pp.23-24 cross checked by report on Vidhan Sabha elections, Punjab, 1985, Chief Electoral Officer, Punjab, Chandigarh.

Table XVII: Dalits' Political Parties and their Votes in Punjab, 1952-1980

Year	*Party*	*Votes*
1952	SCF	145,529
1957	SCF	277620
1962	RPI	111441
1967	RPI	76089
1968-69	RPI	71301
1972	RPI	12574
1977	RPI	16313
1980	RPI	2904

Source: Data collected from the BSP office, 2015. Jalandhar.

Table XVIII: Caste-wise Percentage of Scheduled Castes in Punjab

Castes	*Population, 1991*	*Percentage*	*Population, 2001*	*Percentage*	*Population, 2011*	*Percentage*
Ad Dharmi	915098	15.93	1045126	14.86	1017192	11.48
Balmiki, Chuhra, Bhangi	640210	11.14	785464	11.17	866953	9.78
Bangali	4175	0.07	7765	0.11	4690	0.05
Barar, Burar, Berar	10535	0.18	8679	0.12	8451	0.09
Batwal, Barwala	13511	0.23	18930	0.26	19979	0.22
Bauria, Bawaria	78429	1.36	102232	1.45	125259	1.41
Bazigar	162804	2.83	208442	2.96	241125	2.72
Bhanjra	4688	0.081	3370	0.04	3659	0.041
Chamar, Jatia Chamar, Rehgar R	1484268	25.84	1839032	26.16	2078132	23.45
Chanal	762	0.01	3038	0.04	97	0.001
Dagi	631	0.01	98	0.001	322	0.003
Darain	1389	0.02	821	0.01	865	0.009
Deha, Dhaya, Dhea	6730	0.11	8516	0.12	10560	0.11
Dhanak	57997	1.00	66646	0.94	89406	1.00
Dhogri, Dhangri, Siggi	781	0.01	3565	0.05	391	0.004
Dumna, Mahasha, Doom	158357	2.75	181810	2.58	202710	2.28
Gagra	761	0.01	240	0.003	799	0.009
Gandhila, Gandil, Gondla	3216	0.05	3283	0.04	3513	0.039

(contd...)

Kabirpanthi, Julaha	65028	1.13	73705	1.04	84711	0.95
Khatik	10384	0.18	12103	0.17	14482	0.16
Kori, Koli	6521	0.11	16701	0.23	24921	0.28
Marija, Marecha	1954	0.03	104	0.001	260	0.002
Mazhabi, Mazhabi Sikh	1765798	30.74	2220945	31.59	2633921	29.72
Megh	105157	1.83	124210	1.76	141023	1.59
Nat	1413	0.02	1071	0.01	3902	0.04
Od	13015	0.22	19478	0.27	32061	0.36
Pasi	9113	0.15	19247	0.27	39111	0.44
Perna	189	0.003	28	0.0003	68	0.0007
Pherera	956	0.01	06	0.00008	80	0.0009
Sanhai	435	0.007	286	0.004	359	0.004
Sanhal	578	0.01	656	0.009	1538	0.01
Sansi, Bhedkut, Manesh	81062	1.41	105337	1.49	122201	1.37
Sansoi	623	0.01	1096	0.01	456	0.005
Sapela	2333	0.04	3888	0.05	5872	0.066
Sarera	12321	0.21	15228	0.21	14419	0.16
Sikligar	8727	0.15	7528	0.10	11807	0.13
Sirkiband	28940	0.50	73126	1.04	57555	0.64
Mochi					8763	0.09
Mahatam, Rai Sikh					516695	5.83
Rest	83639	1.45	46923	0.66	471871	5.32
Total	**5742528**	**28.35**	**7028723**	**28.85**	**8860179**	**31.9**

Source: Census Bhawan, Data Enumerated by the Author, 2017. Sector 19A, Chandigarh.

APPENDIX IV

Graph 1: Vote Percentages of the BSP in Uttar Pradesh Assembly Elections, 1993-2017

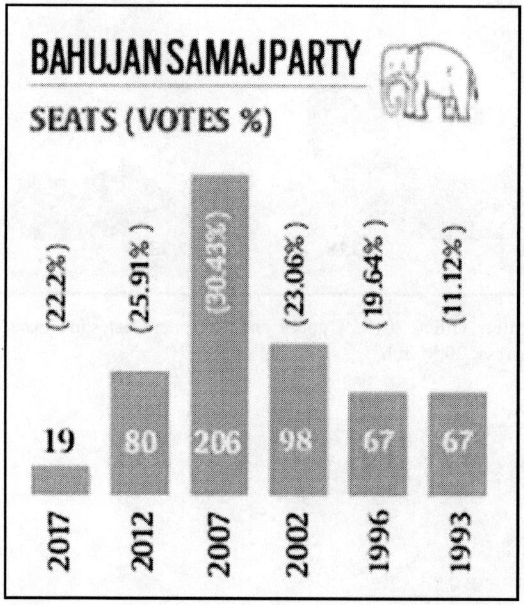

Source: Election Commission of India, 2017, New Delhi.

Pie Chart 2: Vote Percentages of the Major Castes in Uttar Pradesh Assembly Election, 2017

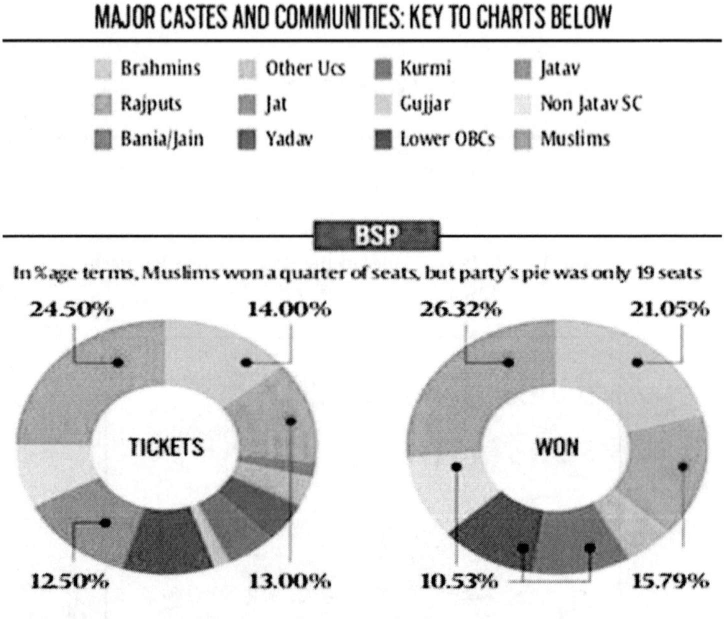

Source: Verniers, Gilles. 2017. 'Upper Hand for Upper Castes in House.' The Indian Express: 20 March.

Selected Bibliography

Primary Sources

- Aley, Monohar. 1997. *The Editorials of Kanshi Ram.* Hyderabad: Bahujan Publishers.
- Ambedkar, B.R. 1982-90. *Caste in India, Speeches and Writings of Dr Baba Saheb Ambedkar.* Vol. 1, Bombay: Government of Maharashtra.
- Census of India, 1991, 2001 and 2011.
- *Election Commission of India (n.d). Statistical Report on General Elections, 1992 and 1996 to the Legislative Assembly Elections of Punjab.*
- *Election Commission of India (n.d). Statistical Report on General Elections, 1996 to the 16th Loksabha,* Vol. 1-3.
- *Election Data of General Assembly Elections to the Punjab Vidhan Sabha.* 1985-2017. Sector 17 E, Chandigarh: Panjab Chief Elections Commission.
- Government of Punjab. 2004. *Human Development Report 2004.* Chandigarh: Government of Punjab.
- *Handbook on National Commission for SCs and STs,* 2011. Delhi: Loknayak Bhawan.
- *Major Decisions and Achievements of U.P. Government under the Dynamic Leadership of Ms. Mayawati and Steps Taken to Perpetuate the Memory of Great Heroes of Social Change.* 1997. Lucknow: Information and Relations Department.
- Moon, Vasant, ed. 1997. *Dr Baba Saheb Ambedkar: Writings and Speeches.* Vol. 15, Bombay: Education Department, Government of Maharashtra.
- *National Commission for Scheduled Castes and Scheduled Tribes, A Handbook.* 2014. New Delhi: Government of India Press.
- *Parliament of India, Loksabha. 1952-2014. Who's Who.* New Delhi: Loksabha Secretariate.
- *Punjab Legislative and Parliamentary Debates, 1984-2017.*
- *Punjab Vidhan Sabha, Who's Who, 1952-2017.* Chandigarh: Vidhan Sabha Secretariate.
- Reports of Election Commission of India.

- Reports of State Election Commission of Punjab.
- *Republican Party of India, Manifesto,* 1967. New Delhi: BSP Office.

B. Books/Pamphlets

- Ahir, D.C. 1992. *Dr Ambedkar and Punjab.* New Delhi: D.K. Publishers and Distributors.
- Ahir, D.C. and A.K. Narain, eds. 1994. *Buddhism and Social Change.* Delhi: B.R. Publishing Corporation.
- Akhtar, Mohammad Jamil. 1999. *Iron Lady, Kumari Mayawati.* New Delhi: Bahujan Sangathak.
- Anand, Mulk Raj, ed. 1990. *Annihilation of Caste: Undelivered Speeches of Dr B.R. Ambedkar*. Delhi: Arnold Publishers.
- Anand, Mulk Raj and Eleanor Zelliot, eds. 1992. *An Anthology of Dalit Literature.* New Delhi: Gyan Prakashan.
- Anand, S., ed. 2014. *Annihilation of Caste.* New Delhi: Narayana Publishing Publications Pvt. Ltd.
- Arora, S.C. 1990. *Turmoil in Punjab Politics.* New Delhi: Mittal Publications.
- Aryama and Sukhadeo Thorat, eds. 2007. *Ambedkar in Retrospect, Essays on Economies, Politics and Society.* New Delhi: Rawat Publications.
- Badajatya, Suraj. 2014. *Babu Mangoo Ram*. New Delhi: Anamica Publishers.
- Baker, Sophie. 1990. *Caste at Home in Hindu India.* London: Jonatham Cape.
- Bakshi, S.R. 1992. *Jagjivan Ram–the Harijan Leader.* Delhi: Anmol Publications.
- Bal, Gurpreet. 1995. *Development and Change in India: A Case Study of Blacksmiths*. New Delhi: National Book Organisation.
- Balley, Lahori Ram. 1997. *Dr Ambedkar: Jeewan Atey Mission (Punjabi).* Jalandhar: Bheem Patrika Prakashan.
- Basu, Swaraj, ed. 2016. *Reading on Dalit Identity: History, Literature and Religion.* Hyderabad: Orient Blackswan.
- Beteille, Andre. 1965. *Caste, Class and Power.* California: University of California Press.
- ———. 2012. *Democracy and its Institutions*. New Delhi: Oxford University Press.
- Bhambhri, C.P. 1993. *Politics in India, 1992-93.* Delhi: Shipra Publications.
- Bob, Clifford. 2008. *Dalit Rights and Human Rights*. New Delhi: Critical Quest.
- Bose, Ajay. 2008. *Behenji, a Political Biography of Mayawati.* New Delhi: Penguin Viking.

- Brar, Bhupinder, Ashutosh Kumar and Ronki Ram, eds. 2008. *Globalisation and the Politics of Identity in India.* New Delhi: Pearson Longman.
- Brass, Paul R. 1965. *Factional Politics in an Indian State: the Congress Party in Uttar Pradesh.* Berkeley: University of California Press.
- ———. 1974. *Language, Religion and Politics in North India.* Cambridge: Cambridge University Press.
- ———. 1975. *Struggle for Justice to Dalit Christians.* New Delhi: Vikas Publications.
- ———. 1994. *The politics of India since Independence.* Cambridge: Cambridge University Press.
- Chand, Moon. 1992. *'BAMCEF at a Glance' in the Bahujan and their Movements.* New Delhi: Bahujan Publication Trust.
- ———. 1992. *The Bahujan and their movements.* New Delhi: Bahujan Publication Trust.
- Chandra, Kanchan. 1999. *Post-Congress Politics in Uttar Pradesh: The Ethnification of the Party System and its Consequences.* New Delhi: Sage Publications.
- Channa, Subhadra Mitra and Joan P. Mencher. 2013. *Life as a Dalit: Views from the Bottom on Caste in India.* New Delhi: Sage Publications.
- Chatterjee, Debi. 2004. *Up Against Caste.* New Delhi: Rawat Publications.
- Deshpande, Satish, ed. 2016. The problem of Caste. New Delhi: Orient Blackswan.
- Dhami, M.S. 1995. *Caste, Class and Politics in Rural Punjab: A Case Study of Sangrur District.* Delhi: Deep and Deep Publications.
- Dirks, Nicholas B. 2002. *Caste of Mind: Colonialism and the Making of Modern India.* Delhi: Permanent Black.
- Dube, Ishita Banerjee, ed. 2008. *Caste in History.* New Delhi: Oxford University Press.
- Dube, Saurabh. 2001. *Untouchable, Pasts Identity and Power among a Central Indian Community, 1780-1950.* New Delhi: Visitaar Publications.
- Dubey, Abhay Kumar. 1997. *Kanshi Ram: Ek Alochnatmak Adhyayan.* Delhi: Raj Kamal.
- ———. 2002. *Adhunikta ke Aine me Dalit.* Delhi: Vani Prakashan.
- Fernandes, Walter. 1981. *Caste and Conversion Movement in India.* New Delhi: Indian Social Institute.
- ———. 1996. *The Emerging Dalit Identity.* New Delhi: Indian Social Institute.
- Gill, M.S. 1997. *Quest for Status: A Study of Untouchability in Rural Punjab.* Amritsar: Guru Nanak Dev University.
- Gill, Sucha Singh. 2004. *Socio-Economic Transformation and Scheduled Castes in Regional Context.* Jaipur: Rawat Publications.

- Goore, M.S. 1993. *The Social Context of an Ideology (Ambedkar's Social and Political Thoughts).* New Delhi: Sage Publications.
- Gorringe, Hugo. 2005. *Untouchable Citizens: Dalit Movements and Democratisation in Tamil Nadu.* New Delhi: Sage Publications.
- Grewal, J.S. 1996. *Sikh Ideology: Polity and Social Order.* New Delhi: Manohar Publications.
- Gupta, Dipankar. 1997. *Social Stratification.* Delhi: Oxford University Press.
- ———. 2000. *Interrogating Caste: Understanding Hierarchy and Difference in Indian Society.* New Delhi: Penguin India.
- ———. 2004. *Caste in Question.* New Delhi: Sage Publications.
- Guru, Gopal. 1998. *Dalit Cultural Movement and Dialectics of Dalit Politics in Maharashtra.* Mumbai: Vikas Adhyayan Kendra.
- ———. 2009. *Humiliation Claims and Context.* New Delhi: Oxford University Press.
- Guru, Gopal and Sarukkai Sunder. 2013. *The Cracked Mirror.* New Delhi: Oxford University Press.
- Hanlon, R.O. 1985. *Caste, Conflict and Ideology: Mahatma Jotirao Phule and Low Caste Protest in 19th Century Western India.* Cambridge: Cambridge University Press.
- Hasan, Zoya. 1986. *Gandhi Ji and Harijan.* New Delhi: Shree Publishing and Distributors.
- ———. 1998. *Quest for Power.* Delhi: Oxford University Press.
- ———. 2000. *Politics and the State in India.* Delhi: Sage Publications.
- ———. 2002. *Parties and Party Politics in India.* New Delhi: Oxford University Press.
- ———, ed. 2002. *Representation and Redistribution: The New Lower Caste Politics of North India.* New Delhi: Oxford University Press.
- ———. 2009. *Politics of Inclusion, Caste, Minorities and Affirmative Action.* Delhi: Oxford University Press.
- Ilaiah, Kancha. 1996. *Why I am not a Hindu: A Sudra Critique of Hindutva Philosophy.* Calcutta: Samya.
- ———. 2009. *Post-Hindu India: A Discourse on Dalit Bahujan, Socio-Spiritual and Scientific Revolution.* New Delhi: Sage Publications.
- Jaffrelot, Christophe. 2007. *Hindu Nationalism.* Delhi: Permanent Black.
- ———. 2010. *Religion, Caste and Politics in India.* New Delhi: Primus Books Publishers.
- Jatava, D.R. 1997. *Social Philosophy of B.R. Ambedkar.* Jaipur: Rawat Publications.
- ———. 2001. *Dynamics of Ambedkar Ideology.* Jaipur: Sublime Publications.

- ———. 2005. *Ambedkar Code of Conduct.* Jaipur: ABD Publishers.
- Jayal, Niraja Gopal and Pratap Bhanu Mehta, eds. 2010. *Oxford Companion to Politics in India.* New Delhi: Oxford University Press.
- Jayal, Niraja Gopal, ed. 2011. *Democracy in India.* New Delhi: Oxford University Press.
- Jodhka, Surinder S. 2001. *Community and Identities: Contemporary Discourses on Culture and Politics in India.* New Delhi: Sage Publications.
- ———. 2012. *Changing Caste Ideology, Identity and Mobility.* New Delhi: Sage Publications.
- ———. 2015. Caste in Contemporary India. New Delhi: Routledge.
- John, Sommer G. 2001. *Empowering the Oppressed.* Delhi: Sage Publications.
- John, Webster C.B. 1999. *Religion and Dalit Liberation.* New Delhi: Manohar Publishers and Distributors.
- Judge, Paramjit Singh. 2005. *Religion, Identity and Nationhood.* New Delhi: Rawat Publications.
- ———. 2010. *Changing Dalit Exploration across Time.* Jaipur: Rawat Publications.
- ———, ed. 2014. *Mapping Social Exclusion in India: Caste, Religion and Borderlands.* New Delhi: Cambridge University Press.
- ———, ed. 2014. *Towards Sociology of Dalits.* New Delhi: Sage Publications.
- Juergensmeyer, Mark. 1979. *Religion as a Social Vision: The Movement against Untouchability in 20th Century Punjab.* Berkeley: University of California Press.
- Kishore, Girija. 2003. *Dalit Vimersh.* Shimla: Adhayan Sansthan Rashtarpati Niwas.
- Kishore, Raj. 1994. *Harijan se Dalit.* New Delhi: Vani Prakashan.
- Kohli, Atul. 1992. *Democracy and Discontent: India's Growing Crisis of Governability.* New Delhi: Cambridge University Press.
- ———, ed. 2001. *The Success of India's Democracy.* Cambridge: Cambridge University Press.
- Kotani, H. 1997. *Caste System, Untouchability and the Depressed.* Delhi: Manohar Publishers and Distributors.
- Kshirsagar, K. R. 1994. *Dalit Movement in India and its Leaders.* New Delhi: M.D. Publications Pvt. Ltd.
- Kumar, Ashutosh. 2011. *Rethinking State Politics in India: Regions within Regions.* New Delhi: Routledge.
- Kumar, Vinod and Ashok Kumar. 1996. *Upward Mobility of Depressed Scheduled Castes in Punjab.* Chandigarh: Institute for Development and Communication.

- Kumar, Vivek. 2001. *Dalit Assertion and Bahujan Samaj Party*. Lucknow: Bahujan Sahitya Sansthan.
- ———. 2014. *Caste and Democracy in India: A Perspective from Below.* New Delhi: Gyan Publishing.
- Lal, Shyam and K.S. Saxsena. 1998. *Ambedkar and National Building.* Jaipur: Rawat Publications House.
- Lapalombra, Joseph and Myron Weinor. 1966. *Political Parties and Political Development*. Princeton: Princeton University Press.
- Lench, Owen M. 1969. *The Politics of Untouchability.* London: Columbia University Press.
- Lohia, Ram Manohar. 1964. The Caste System. Hyderabad: Navahind.
- Mangubhai, Jayshree P. 2014. *Human Rights as Practice: Dalit Women Securing Livelihood Entitlements in South Asia.* New Delhi: Oxford University Press.
- Massey, James H. 1995. *Dalits in India: Religion as a Source of Bondage Liberation with Special Reference to Christians.* New Delhi: Manohar Publications.
- Mauraya, C.L. 1996. *BSP Supremo Kanshi Ram Ke Samne*. Allahabad: Kushwha Publishers.
- Mayawati. 2000. *Bahujan Samaj Aur Uski Rajniti.* New Delhi: Bahujan Samaj Party Office.
- Meera Verma, Mrinal Mehta and Rumki Basu. 2004. *Essays on Indian Government and Politics.* New Delhi: Jawahar Publishers and Distributors.
- Mehta, Pratap Bhanu. 2003. *The Burden of Democracy*. New Delhi: Penguin.
- Mendelson, Oliver and Marika Vicziancy. 1998a. *From Untouchable to Dalit*. New Delhi: Cambridge University Press.
- ———. 1998b. *The Untouchables: Subordination, Poverty and the State in Modern India.* Cambridge: Cambridge University Press.
- Murugkar, Lata. 1991. *Dalit Panther Movement in Maharashtra*. Bombay: Bombay Popular Prakashan.
- Nahar, Emanual, ed. 2016. *Social Exclusion and Discrimination with Weaker Sections of Society: An Inclusive Policy.* New Delhi: Kalpaz Publications.
- ———, ed. 2017. *Dr B.R. Ambedkar's Philosophy in Contemporary India.* New Delhi: Kalpaz Publications.
- Narayan, Badri. 2014. *Kanshi Ram – Leader of Dalits*. New Delhi: Penguin/ Viking.
- Omvedt, Gail. 1993. *Reinventing Revolution: India's New Social Movements.* New York: Sharpe.
- ———. 1997. *Dalit Visions: The Anti-Caste Movement and the Construction of an Indian Identity.* Hyderabad: Orient Longman.

- ———. 2003. *Buddhism in India: Challenging Brahmanism and Caste.* New Delhi: Sage Publications.
- ———. 2010. *Dalit Vision.* New Delhi: Orient Blackswan Pvt. Ltd.
- ———. 2016. *Understanding Caste, From Buddha to Ambedkar and Beyond.* New Delhi: Orient Blackswan.
- Oommen, T.K. 1990. *Protest and Change: Studies in Social Movements.* Vol. 5, New Delhi: Oxford University Press.
- Pabla, A.S. 2008. *Warriors of Untouchables: Ambedkar and Gandhi.* New Delhi: Cyber Tech Publications.
- Pai, Sudha. 2000. *State Politics, New Dimensions.* New Delhi: Shipra Publications.
- ———. 2007. *Political Process in Uttar Pradesh: Identity, Economic Reforms and Governance.* New Delhi: Pearson/Longman.
- ———. 2010. *Developmental State and Dalit Question in Madhya Pradesh: Congress Response.* New Delhi: Routledge.
- ———. 2013. *Dalit Assertion (Oxford India Short Introduction).* New Delhi: Oxford University Press.
- Palkhiwala, Nani A. 1994. *We, the Nation, the Lost Decades.* Calcutta: UBS Publishers.
- Pinto, Ambrose, ed. 1999. *Dalit: Assertion for Identity.* New Delhi: Indian Social Institute.
- Pradeep K. Chhibber. 1999. *Democracy without Association.* New Delhi: Vistaar Publications.
- Puri, Harish K. and Paramjit S. Judge, eds. 2000. *Social and Political Movement, Readings on Punjab.* Jaipur: Rawat Publications.
- Rajan, Ambeth. 1994. *My Bahujan Samaj Party.* New Delhi: ABCDE Publications.
- Ram, Kanshi. 1992. *Bahujan Samaj Ke liye Asha ki kiran.* New Delhi: Bahujan Publications.
- ———. (n.d.). 2007. *Swatantra Bharat Mein Bahujan Samaj Ashrit Kyon.* (BSP Booklet).
- Ram, Nandu. 1988. *The Mobile Scheduled Castes, Rise of a New Middle Class.* Delhi: Hindustan Publishing Corporation.
- Ram, Ronki. 2012. *Dalit Pachhan, Mukti ate Shaktikaran.* Patiala: Publication Bureau, Punjabi University.
- Rao, Yagati Chinna, ed. 2009. *Dividing Dalits.* Jaipur: Rawat Publications.
- Rodrigues, Valerian, ed. 2002. *The Essential Writings of B.R. Ambedkar.* Delhi: Oxford University Press.
- Rudolph, Lloyd I. and Susanne Hoeber Rudolph. 2008. *Explaining Indian Democracy, a Fifty Years Perspective, 1956-2006.* London: Oxford University Press.

- Sadasivan, S.N. 1977. *Party and Democracy in India.* New Delhi: Tata Mcgraw-Hill Publishing Company Limited.
- Sandhu, Davinder Pal. 1992. *Sikhs in Punjab Politics, Study of Minority.* New Delhi: Patriot Publishers.
- Sarkar, Sumit and Tanika Sarkar, ed. 2014. *Caste in Modern India.* New Delhi: Permanent Black.
- Satyanarayana, A. 2005. *Dalits and Upper Castes.* New Delhi: Kanishka Publishers Distributors.
- Shah, Ghanshyam. 1990. *Social Movements in India: A Review of Literature.* Delhi: Sage Publications.
- ———. 1992. *Dalit Movement in India.* Delhi: Sage Publications.
- ———, ed. 1997. *Social Transformation in India.* New Delhi: Rawat Publications.
- ———. 2002. *Caste and Democratic Politics in India.* New Delhi: Permanent Black.
- Sharma, K.L. 1994. *Social Stratification and Mobility.* Jaipur: Rawat Publications.
- ———. 1997. *Caste and Class in India.* Jaipur: Rawat Publications.
- Sharma, Satish K. 1985. *Social Movements and Social Change: A Study of Arya Samaj and Untouchability in Punjab.* New Delhi: B. R. Publishers.
- Sharma, Ussula. 1994. *Contextualizing Caste.* Oxford: Blackwell Publishers.
- Shourie, Arun. 1997. *Worshipping False Gods.* Delhi: ASA Publications.
- Shyamlal. 1981. *Caste and Political Mobilisation: The Bhangis.* Jaipur: Panchsheel Prakashan.
- ———. 2008. *Ambedkar and Dalit Movement.* New Delhi: Rawat Publications.
- Sigmund, Neumann. 1956. *Modern Political Parties, Approaches to Comparative Politics.* Chicago: University of Chicago Press.
- Simon, R. Charsley and G.K. Karnath. 1998. *Challenging Untouchability, Dalit Initiative and Experience from Karnataka.* New Delhi: Sage Publications.
- Singh, Davinder. 1993. *Akali Politics in Punjab (1964-1985).* New Delhi: National Book Organisation.
- Singh, Ekta. 2005. *Caste System in India.* Delhi: Kalpaz Publications.
- Singh, Gobinder. 1986. *Religion and Politics in Punjab.* New Delhi: Deep & Deep Publications.
- Singh, Gurharpal. 2000. *Ethnic Conflict in India: A Case Study of Punjab.* New Delhi: MacMillan Press.
- Singh, Lakhwinder. 1994. *Party Politics in Punjab.* New Delhi: Harnam Publications.

- Singh, R.K. 1994. *Kanshi Ram aur B.S.P. (Hindi).* Allahabad: Kushwala Book Distributors.
- Sivaprakasam, M.N. 2002. *Dalits and the Social Mobilisation.* New Delhi: Rajat Publications.
- Srinivas, M.N. 1996. *Caste: its Twentieth Century Avtar.* Delhi: Penguin Books.
- ———. 2001. *Adhunik Bharat me Jati.* Delhi: Raj Kamal Prakashan.
- Srivastav, Jitender and Ravinder Kalia, eds. 2012. *Premchand, Dalit Jivan ki Kahaniyan.* New Delhi: Bharatiya Gyanpith.
- Thorat, Sukhadeo. 2004. *Hindu Social System & Human Rights of Dalits.* New Delhi: Critical Quest.
- ———. 2016. *Dalits in India: Search for a Common Destiny.* New Delhi: Sage Publications.
- Thorat, Sukhadeo and Umakant, eds. 2004. *Caste, Race and Discrimination, Discourses in International Context.* New Delhi: Rawat Publications.
- Thorat, Sukhadeo and Narender Kumar, eds. 2008. *B.R. Ambedkar, Perspectives on Social Exclusions and Inclusive Polices.* New Delhi: Oxford University Press.
- Thorat, Sukhadeo and Katherene Newman, eds. 2009. *Blocked by Caste: Economic Discrimination in Modern India.* New Delhi: Oxford University Press.
- Virdi, S.L. 2004. *Bahujan Manifesto.* Calgary: Guru Ravi Dass Society of Calgary.
- Viswanathan, S. 2005. *Dalits in Dravidian Land.* Channai: Navayana.
- Wallace, Paul. 1990. *Religion and Ethnic Politics: Political Mobilisation in Punjab.* Delhi: Oxford University Press.
- Wallace, Paul and Surinder Chopra, eds. 1981. *Political Dynamics of Punjab.* Amritsar; Guru Nanak Dev University.
- Weber, Max. 1958. *The Religion of India: The Sociology of Hinduism and Buddhism.* Translated by H.M Gerth, (Don Gelncoe, Ill: Freepress).
- Weiner, Myron. 1957. *Party Politics in India.* Princeton: Princeton University Press.
- ———. 1967. *Party Building in a new Nation.* Chicago: University of Chicago Press.
- ———. 1984. *India at the Polls, 1980.* Delhi: Munshiram Manoharlal Publishers.
- Wiener, Myron and Rajni Kothari, eds. 1965. *Indian Voting Behaviour.* Calcutta: Firma K. L. Mukhopadhya.
- Weiner, Myron and Field J.O., eds. 1975. *Electoral Politics in Indian States, Parties System and Cleavages.* Delhi: Manohar Book Service.

- Yadav, Narender. 2003. *Out Caste (A Memoir).* Delhi: Penguin books.
- Zelliot, Eleanor. 1969. *Dr Ambedkar and the Mahar Movement.* University of Pennsylvania.
- ———. 1972. *Gandhi and Ambedkar: A Study in Leadership.* Tucson: University of Arizona Press.

C. Articles and Research Papers

- Aloysius, G. 1999. 'Caste in and above History.' *Sociological Bulletin* 48 (1-2): 151-175.
- Baixas, Lionel. 2007. 'The Dera Sacha Sauda Controversy.' *Economic and Political Weekly* XLII (40): 4059-4065.
- Bal, Gurpreet. 1998. 'Communities and Culture in Entrepreneurship Development in India.' *The Journal of Entrepreneurship* 7 (2): 171-182.
- Balasubramanian, J. 2011. 'Dalits and Lack of Diversity in the Newsroom.' *Economic and Political Weekly* XLVI (11): 21-25.
- Balley, Lahori Ram. 2003. 'Forward.' In *Why Ambedkar Embraced Buddhism and Not Sikhism,* edited by K.C. Sulekh, 3-4. Jalandhar: Bheem Patrika.
- Bandyopadhyay, Sekhar. 2000. 'Transfer of Power and the Crises of Dalit Politics in India, 1945-47.' *Modern Asian Studies* 34 (4): 893-942.
- Bandyopadhyay, Suraj. 2004. 'Differentiation and Formation of Hierarchy: A Methodological Note on Social Stratification.' *Contributions to Indian Sociology* 38 (1-2): 247-259.
- Barrier, Gerald. N. 1995. 'Tradition and Sikh Identity in the Modern World.' *International Journal of Punjab Studies* 2 (1): 103-113.
- Basu, Raj Sekhar. 2014. Life as a Dalit: Views from the Bottom on Caste in India: Postcards from Below.' *Economic and Political Weekly* XLIX (46): 35-37.
- ———. 2017. 'Reading on Dalit Identity: History, Literature and Religion – A Voice to Dalit Cause.' *Economic and Political Weekly* LII (4): 33-37.
- Basu, Swaraj. 2004. 'Dynamics of a Caste Movement: The Raj Bansis of North Bengal.' *Indian Social Science Review* 6 (2): 236-240.
- Bayly, Susan. 2014. 'Western Orientalists and the Colonial Perception of Caste.' In *Caste in Modern India*, edited by Sumit Sarkar and Tanika Sarkar, 47-87. New Delhi: Permanent Black.
- Beteille, Andre. 2002. 'Hierarchical and Competitive Inequalities.' *Sociological Bulletin* 51 (1): 51-60.
- ———. 2009. 'Sociology and Ideology.' *Sociological Bulletin* 58 (2): 196-212.
- Bhambhri, C.P. 1999. 'Dialectics of Caste and Casteism.' *Economic and Political Weekly* XXXIV (36): 4-10.

- Bharti, Dwarka. 2004. 'Protection of Dalit Sensibilities in Punjabi Dalit Literature.' In *Dalits in Regional Context,* edited by Harish K. Puri, 307-316. Jaipur: Rawat Publications.
- Brass, Paul. 1997. 'General Election, 1996 in U.P.' *Economic and Political Weekly* XXVIII (38): 2403-11.
- Caton, Brian P. 2014. 'Social Categories and Colonisation in Punjab, 1849-1920.' In *Caste in Modern India*, edited by Sumit Sarkar and Tanika Sarkar, 113-136. New Delhi: Permanent Black.
- Chahal, S.K. 2009. 'Initiating a Movement of the Down-trodden: An Overview of the Early Phase of Dr B.R. Ambedkar's Politics, 1918-1931. *Punjab University Research Journal (Arts)* XXXVI (1-2): 113-128.
- Chandhoke, Neera. 2016. 'Debating India: Essays on Indian Political Discourse –Dialogical Dreams: Political Discourse in India.' *Economic and Political Weekly* LI (38): 33-38.
- Chandra, Kanchan. 2000. 'Elite Incorporation in Multi-Ethnic Societies.' *Asian Survey* 40 (5): 836-885.
- ———. 2001. 'Ethnic Bargains, Group Instability and Social Choice Theory.' *Politics and Society* 29 (3): 337-362.
- Chandra, Kanchan and Chandrika Parmar. 1997. 'Party Strategies in the UP Assembly Election 1996.' *Economic and Political Weekly* XXXII (5): 214-21.
- Chatterjee, Debi. 2005. 'Up Against Caste: Comparative Study of Ambedkar and Pariyar.' *Indian Social Science Review* 7 (1): 171-176.
- Chatterjee, Partha. 2010. 'The State.' In *Politics in India*, edited by Niraja Gopal Jayal and Pratap Bhanu Mehta, 5-14. New Delhi: Oxford University Press.
- Chavan, Dilip. 2010. 'Relevance of the Caste-based Census.' *Mainstream* XLVIII (24): 29-30.
- Chinnaiah, Jangam. 2005. 'Caste and Dalit Emancipation.' *Economic and Political Weekly* XXXX (28): 3021-23.
- D.N. 1991. 'Gandhi, Ambedkar and Separate Electorates Issue.' *Economic and Political Weekly* 26 (21): 1329.
- Desai, Sonalde and Amaresh Dube. 2011. 'Caste in 21st Century India: Compelling Narratives.' *Economic and Political Weekly* XLVI (11): 21-25.
- Deshpande, Anirudh. 1997. 'Casteism, Communalism and Politics.' *Economic and Political Weekly* XXXII (40): 2578-79.
- Dhami, M.S. 1978. 'The Punjab Assembly Elections – June 1977: A Micro Study of three Assembly Constituencies.' *Punjab Journal of Politics* 11 (2): 1-45.
- Dixit, Arun and Sona Dixit. 2005. 'Ambedkar and Human Rights.' *Mainstream* XXXXIII (17): 21-23.

- Duncan, J. 1997. 'New Political Equations in North India: Mulayam, Mayawati and Government Instability in Uttar Pradesh.' *Asian Survey* 37 (10): 10.
- ———. 1999. 'Dalits and Politics in Rural North India: The Bahujan Samaj Party in Uttar Pradesh.' *The Journal of Peasant Studies* 24 (4): 54.
- Fazal, Tanweer. 2017. 'Scheduled Castes, Reservations and Religion: Revisiting a Juridical Debate.' *Contributions to Indian Sociology* 51(1): 1-24.
- Gorringe, Hugo. 2005. 'You Build Your House, We'll Build Ours: The Attractions and Pitfalls of Identity Politics.' *Social Identities* 11 (6): 653-672.
- ———. 2008. 'The Caste of the Nation: Untouchability and Citizenship in South India.' *Contributions to Indian Sociology* 42 (1): 123-149.
- ———. 2016. 'Drumming out Oppression, or Drumming in it? Identity, Culture and Contention in Dalit Politics.' *Contributions to Indian Sociology* 50 (1): 1-26.
- Gosal, R.P.S. 2004. 'Distribution and Relative Concentration of Scheduled Caste Population of Punjab.' In *Dalits in Regional Context,* edited by Harish K. Puri, 21-42. Jaipur: Rawat Publications.
- Gudavarthy, Ajay. 2016. 'Brahmanism, Liberalism and the Post Colonial Theory.' *Economic and Political Weekly* LI (24): 15-17.
- Gundimeda, Sambaiah. 2009. 'Dalits Praja Rajyam Party and Caste Politics.' *Economic and Political Weekly* XLIV (21): 50-54.
- Gupta, Dipankar. 2004. 'Introduction, the Certitudes of Caste: When Identity Trumps Hierarchy.' *Contributions to Indian Sociology* 38 (1-2): 1-15.
- ———. 2016. 'Social Science and Democracy.' *Economic and Political Weekly* LI (4): 31-36.
- Gupta, Smita. 2009. 'BSP at the Crossroads.' *Economic and Political Weekly* XLIV (26-27): 19-23.
- Guru, Gopal. 1993. 'Dalit Movement in Mainstream Sociology.' *Economic and Political Weekly* XXVIII (14): 570-573.
- ———. 1997. 'Understanding Dalit Protest in Maharashtra.' *Economic and Political Weekly* XXX11 (30): 1879-1880.
- ———. 2001. 'The Language of Dalit Bahujan Political Discourse.' In *Dalit Identity and Politics,* edited by Ghanshyam Shah, 97-107. New Delhi: Sage Publications.
- ———. 2005. 'Understanding the Category 'Dalit.' In *Atrophy in Dalit Politics,* edited by Gopal Guru, 66-77. Mumbai: Vikas Adhyayan Kendra.
- ———. 2008a. 'Democracy in Search of Dignity', In *Human Rights and Peace in India,* edited by Ujjwal Singh, 74-89. New Delhi: Sage Publications.

- ———. 2008b. 'Untouchability in Rural India: Confronting Untouchability.' *Economic and Political Weekly* XLIII (28): 31-33.
- ———. 2009. 'Rejection of Rejection: Foregrounding Self-respect.' In *Humiliating: Claims and Context*, edited by Gopal Guru, 209-225. New Delhi: Oxford University Press.
- ——— 2010. 'Social Justice.' In *Politics in India*, edited by Niraja Gopal Jayal and Pratap Bhanu Mehta, 361-377. New Delhi: Oxford University Press.
- ———. 2011. 'Liberal Democracy in India and the Dalit Critique.' *Social Research* 78(1): India's World, Spring.
- Guru, Gopal and Geetha, V. 2000. 'New Phase of Dalit-Bahujan Intellectual Activity.' *Economic and Political Weekly* XXXV (3): 130-134.
- Hasan, Zoya. 2001. 'Transfer of Power? Politics of Mass Mobilisation in UP.' *Economic and Political Weekly* 36 (46-47): 4401-4409.
- Heath, Anthony and Yogendra Yadev. 1999. 'United Colours of Congress, Social Profile of Congress Voters, 1996 and 1998.' *Economic and Political Weekly* XXXIX (34): 2522-2523.
- Heering, Alexandra D. 2016. 'Dalit and Memories, Remembrance of Day Past.' *Economic and Political Weekly* LI (11): 70-77.
- Ilaiah, Kancha. 1994a. 'BSP and Caste as Ideology.' *Economic and Political Weekly* 29 (12): 668-69.
- ———. 1994b. 'Caste and Contradictions.' *Economic and Political Weekly* XXIX, (43): 756-766.
- Jaffrelot, Christophe. 1992. 'Hindu Nationalism Strategic Syncretism in Ideology Building.' *Indian Journal of Social Science* 5 (4): 373-393.
- ———. 2000. 'The Rise of the Other Backward Classes in North India.' *Journal of Asian Studies* 59 (1): 86-108.
- ———. 2014. 'Hindu Nationalism and Democracy.' In *Democracy in India*, edited by Niraja Gopal Jayal, 509-534. New Delhi: Oxford University Press.
- Jeffrey, Craig, Patricia Jeffrey and Roger Jeffery. 2008. 'Dalit Revolution? New Politicians in Uttar Pradesh, India.' *The Journal of Asian Studies* 67 (4): 1365-1396.
- Jodhka, Surinder S. 1997. 'Crisis of the 1980s and the Changing Agenda of Punjab Studies: A Survey of Some Recent Research.' *Economic and Political Weekly* XXXII (6): 273-79.
- ———. 2000. 'Prejudice' Without Pollution? Scheduled Caste Population in Contemporary Punjab.' *Journal of Indian School of Political Economy* 12 (3&4): 381-403.
- ———. 2003a. 'Caste Occupation Divide Gets Sharper in Punjab.' *Economic and Political Weekly* XXXVII (19): 1813-23.

- ———. 2003b. 'Caste Tension in Punjab.' *Economic and Political Weekly* XXIII (28): 2923-26.
- ———. 2006. 'Religion and Communities: Social Identities in Contemporary Punjab.' In *Religion, Culture and Politics in India,* edited by Rajendra Vora and Anne Feldthans, 299-316. Delhi: Manohar Publications.
- ———. 2010a. 'Caste and Politics.' In *Politics in India,* edited by Niraja Gopal Jayal and Pratap Bhanu Mehta, 154-167. New Delhi: Oxford University Press.
- ———. 2010b. 'Dalits in Business: Self-Employed Scheduled Castes in North-West India.' *Economic and Political Weekly* XLV (11): 41-42.
- Jodhka, Surinder S. and Murli Dhar. 2003. 'Cow, Caste and Communal Politics.' *Economic and Political Weekly* XXXVIII (3): 174-80.
- Judge, Paramjit Singh. 1997. 'Green Revolution and the Bahujan Samaj Party in Punjab.' In *Dimensions of Social Change: Essays in Honour of Professor P.N. Pimpley,* edited by Paramjit S. Judge and Satish K. Sharma, 48-65. Jaipur: Rawat Publications.
- ———. 2002a. 'Punjabis in England: Ad-Dharmi Experience.' *Economic and Political Weekly* XXXXII (31): 3244-50.
- ———. 2002b. 'Religion, Caste and Communalism in Punjab.' *Sociological Bulletin* 51 (2): 175-94.
- ———. 2003. 'Hierarchical Differentiation among Dalits.' *Economic and Political Weekly* XXXVIII (28): 2990-2991.
- ———. 2004a. 'Politics of Sikh Identity and the Fundamentalist Assertion.' *Economic and Political Weekly* XXXIX (35): 3947-3954.
- ———. 2004b. 'Symbols, Community and State: The Sikhs and the Operation Blue Star.' *Punjab Journal of Politics* XXVII (1): 1-25.
- Judge, Paramjit S. and Gurpreet Bal. 2008. 'Understanding the Paradox of Changes among Dalits in Punjab.' *Economic and Political Weekly* XXXXIII (41): 49-54.
- Judge, Paramjit S. and Manjit Kaur. 2010. 'The Politics of Sikh Identity: Understanding Religious Exclusion.' *Sociological Bulletin* 59 (3): 345-367.
- Juergensmeyer, Mark. 1981. 'Political Origins of a Punjabi Lower Caste Religion.' In *Political Dynamics of Punjab,* edited by Paul Wallace and Surendra Chopra, 209-227. Amritsar: Guru Nanak Dev University.
- ———. 2000. 'Ad-Dharm Movement.' In *Social and Political Movement: Readings on Punjab*, edited by Harish K. Puri and Paramjit S. Judge, 221-232. New Delhi: Rawat Publications.
- ———. 2004. 'Cultures of Deprivation: Three Case Studies in Punjab.' In *Dalits in Regional Context*, edited by Harish K. Puri, 43-61. New Delhi: Rawat Publications.

- Kailash, K.K. 2007. 'Middle Game in Coalition Politics.' *Economic and Political Weekly* 42 (4): 307-317.
- ———. 2009. 'Alliances and Lessons of Election 2009.' *Economic and Political Weekly* 44 (39): 52-57.
- ———. 2012. 'The More things Change, the More they Stay the Same in India: the Bahujan and Paradox of the "Democratic Upsurge".' *Asian Survey* 52 (2): 321-347
- Kalladayil, Simon and J.S. Sekhon. 2008. 'Christianity in Punjab: An Empirical Outlook.' *Punjab Journal of Politics* XXXII (33): 31-47.
- Kapoor, S.D. 2016. 'On the Ambedkar – Gandhi Debate.' *Economic and Political Weekly* LI (10): 75-76.
- Kapur, Divesh, Chander Bhan Prasad, Lant Pritchett and D Shyam Babu. 2010. 'Rethinking Inequality: Dalit in Uttar Pradesh in the Market Reform Era.' *Economic and Political Weekly* XLV (35): 39-49.
- Kaur, Manjot. 2006. 'Caste Occupational Change and Social Mobility: A Case Study of Thathiars.' *Punjab Journal of Politics* 27 (2): 95-112.
- Kaur, Ravinder. 2000. 'Sikh Identity: Issues and Development.' *Indian Social Science Review* 2 (1): 193-203.
- ———. 2008. 'Narrative Absence: An Untouchable Account of Partition Migration.' *Contributions to Indian Sociology* 42 (2): 281-307.
- Kaviraj, Sudipta. 2000. 'Democracy and Social Inequality.' In *Transforming India: Social and Political Dynamics of Democracy,* edited by Francine R. Frankel, Zoya Hasan, Rajeev Bhargava and Balveer Arora, 89-119. New Delhi: Oxford University Press.
- Kolge, Nishikant. 2017. 'Was Gandhi a 'Champion of the Caste System'?' *Economic and Political Weekly* LII (13): 42-50.
- Kumar, Arvind. 2017. 'Questioning 'the Dalit Question'.' *Economic and Political Weekly* LII (4): 71-73.
- Kumar, Ashutosh.1993. 'Caste, Agrarian Relations and Agrarian Conflict in India.' *Punjab Journal of Politics* XVII (2): 45-56.
- ———. 2005. 'Electoral Politics in Punjab: 1966-2004.' *Journal of Punjab Studies* 12(1): 111-128.
- ———. 2008. Dissonance between Economic Reforms and Democracy.' *Economic and Political Weekly* 43(1): 54-60
- ———. 2009. 'Punjab: Resurgence of the Congress.' *Economic and Political Weekly* 44 (39): 183-186.
- ———. 2014a. 'Parliamentary Elections in Punjab: Explaining the Electoral Success of Aam Aadmi Party.' *Journal of Punjab Studies* 21(1):113-127.
- ———. 2014b. 'Deras as Sites of Electoral Mobilisation in Indian Punjab: Explaining why Political Parties do flock to the Deras,' *Asian Ethnicity* 17(3): 335-350.

- Kumar, Ashutosh and J.S. Sekhon, 2009. 'Punjab: Resurgence and Campaigning Paid Dividends.' *Economic and Political Weekly* XLIV (39): 26 September.
- Kumar, Lovedeep. 2008. 'Dalit Leadership in Punjab Legislative Assembly 1967-2002: A Socio-Economic Profile.' *Indian Association of Social Science Institutions (IASSI)* 27 (1&2): 104-114.
- Kumar, Pradeep. 1998. 'Hindus and Others, Sociology of Dalit Bahujans.' *Mainstream* XXXVI (25): 21-25.
- ———. 1999a. 'Bahujan Samaj Party: Breaking Ground in Uttar Pradesh.' *Mainstream* XXXVII (25): 18-25.
- ———. 1999b. 'Dalit and the BSP in Uttar Pradesh: Issues and Challenges.' *Economic and Political Weekly* XXXIV (14): 822-26.
- ———. 2001. 'Reservations within Reservations.' *Economic and Political Weekly* XXXVI (37): 3505-3507.
- Kumar, Vivek. 2005. 'Situating Dalits in Indian Sociology.' *Sociological Bulletin* 54 (3): 514-33.
- ———. 2007. 'Behind the BSP Victory.' *Economic and Political Weekly* XLII (24): 2237-2239.
- ———. 2016a. 'How Egalitarian is Indian Sociology?' *Economic and Political Weekly* LI (25): 33-39.
- ———. 2016b. 'Discrimination on Campuses of Higher Learning, a Perspective from Below.' *Economic and Political Weekly* LI (6): 12-15.
- Kumbhar, Sitaram. 2016. 'Everyday Dalit Experiences of Living and the Denials.' *Economic and Political Weekly* LI (35): 13-15.
- Lal, Madan and Jagrup Singh. 2005. 'Political Sociology of Religious Sects in Punjab.' *Punjab Journal of Politics* XXXIX (1): 141-155.
- Lindt, Benjamin. 2013. 'Towards a Comprehensive Model of Caste.' *Contributions to Indian Sociology* 47 (1): 85-112.
- Lobo, Lancy. 2001. 'Visions, Illusions and Dilemmas of Dalit Christians in India.' In *Dalit Identity and Politics,* edited by Ghanshyam Shah, 242-257. New Delhi: Sage Publications.
- Louis, Prakash. 2007. 'Dalit Christian.' *Economic and Political Weekly* XLII (16): 1410-1414.
- Louis, Prakash and Surinder S. Jodhka. 2003. 'Conflict and Dalit Identity in Rural Punjab.' *Social Action* 53: October-December.
- Madan, T.N. 2006. 'Sociology of Hinduism: Reading 'Backwards' from Srinivas to Weber.' *Sociological Bulletin* 55 (2): 267-281.
- Malik, Yogender. 1986. 'The Akali Party and Sikh Militancy: More for Greater Authority or Secessions in Punjab.' *Asian Survey* XXVI (3): 352-353.

- Mendelson, Oliver. 1993. 'The Transformation of Authority in Rural India.' *Modern Asian Studies* 27 (4): 804-42.
- Mishra, Amresh. 1993. 'UP Dalit Assertion: Possibilities and Limitations.' *Economic and Political Weekly* XXXVIII (50): 2701-2702.
- Mishra, Shiv Kumar. 2009. 'Mayawati Gimmicks.' *Mainstream* XLVII (20): 1-7 May.
- Misra, Chaturanan. 2005. 'The Caste Factor.' *Mainstream* XXXXIII (28): 11-12.
- Nahar, Emanual. 2006. 'Dalit Christians in Punjab: An Analytical Study.' Seminar on *'Dalits in Punjab Politics.'* Sponsored by ICSSR, Jalandhar: TRINITY College. 18 February.
- ———. 2007. 'Restoration of Human Rights and Dignity to Dalits.' *Diviner* 4 (2): 167.
- ———. 2017. 'Dr B.R. Ambedkar's Philosophy in Contemporary India.' In B.R. *Ambedkar's Philosophy in Contemporary India,* edited by Emanual Nahar, 31-48. New Delhi: Kalpaz Publications.
- Nahar, Emanual and Priyanka. 2016. 'Politics of Social Exclusion: A Study of Dalit Christian in the State of Punjab.' In *Social Exclusion and Discrimination with Weaker Sections of Society: An Inclusive Policy,* edited by Emanual Nahar, 23-34. New Delhi: Kalpaz Publications.
- Narayan, Badri. 2004. 'Inventing Caste History: Dalit Mobilisation and Nationalist Past.' *Contributions to Indian Sociology* 38 (1-2): 193-221.
- Naudet, Jules. 2008. 'Paying Back to Society: Upward Social Mobility among Dalits.' *Contributions to Indian Sociology* 42 (3): 413-443.
- Nayar, Kuldeep. 2016. 'Segregation in Democracy.' *Mainstream* LIV (34): 13-16.
- Pai, Sudha. 1993. 'Emergence of New Social Forces in UP.' *Mainstream* XXXII (5): 3-5.
- ———. 1996a. 'Transformation of the Indian Party System: An Analysis of the 1996 Loksabha Elections.' *Asian Survey* 34 (12): 1170-83.
- ———. 1996b. 'Trends in the Party System: Loksabha Elections in UP.' *Mainstream* 34 (28): 9-11.
- ———. 1997. 'Dalit Assertion in UP: Implications for Politics.' *Economic and Political Weekly* XXXII (37): 2312-2314.
- ———. 1998. 'The BSP in Uttar Pradesh' (Special Issue on Dalit) Seminar No. 471, November: 38-42.
- ———. 1999. 'BSP's New Electoral Strategy Pays off.' *Economic and Political Weekly* XXXII (44): 3099 -3101.
- ———. 2002. 'Electoral Identity Politics in Uttar Pradesh.' *Economic and Political Weekly* XXXVII (14): 1334-1341.

- ———. 2003a. 'BSP's Prospect in the Assembly Election.' *Economic and Political Weekly* XXXIIX (30): 3135-38.
- ———. 2003b. 'Deprivation and Development in UP: the Economic Agenda of the BSP.' *Man and Development* 25 (1): 35-54.
- Pai, Sudha and Jagpal Singh. 1998. 'Politicisation of Dalits and Most Backward Castes: A Study of Social Conflict and Political Preference in Village of Meerut District.' *Economic and Political Weekly* XXXII (23): 1356-62.
- Palshikar, Suhas. 2017. 'India's Second Dominant Party System.' *Economic and Political Weekly* LII (12): 12-15.
- Patil, Sharad. 2009. 'Search for Aborigines, or Sudra Varna, or Caste-Ending Equality?' *Mainstream* XLVII (11): 31.
- Pettigrew, Joyce. 1977. 'Socio-Economic Background of the Emigration of Sikhs from Doaba.' *Punjab Journal of Politics* 1 (1): 23-48.
- Pinto, Ambrose. 2010. 'Should Dalit Christian/Muslims be Excluded from Reservation?' *Mainstream* XLVII (17): 33-34.
- Puri, Harish. K. 2003. 'Scheduled Castes in Sikh Community: A Historical Perspective.' *Economic and Political Weekly* XXXIII (26): 2693-2713.
- Ram, Ronki. 2001. 'From Servitude to Assertion: Ambedkar's Subaltern Approach to Nationalism and Dalit Liberation.' *Social Sciences Research Journal* 9 (2): 146-170.
- ———. 2004a. 'Dalit Sikhs.' *Dalit International Newsletter* 9 (3): 5-7.
- ———. 2004b. 'Role of Ad-Dharmis: Chamar Protest in Punjab is linked to Talhan Caste Violence.' *Dalit Voice* 23 (4): 11-12.
- ———. 2007. 'Babu Mangoo Ram and Emancipation of Dalits PART-2.' Accessed from: *http://worldsikhnews.com/index2.php*.
- ———. 2009a. 'Bhakti as Social Protest: Guru Ravidass and the Rise of Dalit Consciousness in Punjab. *India Journal of Politics* 43 (4): 43-64.
- ———. 2009b. 'Regional Specificities and Caste Hierarchies in Punjab.' *Indian Journal of Politics* 43 (2): 15-29.
- ———. 2011. 'Beyond Conversion and Sanskritisation: Articulating an Alteranative Dalit Agenda in East Punjab' *Modern Asian Studies:* 1-64. Accessed from: *http://journals.cambridge.org*.
- ———. 2016. 'Structures of Social Exclusion, Dera Culture and Dalit Social Mobility in Contemporary East Punjab.' *Contemporary Voice of Dalit* 8 (2): 186-195.
- ———. 2017. 'The Genealogy of a Dalit Faith: The Ravidassia Dharm and Caste Conflict in Contemporary Punjab.' *Contributions to Indian Sociology* 51 (1): 52-78.
- Ramaiah. 1998. 'The Plight of Dalits: A Challenge to the Social Work Professions.' *Indian Journal of Social Work* 59 (1): 52.

- Rao, Y. Chinna. 2003. 'The Rise and Growth of Dalit Movement in Andhra, 1906-1946', *Indian Social Science Review* 5 (1): 117-155.
- Rawat, Ramnarayan. 2001. 'Partition, Politics and Achhut Identity: A Study of Scheduled Castes' Federation and Dalit Politics in U.P. 1946-48.' In *The Partition of Memory: Afterlife of the Division of India,* edited by Suvir Kaul, 111-139. Delhi: Permanent Black.
- Robinson, Rowena. 2004. 'Sociology of Christianity, Conversion and Secularism in India: Some Reflection.' *Sociological Bulletin* 54 (3): 473-496.
- Rudolph, Lloyd and Susanne H. Rudolph. 1958. 'Survey in India, Field Experience in Madras State.' *The Public Opinion Quarterly* 22 (3): 235-245.
- Rupavath, Ramdas. 2016. 'Confronting Everyday Humiliation.' *Economic and Political Weekly* LI (31): 16-19.
- Saberwal, S. 1973. 'Receding Pollution: Intercaste Relations in Urban Punjab.' *Sociological Bulletin* 22 (2): 234-59.
- Sachar, Rajinder. 2010. Caste in Census 2011 – Is it Necessary?' *Mainstream* XLVIII (23): 5.
- Sagar, Tarsem. 2006. 'Dalit Politics in Punjab: Some Observation.' A paper presented at the Seminar on '*Dalit in Punjab Politics'*, held on 18th February at Trinity College, Jalandhar.
- Sahay, Gaurang R. 2004. 'Hierarchy, Difference and the Caste System: A Study of Rural Bihar.' *Contributions to Indian Sociology* 38 (1-2): 113-137.
- Samarendra, Padmanabh. 2016. 'Religion and Scheduled Caste Status.' *Economic and Political Weekly* LI (31): 13-16.
- Sarkar, Jayabrata. 2010. 'Losing the 'Dalit' Plot in Sarvajan Politics.' *Mainstream* XLVIII (16): 7-9.
- Sarukkai, Sunder. 2007. 'Dalit Experience and Theory.' *Economic and Political Weekly* XLII (40): 4043-4049.
- Saxena, Ravi. 2009. 'Dalit Question: Reading Godan and Joothan as Narratives of Dalit Protest.' *Punjab University Research Journal (Arts)* XXXVI (1&2): 90-112.
- Sekhon, Jagrup Singh. 2004. 'Punjab: By Elections or Referendum.' *Punjab Journal of Politics,* XXVIII (2): 97-110.
- ———. 2006. 'Dalits in Punjab: An Overview.' Seminar on 'Dalits in Punjab Politics.' sponsored by ICSSR, Jalandhar: Trinity College, 18 February.
- Shah, A.M. 2002. 'The 'Dalit' Category and its Differentiation.' *Economic and Political Weekly* XXXVII (14): 1317-1319.
- ———. 2007. 'Purity, Impurity, Untouchability: Then and Now.' *Sociological Bulletin* 56 (3): 355-369.

- ———. 2017. 'The Mirage of a Casteless Society in India.' *Economic and Political Weekly* LII (9): 61-66.
- Shah, Ghanshyam. 2000. 'Hope and Despair: A Study of Untouchability and Atrocities in Gujarat.' *Journal of Indian School of Political Economy* XII (3 and 4): 459-72.
- ———. 2002. 'Caste, Hindutva and Hideousness.' *Economic and Political Weekly* XXXVII (15): 1391-1393.
- Sharma, Shalini and Simran K. Sidhu. 2012. 'Dalit Assertion through Grass Root Leadership in Doaba Region of Punjab.' *Guru Nanak Journal of Sociology* 33(1&2): 74-83.
- Shen and Mohan Jharta. 2007. 'Religious Conversion of Dalits from Hinduism to Christianity: A Sociological Perspective.' *Guru Nanak Journal of Sociology* 28 (1-2): 97-111.
- Shukla, Surinder K. 1994. 'Democracy in India: Issues and Problems.' *Indian Journal of Political Science* 55 (4): 401- 410.
- Singh, Bhupinder. 2001. 'Impact of the 1997 Assembly Elections on the Political Development in Punjab.' *Punjab Journal of Politics* XXV (2): 163-173.
- Singh, Jagpal. 1998. 'Ambedkar and Assertion of Dalit Identity, Socio-cultural Protect in Meerut District of Uttar Pradesh.' *Economic and Political Weekly* XXXIII (40): 2611-18.
- Singh, Jatinder. 2015. 'Punjab at the Crossroads, Searching for Democracy.' *Economic and Political Weekly* 50(48): 12-14.
- Singh, Maanvender. 2016. 'Reservation amidst the Din of 'Development.' *Economic and Political Weekly* LI (38): 65-69.
- Singh, Nirmal. 2007. 'Dalits under the Caste Structure and the Role of the State.' In *Social Legislation and Social Change*, edited by Dr Manjit Singh, 76-86. Patiala: Twenty First Century Publications.
- ———. 2011. 'Dr Ambedkar and the Renewing Scenario of Dalit Identity.' In *Dr Ambedkar's Philosophy of Social Justice,* edited by Dr S.S Randhawa and Sardool Singh, 65-83. Chandigarh: Salaria Publication House.
- ———. 2013a. 'Caste System and Equality in India.' *Third Concept* 27 (314): 28-31.
- ———. 2013b. 'Caste Ridden Society in Democratic India.' *NAM Today* XXXIII (1): 14-18.
- ———. 2013c. 'Dalit Women in the Democratic India.' *Emerging Trends in Social Sciences* 2 (7): 79-81.
- ———. 2013d. 'Towards a Casteless Democratic India.' *Diviner* 10 (2): 145-155.
- ———. 2014. 'BSP in Punjab: Analysing its Failure.' *Economic and Political Weekly* XLIX (48): 17-19.

- ———. 2015. 'Human Rights Upsurge in a Caste Ridden Democratic India.' In *Law Review,* edited by Emanual Nahar and Amritpal Kaur, 131-139. Gurgaon: LexisNexis.
- ———. 2016. 'Ambedkar's Quest of a Mere Democratic India.' In *Social Exclusion and Discrimination with Weaker Sections of Society: an Inclusive Policy,* edited by Emanual Nahar, 83-93. New Delhi: Kalpaz Publications.
- ———. 2017. 'Ambedkar's Vision of a Mere Democratic India.' In *Dr B.R. Ambedkar's Philosophy in Contemporary India,* edited by Emanual Nahar, 159-168. New Delhi: Kalpaz Publications.
- ———. 'BSP in Uttar Pradesh.' *Mainstream* LV (42): 18-21.
- Singh, Shyam. 2011. 'BSP's Route to 2012.' *Mainstream* XXIX (15): 6-9.
- Singh, Sukhdev and B.R. Jindal. 2005. 'Social Change in Rural Punjab: A Study of Untouchability and Caste Relations.' *Guru Nanak Journal of Sociology* 26 (2): 71-91.
- Sinharay, Praskanva. 2016. 'Dalit Question in the Upcoming West Bangal Assembly Election.' *Economic and Political Weekly* LI (9): 17-20.
- Sonawane, Rakshit. 2016. 'Joining the Mainstream or Losing Steam?' *Economic and Political Weekly* LI (25):29-31.
- Srivastava, Arun. 2016. 'Sangh Reprisal against Dalit in Modi Raj.' *Mainstream* LIV (34): 31-33.
- Srivastava, Vinay Kumar. 2016. 'Speaking of Caste: Merit of the Principle of Segmentation.' *Sociological Bulletin* 65 (3): September-December: 317-388.
- Teltumbde, Anand. 2001. 'Dalit Capitalism and Pseudo Dalitism.' *Economic and Political Weekly* XLVI: 10-11.
- ———. 2007. 'Uttar Pradesh: A Mayawi Revolution.' *Economic and Political Weekly* XLII (23): 2147-2149.
- ———. 2010a. 'Categorisation: A Poisonous Proposition.' *Economic and Political Weekly* XLV (35): 28-30.
- ———. 2010b. 'Mayawati's Mega Service to the Nation.' *Economic and Political Weekly* XLV (15): 12.
- ———. 2015. 'Organiser on Ambedkar, Repeating a Big IIT-MLie.' *Economic and Political Weekly* 50 (28): 10-11.
- ———. 2016a. 'Brahminical Arrogance.' *Economic and Political Weekly* LI (2): 10-11.
- ———. 2016b. 'Dalit Cry on the Eve of the Ambedkar Festival.' *Economic and Political Weekly* LI (19): 10-11.
- ———. 2016c. 'Dalit Protest in Gujrat.' *Economic and Political Weekly* LI (32): 10-11.
- ———. 2016d. 'Two Years of an Ambedkar Bhakt and the Plight of Dalits.' *Economic and Political Weekly* LI (23): 10-11.

- ———. 2016e. Modi's Faux Pas on Ambedkar.' *Economic and Political Weekly* LI (16): 23-25.
- ———. 2017a. 'Robbing Rohith of his Dalitness'. *Economic and Political Weekly* LII (9): 10-11.
- ———. 2017b. 'End of the Dalit Chimera.' *Economic and Political Weekly* LII (18): 10-11.
- Thorat, Sukhadeo and Katherine S. Newman. 2007. 'Caste and Economic Descrimination: Causes, Consequences and Remedies.' *Economic and Political Weekly* XLII (41): 4121-4125.
- Thorat, Sukhadeo and Nidhi Sadhna. 2009. 'Caste and Ownership of Private Enterprises.' *Economic and Political Weekly* XLIV (23): 13-17.
- Trivedi, Mridula. 2007. 'Social Mobility and Class Formation among the Bhils of Rajasthan.' *Guru Nanak Journal of Sociology* 28 (1-2): 47-57.
- Uniyal, Lalit. 1996. 'Kanshi Ram.' *Mainstream* XXXIV (8): 28-29.
- Varshney, Ashutosh. 2000. 'Is India Becoming More Democratic?' *The Journal of Asian Studies* 59 (1): 3-25.
- Verma, A.K. 2005. 'BSP's Strategy in Uttar Pradesh.' *Economic and Political Weekly* XXXX (26): 2647-48.
- ———. 2007. 'Mayawati's Sandwich Coalition.' *Economic and Political Weekly* XLII (22): 2039-2043.
- Verma, P.S. 2001. '*Dalit Mobilisation in Punjab.*' Paper presented in Punjab University on 27-28 February at ICSSR Complex, Panjab University Chandigarh.
- Vij, Shivam. 2010. 'Can the Congress Win over UP's Dalits?' *Economic and Political Weekly* XLV (19): 21.
- Wallace, Paul. 1990. 'Religious and Ethnic Politics: Political Mobilisation in Punjab.' In *Dominance and State Power in Modern India,* edited by Francine Frankel and M.S.A. Rao, 416-481. Delhi: Oxford University Press.
- Wankhede, Harish S. 2010. 'Dalit Symbolism and the Democratisation of Secular Spaces.' *Mainstream* XLVIII (12): 29-32.
- Weiner, Myron. 2001. 'The Struggle for Equality: Caste in Indian Politics.' In *The Success of India's Democracy,* edited by Atul Kohli, 193-225. Cambridge: Cambridge University Press.
- Yadav, Yogendra. 1993. 'Political Change in North India interpreting Elections, 1993-95.' *Economic and Political Weekly* XXVIII (51): 2767-74.
- Zelliot, Eleaner. 1988. 'Congress and the Untouchables, 1917-1950.' In *Congress, and the Indian Nationalism: Pre-independence Phase,* edited by Richard Sisson and Stanley A. Wolpert, 182-198. Berkeley: University of California Press.

- ———. 2001. 'Dalit Traditions and Dalit Consciousness.' In *Democratic Governance in India: Challenges of Poverty, Development and Identity,* edited by Niraja Gopal Jayal and Sudha Pai, 232-252. New Delhi: Sage Publications.

D. Newspapers/News Websites and Magazines

- Anandan, Sujata M. 1999. 'Kanshi Ram Mission of the Few.' *Outlook*: 6 September.
- Bains, Harcharan. 2017. 'Punjab poll: It's Time to Look beyond Bitterness.' *Tehelka* 14 (6): 31 March.
- Bhardwaaj, Satyendra. 2007. 'UP mein ab Mayaraaj.' *Vichar Saransh*: 15 June.
- Bhargava, Rajeev. 2017. 'The Legitimation Crisis of Indian Democracy.' *The Hindu*: 2 April.
- Bhuson, Bharat. 1997. 'Kanshi Ram's Shrinking Agenda.' *Hindustan Times*: 9 October.
- C. G., Manoj and Liz Mathew. 2017. 'Indian National Congress.' *The Indian Express*: 19 March.
- Chandra, Kanchna. 2017. 'Back to the Bahujan Model?' *The Hindu*: 4 April.
- Chidambaram, P. 2017. 'India at 70: The Curse of Caste.' *The Indian Express*: 27 August.
- Chishti, Seema. 2009. 'The Longest Campaign.' *The Indian Express:* 30 July.
- Devi, Vasanthi. 2000. 'Dalits and the State.' *Frontline:* 21 July.
- Devji, Faisal. 2016. 'Gandhi and Ambedkar, A False Debate.' *The Hindu*: 22 February.
- Dorairaj, S. 2009. 'No Entry.' *Frontline* 26 (15): 31.
- Guha, Ramachandra. 2010. 'Ambedkar's Desiderata.' *Outlook* L (4): 22-30.
- Gupta, Dipankar. 2007. 'The Threat from Within.' *Hindustan Times*: 28 July.
- ———. 2016. 'A Tale of Two Reservations.' *The Times of India*: 27 February.
- Gupta, Smita. 2016. 'Dalit-Hindutva Paradox.' *The Hindu*: 9 February.
- Gopal, Guru. 1998. 'Crocodile Tears for Dalits.' *The Hindu*: 15 February.
- ———. 2010. 'India in Transition, Dalits Demand More State Intervention.' *Frontline,* access at: *http://casi.ssc.upenn.edu/iit/guru.*
- ———. 2017. 'Dalits: In a State of Unfreedom.' *Frontline* 34 (17): 1 September.
- Hasan, Zoya. 2017a. 'Saffron Storm in Uttar Pradesh.' *The Hindu*: 16 March.

- ———. 2017b. 'The Coming of a Hindu State.' *India Today*: 23 March.
- Hiteshi, Bharat. 2017. 'How Amarinder Trounced his Rivals Single-handedly.' *Tehelka* 14 (6): 31 March.
- Ilaiah, Kancha. 2007. 'Inverted Pyramid: the New Order Power Equation.' *Tehelka* 4 (20): 26 May.
- Jayaram, Ravi Shankar. 2016. 'The BSP is Showing Sign of a Political Revival.' *Hindustan Times:* 11 July.
- Jha, Srinand. 2017. 'UP Elections 2017, Mayawati's Dalit Vote Base is slipping away Fast.' *Hindustan Times*: 14 March.
- Jodhka, Surinder S. 2003. 'Caste Occupation Divide Gets Sharpner in Punjab: Agrarian Technology has Reshaped Social Relations.' *The Tribune*: 18 July.
- ———. 2017a. 'Because Caste did'nt Go away.' *The Indian Express*: 11 April.
- ———. 2017b. 'Why do People Go to the Dera?' *The Wire*: 27 August.
- Koppikar, Smruti. 2010. 'Bhim, Eklavya.' *Outlook* L (4): 36-37.
- Kumar, Ajay. 1987. 'Some Questions on the BSP.' *The Times of India:* 6 April.
- Kumar, Vivek. 2000. 'BSP Honeymooning with the Media.' *The Pioneer*: 11 July.
- Kureel, Manoj. 2008. 'Elephant that Can't Remember.' *Tehelka* 5 (3): 26 January.
- Mannathukkaren, Nissim. 2017. 'Transcending Democracy beyond Elections.' *The Hindu*: 1 April.
- Mathur, Mudit. 2017a. 'Brand Modi: Trusted or Thrusted?' *Tehelka* 14 (6): 31 March.
- ———. 2017b. 'BJP Plays Caste Card Well.' *Tehelka,* 14 (6): 31 March.
- ———. 2017c. 'Mayawati Eyes win through Revamp in Social Engineering.' *Tehelka* 14 (5): 2 March.
- Misre, Yogesh. 2007. 'Ratno ki Maya.' *Outlook Weekly*: 4 June.
- Naidu, M. Venkaiah. 2017. 'The Voter's new Religion.' *The Indian Express*: 16 March.
- Naim, Shahira. 2009. 'UP Rejects Social Engineering, Votes for Development.' *The Tribune:* 22 May.
- ———. 2010. 'Maya is reasserting her Dalit Identity.' *The Tribune:* 16 March.
- Nanda, Meera. 2007. 'It's a Long Wait to Revolution, Mayaji.' *Tehelka:* 23 June.
- Nayar, Kuldeep. 2012. 'Ignored Cause of Dalit Uplift.' *The Tribune*: April 25.

- Nirupama, Subramanian. 2016. 'Kejriwal in Punjab Today, Why is he Seeking Dalit Vote?' *The Indian Express*: 15 March.
- Nooruzzaman, Syed. 2009. 'Congress vs BSP in UP.' *The Tribune*: 1 August.
- Omvedt, Gail. 1999a. 'Ambedkar's New Buddhism.' *The Hindu*: 25 February.
- ———. 1999b. 'Dalit Politics.' *The Hindu*: 1 April.
- Paswan, Sanjay. 2017. 'A New Dalit Agenda.' *The Indian Express*: 5 May.
- Prasad, K.V. 2007. 'BSP Hopes to Make its Presence Felt in Punjab.' *The Hindu*: 25 February.
- Pubby, Vipin. 2009. 'Why Dera a Flash Point? Sets off Sparks across State' *The Indian Express*: 25 June.
- Raj, Udit. 2016. 'Not Without Reservations.' *The Indian Express*: 13 May.
- Rai, Upendrra. 2017. 'Great Power comes with Greater Responsibility.' *Tehelka* 14 (6): 31 March.
- Ram, Mangoo. 1971. 'Meri Videsh Yatra and Mera Jivan Birtant.' *Ravidass Patrika*: 6 April.
- Ram, Ronki. 2004. 'The Dalit Sikhs.' *Newsletter* 9 (3): 5-7.
- ———. 2007a. 'Catastrophe in Making: Religion, Deras, and Dalits in Punjab.' *World Sikh News:* 13-19 June.
- ———. 2007b. 'Conflict of New Assertion.' *Tehelka* 4 (27): 8-14 July.
- ———. 2007c. 'The Elephant and the Broken Pyramid: Mayawati's Victory Promises a New Construct for our Democracy.' *Tehelka* 4 (21): 27 May-2 June.
- Ramakrishnan, Venkitesh. 2007a. 'Dalit Power.' *Frontline* 24 (10): 19 May.
- ———. 2007b. 'Heat and Dust.' *Frontline* 24 (10): 4 May.
- ———. 2007c. 'The New Behenji.' *Frontline* 24 (8): 21 April.
- ———. 2007d. 'Winning Formula.' *Frontline* 24 (10): 19 May.
- ———. 2008a. 'Going Strong.' *Frontline* 24 (10): 9 May.
- ———. 2008b. 'Mayawati's Turn.' *Frontline* 25 (2): 1 February.
- ———. 2009. 'Battle for Turf.' *Frontline* 26 (2): 14 August.
- ———. 2017. 'Arithmetic of Success.' *Frontline* 34 (6): 31 March.
- Rana, O.P. 2009. 'Kya Baspa Punjab Andar Teesra Rajnitik baddal Ban Skegi.' *Nwa Jmana:* 3 May.
- ———. 2010a. 'Baspa ate Punjab da Tija Siyasi Baddal.' *Punjabi Tribune:* 8 May.
- ———. 2010b. 'Baspa di Bewfai da Shikar, Kanshi Ram Prokar.' *Nwa Jmana*: 12 August.
- Sandhu, Nirmal. 2003. 'Why Talhan Happened.' *The Tribune*: 17 June.

- Sethi, Sunil. 1997. 'When Dalit Women Find their Voice.' The *Times of India*: 28 July.
- Sharan, Shankar. 2016. 'Dalit Vimarsh ki Dasha-Disha.' *Dainik Bhashkar*: 18 August.
- Singh, Gurmukh. 1995. 'Power to Maya.' *The Times of India*: 11 June.
- Singh, I. P. 2011. 'Ban on Movie – an Eye on Dalit Votes.' *The Times of India*: 13 August.
- Singh, Jangveer. 2001. 'Dalits barred from Temple.' *The Tribune*: 20 May.
- Singh, Krishan Prataap. 2010. 'Uttar Pradesh me Baspa-Congress dwend ki Disha.' *Dainik Tribune*: 9 April.
- Singh, Manjit. 2011. 'Making the Punjab Dalit Vote Count.' *Hindustan Times*: 1 November.
- Singh, Narinderpal. 2007. 'Shiromani Committee and Caste.' *Desh Sewak*: 1 July.
- Singh, Nihal. 2008. 'Importance of Being Maya, Rise of Dalit Leader can't be ignored.' *The Tribune*: 8 June.
- ———. 2017. 'Congress Electoral Debacle.' *The Tribune*: 18 March.
- Singh, Ramendra. 2017. 'SP, BSP Lose Strongholds too.' *The Indian Express*: 12 March.
- Singh, Sanjay. 2009. 'Division among SCs in Bihar Complete.' *The Tribune*: 30 July.
- Sinha, Anil. 2017. 'Saffron Spreads over Ganga-Yamuna Waters.' *Tehelka* 14 (6): 31 March.
- Subrahmanian, Vidya. 2007. 'Wrong Again.' *Frontline* 24 (10): 15-17.
- Subramanian, Nirupama. 2016. 'Kejriwal in Punjab Today: Why is he seeking Dalit vote?' *The Indian Express*: 15 March.
- Swami, Praveen. 2003. Dalits Battle in a Punjab Village.' *Frontline* 20 (9): 26.
- Thakur, Sankarsan. 2007. 'Future Shock.' *Tehelka* 4 (20): 26 May.
- Thukral, Gobind. 2009. 'Show of Strength, Dalits Assert their Identity in Punjab.' *The Tribune*: 22 June.
- Trivedi, Divya. 2017. 'No Truck with the BJP.' *Frontline*: 17 March.
- Varshney, Ashutosh. 2017. 'A PM Like Indira.' *The Indian Express*: 16 March.
- Verniers, Gilles. 2017. 'Upper Hand for Upper Castes in House.' *The Indian Express*: 20 March.
- Virdi, Harcharan Das. 2001. 'Ad-Dharm and Ad-Dharmi Quam (Punjabi).' *Begumpura Times Quarterly* 3 (2): 10-15.
- Virdi, S.L. 2003. 'Bharat De Dalitan Di Asseem Dastan Da Dastavej.' *Begumpura Shaher:* 11 August.

- Wyatt, Anrade. 1997. 'BSP Marks a Defining Movement.' *India Today*: 20 January.
- Yadav, Shyamlal. 2017. 'UP: A Political History.' *The Indian Express*: 10 March.
- Yadav, Yogendra. 2017. 'I don't share this Optimism.' *The Tribune*: 1 September.
- Hasan, Zoya. 2007. 'What Next?' *Frontline*, 24 (10), 1 June: 18-21.

Index

C

L

M

R

S